Let the Seller Beware

The 32 Buyer Outs in the Texas Real Estate Contract

3rd Edition

Revised for 2019

Reba Saxon

Published by

VILLAGE SCRIBES PUBLISHING

ISBN: 9780983143635

About the Author

Reba Saxon has been in the real estate industry for many years, first as the child of a Realtor® in Louisiana, then as an agent in Colorado in 1980 (when interest rates were 18%), but mostly in Texas since 2003. She served a 250+-agent real estate office in a management position and performed as a top producer there (but not at the same time). Additionally, Reba is a Certified Real Estate Instructor, on the faculty for the Texas Association of Realtors®, served on the Professional Development Committee at the state level and is serving on the Education Advisory Standards Committee at the Texas Real Estate Commission. As a member of the Professional Standards Committee, she has participated in Ethics hearings between Realtors® and between Realtors® and consumers. She has achieved the following designations through education and personal production:

ABR: Accredited Buyer Representative
CDEI: Certified Distance Education Instructor
CREI: Certified Real Estate Instructor
CRS: Certified Residential Specialist
EcoBroker
EAH: Employer Assisted Housing/Home from Work
GRI: Graduate, Realtor® Institute
GREEN
SFR: Short Sale and Foreclosure Resource
SRES: Senior Real Estate Specialist
TAHS: Texas Affordable Housing Specialist

Reba teaches Legal Updates, Broker Responsibility, and Professional Standards courses as well as several of the designation classes above at Texas REALTOR® associations as well as courses she has authored: Agent Responsibility, Agent Investor, Agent Negotiator, Agent Assistant. She is the owner/broker of Teacher Realty.

TABLE OF CONTENTS

INTRODUCTION
Why this handbook?

Texas real estate contracts are driven by consumer-focused law. In some ways, it is as if the seller is viewed as a giant corporate manufacturer of this large product to be sold for many thousands of dollars, vs the poor, defenseless buyer, whom we must protect. To provide this protection, there are more than thirty "outs" for buyers in our residential contract and related addenda. There are only three for the Seller!

Most agents are familiar with the option period that can be purchased by the Buyer directly from the Seller in Paragraph 23 of the contract. This option period is to allow for inspections and obtaining contractors' estimates for specific repairs the Buyer may want to consider as a part of the purchase. It provides time for any due diligence the Buyer wants to perform. What many real estate agents don't know is that this is only the most obvious "out" and there are many more.

This book outlines and explains the entire Texas Real Estate Sales Contract for the resale of One-to-Four Family Residential properties and includes all related addenda explained by a seasoned negotiator. It will benefit any Agent, Broker, Buyer or Seller of residential property in Texas. Many of the aspects may also apply to contracts available in other states, but this book applies to practice in Texas.

The real estate sales contract is THE most important document in a real estate agent's briefcase. Listing agreements are nice, buyer representation agreements are nice, but their use only indicates the possibility of income. Nobody is going to get paid until a contract is written and closed. It is imperative that you know the contract inside and out, for yourself and for your clients, since the contract conveys property and large sums of money. It is the single most important aspect of our business.

Once I was referred to a client who wished to sell her home in Hutto, Texas. Hutto was once a tiny town eight miles east of Round Rock. During the development boom of the 2000s, Hutto went from less than 300 people to over 20,000, and from a dusty Texas farming town to a sprawling bedroom community for Austin and Round Rock, which is a suburb of Austin as well. There were thousands of newer homes in the area, but this home was quite different: a Craftsman bungalow in the original town, built in 1928. It had character. It had soul. I wanted the experience of working with it. I made an appointment to list the house, but was waylaid and called to say I would be thirty minutes late. The Seller said she had to pick her daughter up in an hour anyway so we rescheduled, because that didn't leave us enough time. My listing appointments run an hour and a half. Doesn't matter if it's their first time to sell or their fifth, somehow whenever I get back in my car and check the clock it's been ninety minutes. It just takes that long to talk about the Seller's needs, thoroughly explain the listing agreement, and discuss the market data that determines the price.

I was sick as a dog on the rescheduled appointment day. I knew that no one would want to even be exposed to me across the table. In fact, I went to a clinic instead and called the

Seller to explain. "Oh, that's ok, just call me when you are better." I must have been *really* sick to miss a listing appointment.

When I called back to reset the appointment, the Seller said, "I appreciate your efforts to try to get this together, Reba, but I am worn out by the process. I was referred to three other Realtors® and have been through this three times already. They are all pretty good, and I am just going to pick one of those. This is an emotional decision for me to sell this house, and I just can't go through it again."

I said, "No, you really need to see me."

"Well, why?" she said. "I mean, do you really know and love Hutto? Because I think whoever sells this house needs to know and love Hutto."

"With all due respect, I don't need to know and love Hutto. Our Buyer's Agents need to know and love Hutto. What I *do* know are the 24 outs for a Buyer in our contract, how to close those loopholes, and how to make sure you don't leave any money on the table."

She said, "…Would 1:30 be okay?" [I've since found 8 more—the longer you study it, the more you know.]

So, while no single buyer would ever encounter all 30+ of the outs available, my goal is to get you to be able to say you *know them all*.

How We Got Here

When I first got into real estate in Texas, I took the 30-hour Law of Contracts class as part of the pre-licensing requirements. During my first year, I also took the twelve days of GRI (Graduate, Realtor® Institute) coursework leading to that designation. Two full days of that series focus on Contracts and Contract Procedures. My husband asked me what we were studying, and when I replied, "Oh, the contract," he asked, "How long can you study the same thing?" The answer is: an entire career. Knowing and negotiating the contract is the most important aspect of practicing real estate. There are over thirty related addenda that may be used. There are several possible special clauses you might want to enter in the Special Provisions Paragraph because there is no approved addendum, but you must avoid "practicing law" by getting creative there. Classes in contracts are generally the most well attended classes in any real estate brokerage office because agents know that they always pick up something that they will use in their business.

A basic understanding of contract law provides for just that, but basic is not nearly enough. The Texas Real Estate Commission (TREC), the regulatory agency for real estate licensees, promulgates contracts for use by those licensees. The best definition I can give for 'promulgates' is 'requires the use of'. The contracts and related addenda are actually written by the Texas Broker-Lawyer Committee, made up of 6 lawyers, 6 brokers, and a member of the public to provide the "Huh?" that leads to better explanations within documents so that the consumer can understand what these professionals are writing and guards against unexplained industry jargon and legalese. When this Broker-Lawyer

Committee finishes drafting a new document or a revision of an existing one, TREC publishes the proposed changes and seeks input from the real estate community for several months before setting the changes in stone. This revision follows this process just completed in the last 6 months of 2017, with the new contract forms required for use in 2018 used in this book.

Following the simple requirements for a valid contract would result in a one-page document that could be written on the back of a paper sack. The Texas contract is now at eight pages plus a two pages for identification of the real estate Brokers and their Agents involved in the transaction, instructing the closing entity on the expected commission payment for the Buyer's Agent from the Listing Agent, and provides places for the receipt of the option fee and the contract to be noted. How did we get from one page to ten pages? Partly through explanatory text added to make things clearer to the parties involved. Additionally, the various other regulatory agencies (Texas Department of Insurance, various taxing authorities) and other laws (Texas Property Code, Texas Water Code) want to get a word in edgewise about their requirements when transferring property. Sometimes (often) there has been a lawsuit and the additional text resulted from reaction to various problems encountered in those litigated transactions, in an effort to prevent those same problems for folks in the future.

The simple requirements for a valid contract are (1) Competent parties (Buyer and Seller who can understand the contract, are not under the influence or otherwise not competent), (2) Legal subject matter (can't be for something illegal) (3) Consideration: a give and take from each side (give money and take property/give property and take money), (4) Mutual Assent (everybody has agreed to all terms, shown with signatures), and (5) Delivery and Acceptance. In most states, there is also a requirement that a real estate contract must be in writing. In Texas, an oral contract can be used to set up the transfer of real estate, but it can't be enforced. We behave according to contracts every day, most of them implied. If there is a transfer of real estate involved, the contract must be expressed in some way, not implied, and writing is preferred.

Several states do not allow real estate Brokers or Agents to complete contracts at all; an attorney is involved in every real estate transaction. But at some point in Texas, I'm guessing that Brokers may have gone to the state legislature and said, "A lot of these real estate sales are the same type of transaction over and over. We could save the public (your constituents) money if we could just be allowed to have a contract--drafted by attorneys, of course--on which we could just fill in the blanks." And it must have been a time when there weren't so many lawyers in the legislature, because they said okay. This would be a nice revenue stream for attorneys, so we are very happy that we can serve our clients in this way, and that they are not forced to use an attorney for a boilerplate real estate transaction. Of course, we encourage them to hire an attorney if they have any questions beyond our limited expertise.

When I managed a large real estate office in the Austin, Texas suburb of Round Rock, part of my job was to resolve agents' problems and conflicts. I would say that 80% of those problems were preventable with additional knowledge in just two areas: Contracts and Agency. Often an agent would come and sit in my office, saying "This problem has happened or is going to happen, what do I do?" And I would patiently point out to them the Paragraph in the contract that showed they didn't need to come up with anything new, it was resolved right there in the contract. If they knew their contract better, they wouldn't have been so upset and stressed out, or there wouldn't have been a problem in the first place. As far as Agency, when an agent told me, "The other side is saying/doing this, what should I do?" my answer was usually, "You don't need to DO anything. You are the Agent for the Broker, who is the Client's agent/representative. You need to make sure that our Client is fully informed, let them make the decision, then you carry out that decision." No judgment calls, no unnecessary shouldering of blame.

As I have taught our sales contract numerous times, I have come to the conclusion that there is negotiation available in many areas that are not used often. If you are acting as an Agent for your Broker's listing, and thus for the Seller, you need to know where to advise your client to stand firm and where to negotiate. If you are a Buyer's Agent, you need to know how to make your client's offer stand out from others and how to reassure your firm's clients that they are very well protected so that they can move forward quickly when you help them find the right house.

This handbook will provide you with those skills. Your Broker will guide you in how he/she wants you to do business in his/her name, but you can at least have the right questions to ask. When you have a contract question, ask your broker, and if he/she is unavailable, you can call the Texas Association of Realtors® (TAR) Legal Hotline.

USING THIS BOOK: The One to Four Family Residential Contract is used as the template, and is included in full about mid-book. The paragraphs are also excerpted and available before each paragraph discussion within the text. Most of the most often-used forms are available at the end of this book as well. The 'BUYER OUTS' are all identified in brackets. To be considered a true 'out', the party must receive the earnest money when all is said and done.

NOTE: A buyer "out" is not necessarily automatic; in many cases it would just give one party cause for a lawsuit. Will they win? No one can say how a particular judge might rule on a particular day, as judges have latitude in what they consider. They can use past case history, the specifics of the particular case, even the 'vibe' they get in the courtroom from the two parties. A judge can definitely determine that fault is present, but whether it rises to the level of total breach and prevents the conveyance of the property is a judge's decision unless the phrase "time is of the essence" is involved.

****

ONE TO FOUR FAMILY RESIDENTIAL RESALE CONTRACT

PARAGRAPH 1: PARTIES

> **1. PARTIES:** The parties to this contract are _____(Seller) and
> _____(Buyer). Seller agrees to sell and convey to Buyer and Buyer agrees to buy from Seller the Property defined below.

PARTIES: The names of the Sellers and Buyers of the property are entered. The title company will be using the first two paragraphs of the contract to draw up the deed, but will confirm names and other titling details with the parties directly. In the past, if a single person was purchasing the property, we might enter "a single person" after their name to signal that there was no spouse who could later claim the property under community property rights, but that is really not necessary today. If the Buyers are a married couple with the same last name, the old way was to add "a married couple" after their names, but today it is assumed that they are married if you do not add that phrase. In fact, it is the title company's responsibility to establish how the new owners want to take title, and making suggestions in this area could constitute the practice of law. I have had a title company's attorney add "and spouse" between the names, which angered a client when she sat at the closing table and saw the deed written that way. She was an attorney for the state, and she didn't like being classified as the "spouse". She said to her husband, "Why do I have to be the 'spouse'? Why can't YOU be the 'spouse'?" I immediately asked, "Do you want to have it changed? We can close later and they can redraw the deed."

"No, it's ok. Let's go ahead." She just wanted to be heard. It's very important that you be at every closing. Every closing. It is disappointing when an agent doesn't attend a closing, or they have an assistant go in their place. There has always been some problem I could solve. From just answering a question to resolving a problem with a phone call to a builder, but mainly to help set the tone of the transaction. You want it to be a business transaction, not the unfamiliar yet high-stakes event it is for buyers who haven't bought a time or two before.

In the case of the Sellers' names, make sure if the property is listed in one person's name that there is not a spouse. Basically, it takes "one to buy, two to sell" when it is a couple's homestead, and community property laws also impact the sale of property depending on marital status at the time of original purchase or acquisition.

If two Buyers are not married, your job would be to alert them that they need to talk to an attorney to determine how to take title to protect themselves and each other if something should happen to one of them.

If there are more Sellers' or Buyers' names than will fit, you may add them in Paragraph 11: Special Provisions.

PARAGRAPH 2: PROPERTY

> **2. PROPERTY**: The land, improvements and accessories are collectively referred to as the "Property".
> **A. LAND:** Lot_____ Block_____, _____ Addition, City of _____, County of _____,Texas, known as _____ (address/zip code), or as described on attached exhibit.

PROPERTY: The legal description of the property is entered here if it fits.

LAND: In a Lot and Block description of a subdivision, available on the county tax assessor's roll record for the property, you may need to reverse the description to make it conform to the blanks indicated. The last line, which reads "street/zip" is just that, since the city and state were entered earlier.

If the legal description doesn't conform to the Lot and Block description but is short enough to fit in the blanks, you could also enter it here for everyone's convenience when looking for it. If the description is longer but would still fit in Paragraph 11: Special Provisions, you can enter "See Paragraph 11" or "See Special Provisions". If it is a piece of property that is not described by Lot and Block description and it is being conveyed using a Metes and Bounds description from a survey, you can enter "See Exhibit A" here, check the "Other" box in Paragraph 22 and enter "Exhibit A" in the blank there to describe what "Other" you are attaching. Then simply take the Field Notes from the survey, write "Exhibit A" across the top of it, and voila, it is "attached" to the contract.

> **B. IMPROVEMENTS:** The house, garage and all other fixtures and improvements attached to the above-described real property, including without limitation, the following permanently installed and built-in items, if any: all equipment and appliances, valances, screens, shutters, awnings, wall-to-wall carpeting, mirrors, ceiling fans, attic fans, mail boxes, television antennas, mounts and brackets for televisions and speakers, heating and air-conditioning units, security and fire detection equipment, wiring, plumbing and lighting fixtures, chandeliers, water softener system, kitchen equipment, garage door openers, cleaning equipment, shrubbery, landscaping, outdoor cooking equipment, and all other property owned by Seller and attached to the above described real property.

IMPROVEMENTS: The legal description above describes the location of the actual land and this subparagraph includes all of the man-made items or improvements when conveyed. Equipment and appliances that are permanently installed and built in are included and described here. "Valances, screens, shutters, awnings, wall-to-wall carpeting, mirrors (be careful to note those newer framed bathroom mirrors hung like pictures), ceiling fans, attic fans, mailboxes (in neighborhoods with kiosk-type mailboxes generally the post office handles the provision of keys with a deposit, they are not delivered by the seller), television antennas, mounts and brackets for televisions and speakers, heating and air-conditioning units, security and fire detection equipment, wiring, plumbing and lighting fixtures, chandeliers..."

If you are the listing agent for an occupied home, be very careful about chandeliers, installed stained glass, etc. Exclusions appear on the listing agreement and should be carefully added to the contract. During a listing presentation, it is wise to ask if any of these types of items will be excluded. I have seen big arguments about custom draperies, for example, when the Buyer has found on their final walk-through that the draperies they expected to be left as attached were in fact removed by the Seller to go along with the matching bedspread in their new house. The resulting commissionectomy I had in order to complete the sale to allow for repurchasing custom draperies was not what I had planned. Ideally, we should have a place for exclusions on the Sellers Disclosure, which the Buyer sees and even signs that they have seen it. But until then, make sure you review your 4-month old listing agreement that you've forgotten the particulars of while you are getting new listings, having more closings, and working with buyers. When you receive an offer on a listing, review the listing agreement for exclusions as part of your system. Best practice: Note any exclusions in the MLS agent remarks, so that the buyer's agent can incorporate it properly into an offer from the beginning.

"... water softener system (same here), kitchen equipment (e.g. built-in microwave), garage door openers, cleaning equipment (built-in vacuum system), shrubbery, landscaping (Listing agents: if you notice that your client is a gardener, make a point of this with them because they will start pulling plants out and potting them up for the move as soon as they have a contract. The Buyer gets to buy exactly what they saw the day they signed that offer, unless specifically excluded in writing.), outdoor cooking equipment (permanent barbecue grill, not portable), and all other equipment owned by Seller and attached to the above described real property."

C. ACCESSORIES: The following described related accessories, if any: window air conditioning units, stove, fireplace screens, curtains and rods, blinds, window shades, draperies and rods, door keys, mailbox keys, above ground pool, swimming pool equipment and maintenance accessories, artificial fireplace logs, and controls for: (i) garage doors, (ii) entry gates, and (iii) other improvements and accessories.

ACCESSORIES: Interesting that the stove is considered to convey in Texas, but not the refrigerator. Refrigerators and even washers and dryers do convey in some parts of the country, so if your Buyers are from another state they may be expecting it. The stove conveys because it is a requirement for habitability but make sure they understand when you are showing an occupied home that the other appliances do not convey.... fireplace screens (the custom and attached kind, not the kind that just sits inside the fireplace opening), curtains and rods, blinds, window shades, draperies and rods (see commissionectomy story above), controls for garage door openers, entry gate controls, door keys, mailbox keys (see discussion about kiosk-style mailboxes above) above ground pool, swimming pool equipment and maintenance accessories (careful here if Seller is moving to a new house with a pool, they may think they can take all of the cleaning equipment with them), and artificial fireplace logs (point this out as well, these things can cost upwards of $500 and Sellers may think they can take them, too).

D. EXCLUSIONS: The following improvements and accessories will be retained by Seller and must be removed prior to delivery of possession:_____

EXCLUSIONS: Again, pay attention to this subparagraph. Generally, Buyer Agents will not be aware of anything to put in here unless they have been warned in the MLS Agent Remarks. Otherwise, exclusions will have to be added to a counter from the Seller.

PARAGRAPH 3: SALES PRICE

---

3. SALES PRICE:
A. Cash portion of Sales Price payable by Buyer at closing .... $_____
B. Sum of all financing described in the attached: __ Third Party Financing Addendum, __Loan Assumption Addendum, __Seller Financing Addendum .... $_____
C. Sales Price (Sum of A and B) ....$_____

SALES PRICE: This section is pretty much self-explanatory. If you are filling it out by computer, you would enter the down payment at A, the sales price at C, and the computer will calculate the difference for you at B for the loan amount. Or, you can enter A and B and the computer will fill in the Sales Price.

PARAGRAPH 4: LICENSE HOLDER DISCLOSURE

---

4. LICENSE HOLDER DISCLOSURE: Texas law requires a real estate license holder who is a party to a transaction or acting on behalf of a spouse, parent, child, business entity in which the license holder owns more than 10%, or a trust for which the license holder acts as a trustee or of which the license holder or the license holder's spouse, parent or child is a beneficiary, to notify the other party in writing before entering into a contract of sale. Disclose if applicable:_____

LICENSE HOLDER DISCLOSURE: This paragraph, added in 2016, removes the need to disclose licensure or familial status in Special Provisions. Enter here instead. A simple statement such as "Buyer Reba Saxon is a Texas-licensed real estate agent." Or "Broker Reba Saxon is representing a family member."

PARAGRAPH 5: EARNEST MONEY

5.EARNEST MONEY: Within 3 days after the Effective Date, Buyer must deliver $_____ as earnest money to _____, as escrow agent, at _____ (address). Buyer shall deliver additional earnest money of $_____ to escrow agent within _____ days after the Effective Date of this contract. If Buyer fails to deliver the earnest money within the time required, Seller may terminate this contract or exercise Seller's remedies under Paragraph 15, or both, by providing notice to Buyer before Buyer delivers the earnest money. If the last day to deliver the earnest money falls on a Saturday, Sunday, or legal holiday, the time to deliver the earnest money is extended until the end of the next day that is not a Saturday, Sunday, or legal holiday. **Time is of the essence for this paragraph.**

EARNEST MONEY: This paragraph states the earnest money to be deposited, the escrow agent (which is a title company, _not_ the person who handles the closing) with whom the earnest money will be held in escrow, and provides for a later additional deposit of earnest money. Why would you want to deposit additional earnest money? Perhaps it is a higher priced house that would normally justify at least a 1% earnest money deposit but the Buyer wants to withhold a portion of those funds until they are sure they will complete the sale, typically after their option period (see Paragraph 23: Termination Option), including inspections and any renegotiations of price following those inspections. So if you were setting up an option period of 7 days, for example, you might enter the additional earnest money to be deposited on day 8. Note: Earnest money is not required for a valid contract. It is just to indicate the earnestness of the potential Buyer to the Seller. In a sale between friends or family members, for example, sometimes earnest money is not offered nor requested.

Additionally, this change in additional earnest money could be used to indicate a lower amount on a Back-Up contract, to be supplemented upon moving into first place, the Amended Effective Date.

This paragraph also includes the first of only three Seller Outs. If the earnest money check bounces or is not delivered in time, the Buyer is in default and the Seller can get out (but not get the earnest money, which at this point doesn't exist). It's not common, but there are times when you have a reluctant Seller who wishes they didn't get into this contract. This is really the only way they can get out, and if they find out that the earnest money bounced and nobody told them, there could be cause for a lawsuit. Because of this, and because of fraud even with cashier's checks, many brokers are recommending that the earnest money be wired.

PARAGRAPH 6: TITLE POLICY AND SURVEY

6.TITLE POLICY AND SURVEY:

　　A. TITLE POLICY: Seller shall furnish to Buyer at __ Seller's __Buyer's expense an owner policy of title insurance (Title Policy) issued by _____(Title Company) in the amount of the Sales Price, dated at or after closing, insuring Buyer against loss under the provisions of the Title Policy, subject to the promulgated exclusions (including existing building and zoning ordinances) and the following exceptions:

　　(1) Restrictive covenants common to the platted subdivision in which the Property is located.

　　(2) The standard printed exception for standby fees, taxes and assessments.

　　(3) Liens created as part of the financing described in Paragraph 3.

　　(4) Utility easements created by the dedication deed or plat of the subdivision in which the Property is located.

　　(5) Reservations or exceptions otherwise permitted by this contract or as may be approved by Buyer in writing.

　　(6) The standard printed exception as to marital rights.

　　(7) The standard printed exception as to waters, tidelands, beaches, streams, and related matters.

　　(8) The standard printed exception as to discrepancies, conflicts, shortages in area or boundary lines, encroachments or protrusions, or overlapping improvements: __(i) will not be amended or deleted from the title policy; or __(ii) will be amended to read, "shortages in area" at the expense of __Buyer __Seller.

　　(9) The exception or exclusion regarding minerals approved by the Texas Department of Insurance.

TITLE POLICY: This paragraph names the title company who will provide title insurance for the buyer and the checkboxes in the first line indicate who will pay for that insurance. Normally, the Seller pays for the Buyer's title insurance, but it is a negotiable point. This insurance provides funding for court cases or settlements necessary to protect the Buyer's interest should someone come along and challenge their ownership of the property in the future. There are exceptions to what it will cover, however, and those are numbered 1-9:

1. They will not sue the Home Owners' Association (HOA) to remove any restrictive covenants that are part of the deed restrictions, like limitations that you may not have more than two cars in your driveway, must use specific exterior materials such as roofing materials and paint colors, nor protect you from HOA power to foreclose if you are refusing to pay dues or fines for not following those restrictions.

2. Of course, they will not sue the taxing authorities that have the legal power to tax you under threat of foreclosure to remove that threat.

3. They will not sue your mortgage company to remove the lien on your property.

4. They will not sue the utility companies to remove easements they have to cross your property or install wires or pipes into it.

5. They will not sue to remove any other deed restrictions you are agreeing to with your acceptance of the deed.

6. They will not sue your spouse to remove his/her claims under community property laws.

7. They will not sue Mother Nature if she takes away part of your property through the actions of tides, storms or erosion, nor the state of Texas should it sue you to remove your improvement that has become illegally sited due to the vegetation line's movement.

8. They will not sue to protect you against claims over boundary lines, encroachments hanging over your property line, etc. NOTE: This exception from coverage can be amended to only exclude "shortages in area," meaning boundary lines improperly surveyed that would make you end up with less land. What this means is that they WILL cover the other areas of this exemption, being encroachments, protrusions or overlapping improvements *if* you pay for the additional coverage. As a Buyers' Agent, you can recommend to your client that they pay the additional charge (10% of the main policy premium) to amend this exception. It's a good idea with rural property, particularly if it abuts a road or highway, just in case there is ever an issue with the county or state about widening the road. Your client would probably not want to take on the state in court to contest their idea of how much of the roadside is theirs.

9. They will not cover settlements of mineral leases; if the property you are assisting with has minerals, you should advise the Buyer/Seller to hire a landman or oil and gas attorney to review the abstract in order to discover possible issues.

B. COMMITMENT: Within 20 days after the Title Company receives a copy of this contract, Seller shall furnish to Buyer a commitment for title insurance (Commitment) and, at Buyer's expense, legible copies of restrictive covenants and documents evidencing exceptions in the Commitment (Exception Documents) other than the standard printed exceptions. Seller authorizes the Title Company to deliver the Commitment and Exception Documents to Buyer at Buyer's address shown in Paragraph 21. If the Commitment and Exception Documents are not delivered to Buyer within the specified time, the time for delivery will be automatically extended up to 15 days or 3 days before the Closing Date, whichever is earlier. If, due to factors beyond Seller's control, the Commitment and Exception Documents are not delivered within the time required, Buyer may terminate this contract and the earnest money will be refunded to Buyer.

COMMITMENT: This subparagraph states that the Title Commitment will be delivered by the Seller to the Buyer within 20 days. The Seller doesn't actually deliver the information, the Seller automatically authorizes the Title Company to deliver it, but we can't require anyone to do anything except the parties to the contract, so it's written as a responsibility of the Seller and it is a task that is actually performed on the Seller's behalf by the title company. Generally all parties will receive the Title Commitment within the first two weeks, now that all of the information is online and so easily accessible. The Title Commitment is the Title Company's commitment to issue a title insurance policy in the amount of the sales price to the Buyer. It is issued by the Title Company after *their* attorney's review of the abstract of title. The abstract is a file of all of the records that have ever been recorded regarding the Property. It includes the chain of title, which is a list of the owners and the deeds or wills that conveyed the property from one to the next. But the abstract also includes all other recorded documents pertaining to the property or those owners, so: marriages, divorces, deaths, taxes, any and everything the abstractors can find. Also note that if something comes up, and the title company can't make that 20-day deadline, the contract automatically extends that deadline by 15 days.

When you receive the Title Commitment, it has several parts, Schedules A, B, C and D. Schedule A identifies the contract by its effective date, provides the date the Title Commitment is delivered, and defines the Title Company, their 'GF' or file number assigned to the transaction, the Buyer, the Seller, and the Property. Schedule B shows what they will not cover, including the standard exceptions explained above and any other clouds on the title that they will not insure against, for example mineral leases. I once sold a property with eight mineral leases listed. They appeared to have expired many years ago, but most had a provision that if there was production on the property the lease automatically extended. People don't want to live on a piece of property where someone else could have the right to come on it and dig or drill. If the Seller will assign any position they have in the leases, that can be a solution. The Buyer should refer to an attorney for advice in this area. Schedule C describes the requirements of the Title Insurance Company in instructions to the escrow agent. They want evidence that the taxes have been paid, a particular kind of deed, proof that the signers are the actual people they are supposed to be, and a few other restrictions that they require be carried out before or at closing. Sometimes they ask for proof of marital status or proof that one of the signers who has a fairly common name is not the John Doe who is wanted for something criminal in another county. I had one title closer's assistant ask me to provide proof that my client was not remarried. Think about that. It's pretty easy to prove that someone *is* married, with a marriage certificate for example, but it's pretty hard to prove that something doesn't exist. There is no Not-Married Certificate. It took me several days to convince her that she was asking for something that was not necessary and in fact didn't exist. Schedule D names the officers and directors of the title closing company, the premium amount, and a form that can be signed by the Buyer before or at closing that deletes an Arbitration Provision. This provision removes the possibility of ever suing the title company; it is an agreement to submit to binding arbitration to settle any disputes. I recommend that my clients seriously consider signing this form indicating they want the Arbitration Provision removed and return it to the title company, as not signing it removes a legal avenue. If you do sign it, it's not saying you couldn't use mediation or arbitration to settle a dispute, it's just saying you won't have to be bound to the decision in arbitration. This is all followed up by the actual Title Commitment in official form.

C. SURVEY: The survey must be made by a registered professional land surveyor acceptable to the Title Company and Buyer's lender(s). (Check one box only)

__(1)Within ___days after the effective date of this contract, Seller shall furnish to Buyer and Title Company Seller's existing survey of the Property and a Residential Real Property Affidavit promulgated by the Texas Department of Insurance (T-47 Affidavit). If Seller fails to furnish the existing survey or affidavit within the time prescribed, Buyer shall obtain a new survey at Seller's expense no later than 3 days prior to Closing Date. If the existing survey or affidavit is not acceptable to Title Company or Buyer's lender(s), Buyer shall obtain a new survey at __Seller's __Buyer's expense no later than 3 days prior to Closing Date.

__(2)Within ___days after the effective date of this contract, Buyer shall obtain a new survey at Buyer's expense. Buyer is deemed to receive the survey on the date of actual receipt or the date specified in this paragraph, whichever is earlier.

__(3) Within ___days after the effective date of this contract, Seller, at Seller's expense, shall furnish a new survey to Buyer.

SURVEY: This is a tricky area. A survey is required in Texas by most lenders and title companies. Who pays for it? It's negotiable. If it's a rural property, it's usually seen as a responsibility on the Seller's side, like 'proving up' what they have. On a property that is in a subdivision, it could be argued that the Buyer would be more responsible since it's their lender who wants it. There are even some states in which a survey is not required by the lender. Often the Seller has an existing survey from when they purchased the property, and if nothing has been changed in the footprint of improvements on the property it will be accepted by the title company and lender. This is dependent upon the age of the survey, supposedly within 10 years, but I have seen them accept surveys going back as far as thirty years. Existing surveys must be accompanied by an affidavit (with signatures attested to by a notary) in which the Sellers swear they have not made any changes. A survey on a residential subdivision property would cost $350-450, but even a small acreage property can easily run over $1000, so it's often seen as a nice gesture by the Seller to provide their existing survey. It also helps to get the Seller off the hook as far as paying for a new one. As a Buyer's Agent, though, you should consider that when FEMA greatly expanded the flood plain maps following Hurricane Katrina (Katrina was in 2005, and the new flood plain maps were published in 2007), many properties that were formerly not in any flood plain ended up there as a result of that redrawing, including subdivision houses 2-3 lots away from a drainage ditch! A survey is required to show that flood plain, so it could be argued that your clients should always have a new survey. Regardless, use of existing surveys is still allowed but the main thing to remember is the T-47 affidavit MUST be included. Or else. (You'll see what I mean). And your professional opinion should be to get a new one.

The first checkbox is for the existing survey situation, and the number of days to provide it is negotiable. Two to three days would be reasonable, since they are saying they already have it. NOTE what it says about the affidavit: "If Seller fails to furnish the existing survey or Affidavit within the time prescribed, Buyer shall obtain a new survey at Seller's expense no later than 3 days prior to Closing Date." Real estate agents are often lax about this affidavit, and it can be costly. It *must* be provided with the survey. I know that when you

18

are at a listing appointment and can take the listing agreement, the Sellers Disclosure, and the survey with you, the fact that the affidavit must be notarized means that it must be left behind to obtain later. But please, have the Seller go to their bank or title company where they can have documents notarized for free and get it done as soon as you have the listing, no later than the next day. Don't get caught paying for a survey that was ordered by a Buyer who would have accepted the one your client has just because you didn't make sure the Seller provided the affidavit. The second checkbox activates the subparagraph stating the Buyer will obtain their own new survey, and the third checkbox is used for just telling the Seller you want them to provide a new one. Which box to check would be part of your overall negotiating strategy--if you feel that you are offering plenty for the house, maybe even a high amount because you may be pressured by other offers, you might ask the Seller to provide it. If you feel that you are offering a great price for your Buyer if it is accepted, you might want to recommend they not push the Seller further on this smaller point and advise the Buyer to pay for a new survey. Or if you know that you are in a multiple offer situation and are pressured by other possible offers, you may want to sweeten your offer by taking care of the Survey.

Regardless which way you recommend, a new survey can sometimes take a minimum of 15 days. Those surveyors seem to always feel like they are just swamped and can't get out to the property until week after next, *then* they have to do the research for easements and *then* draw up the survey. (Never mind that they are done mostly with GPS and CAD now.) If there is an existing survey, you might recommend a double-check for any new easements recorded (or double-check that flood plain). You can sometimes track down the original surveyor and have them recertify the survey. This generally runs less than $100 for a subdivision lot.

D. OBJECTIONS: Buyer may object in writing to defects, exceptions, or encumbrances to title: disclosed on the survey other than items 6A(1) through (7) above; disclosed in the Commitment other than items 6A(1) through (9) above; or which prohibit the following use or activity:_____.
Buyer must object the earlier of (i) the Closing Date or (ii) days after Buyer receives the Commitment, Exception Documents, and the survey. Buyer's failure to object within the time allowed will constitute a waiver of Buyer's right to object; except that the requirements in Schedule C of the Commitment are not waived by Buyer. Provided Seller is not obligated to incur any expense, Seller shall cure any timely objections of Buyer or any third party lender within 15 days after Seller receives the objections (Cure Period) and the Closing Date will be extended as necessary. If objections are not cured within the Cure Period, Buyer may, by delivering notice to Seller within 5 days after the end of the Cure Period: (i) terminate this contract and the earnest money will be refunded to Buyer; or (ii) waive the objections. If Buyer does not terminate within the time required, Buyer shall be deemed to have waived the objections. If the Commitment or Survey is revised or any new Exception Document(s) is delivered, Buyer may object to any new matter revealed in the revised Commitment or Survey or new Exception Document(s) within the same time stated in this paragraph to make objections beginning when the revised Commitment, Survey, or Exception Document(s) is delivered to Buyer.

OBJECTIONS: This subparagraph provides for a limitation on the Buyers' time to object to anything they don't like in the Title Commitment or Survey. Five days is a good starting time frame to have the Buyer review these documents with you and/or an attorney. If there is a problem with the title that would prevent conveyance, the Seller gets an automatic extension of 15 days beyond the Closing Date in the contract to cure them. This could be revealed by the survey, (e.g., determining the property is now in a flood zone) but provides time to order an elevation certificate that proves the actual house foundation is above the flood level. (An elevation certificate trumps the flood zone.) Or perhaps something has turned up in the title examination, maybe an old Mechanics' and Materialmen's Lien (M&M Lien), filed when the Seller refused to pay the final installment to a contractor who performed services on the Property. The Seller now has the time and the inclination, probably, to contact that contractor and resolve the dispute so that the Property can be conveyed. If the Seller is unable to cure the problems with the title within 15 days without expense, the Buyer can cancel the contract and receive the earnest money back. [BUYER OUT #1]

E. TITLE NOTICES:

(1) ABSTRACT OR TITLE POLICY: Broker advises Buyer to have an abstract of title covering the Property examined by an attorney of Buyer's selection, or Buyer should be furnished with or obtain a Title Policy. If a Title Policy is furnished, the Commitment should be promptly reviewed by an attorney of Buyer's choice due to the time limitations on Buyer's right to object.

ABSTRACT OR TITLE POLICY: Here it is stated for the Buyer's acknowledgement that the Broker advises the Buyer to have an abstract of title prepared and examined by an attorney of their selection, or make sure they get title insurance. This warning is important to the Texas Real Estate Commission, and allowing a Buyer to purchase property without being so warned constitutes grounds for license suspension, in addition to liability to be sued by the Buyer at a later date if a title problem comes to light without title insurance or an attorney's advice to proceed without it. The warning is in every TREC contract, though, so as long as you are using a TREC contract the Buyer has been duly warned. When might you not be using a TREC contract? Whenever a Buyer or Seller wants to use one they have written or hired an attorney to write for their use. The only time you will really see this in practice is in the purchase of a new home. Every builder has their own contract because they don't like the way the TREC contract is weighted toward the Buyer. Commercial transactions often use attorney-prepared contracts, as well. But for most residential resale transactions, you will be covered. Just make sure you read any other contract required by a principal in a transaction to make sure that warning is in there. If not, include one of several Texas Association of Realtors® forms that include this warning.

(2) **MEMBERSHIP IN PROPERTY OWNERS ASSOCIATION(S):** The Property __ is __ is not subject to mandatory membership in a property owners association(s). If the Property is subject to mandatory membership in a property owners association(s), Seller notifies Buyer under §5.012, Texas Property Code, that, as a purchaser of property in the residential community identified in Paragraph 2A in which the Property is located, you are obligated to be a member of the property owners association(s). Restrictive covenants governing the use and occupancy of the Property and all dedicatory instruments governing the establishment, maintenance, or operation of this residential community have been or will be recorded in the Real Property Records of the county in which the Property is located. Copies of the restrictive covenants and dedicatory instruments may be obtained from the county clerk. You are obligated to pay assessments to the property owners association(s). The amount of the assessments is subject to change. Your failure to pay the assessments could result in enforcement of the association's lien on and the foreclosure of the Property. Section 207.003, Property Code, entitles an owner to receive copies of any document that governs the establishment, maintenance, or operation of a subdivision, including, but not limited to, restrictions, bylaws, rules and regulations, and a resale certificate from a property owners' association. A resale certificate contains information including, but not limited to, statements specifying the amount and frequency of regular assessments and the style and cause number of lawsuits to which the property owners' association is a party, other than lawsuits relating to unpaid ad valorem taxes of an individual member of the association. These documents must be made available to you by the property owners' association or the association's agent on your request.
If Buyer is concerned about these matters, the TREC promulgated Addendum for Property Subject to Mandatory Membership in a Property Owners Association(s) should be used.

MEMBERSHIP IN PROPERTY OWNERS ASSOCIATION(S): This subparagraph identifies whether the Property is or is not in one or more mandatory POAs. If it is, the Seller must provide a warning of that fact and let the Buyer know that as an owner of property covered by such an Association, membership is mandatory, homeowners are subject to rules and fees that could change, and failure to pay those fees can result in foreclosure on the property by a POA. You should always use the suggested Addendum for Property Located in a Property Owners' Association for two huge reasons. First, it can be used to limit the Buyers' exposure to the transfer fees charged by the POA to provide a resale certificate so the property can be sold. But even more importantly, it gives the Buyer the right to cancel the contract at any time if they do not *ever* receive the information [BUYER OUT #2], and gives a time frame for them to cancel the contract *for any reason* after having a chance to review the restrictions in the community [BUYER OUT #3] or if there is a change in rules between contract and closing [BUYER OUT #4]. These restrictions regulate conformity of appearance in neighborhoods, specifying particular exterior materials that can be used, but may be too restrictive for some Buyers in other ways. If a Buyer would like to put a solar water heater on their roof, one of the most cost-effective green retrofits available to homeowners today, most POAs do not allow them. If a Buyer drives a work truck with signage on it, he/she may be prohibited from overnight parking in the development, or even time enough to run home for a sandwich for lunch. Boat parking, RV parking, all are usually addressed. There are subdivisions that prohibit any parking of cars on the street, which may not be a problem now for your Buyers, but may be a real problem when their 10-year-old turns 16 and can finally drive. So make sure that you have your Buyer review the restrictions and help them to determine if they are going to be good for them.

(3) STATUTORY TAX DISTRICTS: If the Property is situated in a utility or other statutorily created district providing water, sewer, drainage, or flood control facilities and services, Chapter 49, Texas Water Code, requires Seller to deliver and Buyer to sign the statutory notice relating to the tax rate, bonded indebtedness, or standby fee of the district prior to final execution of this contract.

STATUTORY TAX DISTRICTS: If there is any entity that has taxing authority over the Property, the Buyer must be informed about that entity, its tax rates and its financial condition so that they can determine whether there might be an additional tax looming on the horizon.

(4) TIDE WATERS: If the Property abuts the tidally influenced waters of the state, §33.135, Texas Natural Resources Code, requires a notice regarding coastal area property to be included in the contract. An addendum containing the notice promulgated by TREC or required by the parties must be used.

TIDE WATERS: Notes that for coastal areas, the Buyer will receive an additional addendum, usually the ADDENDUM FOR COASTAL AREA PROPERTY which warns them that they will likely lose property due to actions of the water and/or the ADDENDUM FOR PROPERTY LOCATED SEAWARD OF THE GULF INTRACOASTAL WATERWAY; both addenda also specify where improvements may be placed relative to the vegetation line, and warn the Buyer that the State can force the removal of such buildings if the vegetation line moves behind the building due to natural actions of wind and water, to protect the dunes. We saw that happen with Hurricane Ike removing 50' of the beach area on Bolivar Peninsula on the south end of Galveston Island.

(5) ANNEXATION: If the Property is located outside the limits of a municipality, Seller notifies Buyer under §5.011, Texas Property Code, that the Property may now or later be included in the extraterritorial jurisdiction of a municipality and may now or later be subject to annexation by the municipality. Each municipality maintains a map that depicts its boundaries and extraterritorial jurisdiction. To determine if the Property is located within a municipality's extraterritorial jurisdiction or is likely to be located within a municipality's extraterritorial jurisdiction, contact all municipalities located in the general proximity of the Property for further information.

ANNEXATION: Warns the Buyer that if the Property is not currently within the boundaries of a municipality (a taxing authority), it may become so. It also describes the Extra Territorial Jurisdiction (ETJ) area, an area beyond the boundaries of cities that they have dibs on annexing at a later date, just in case some other city might be thinking of it.

---

(6) PROPERTY LOCATED IN A CERTIFICATED SERVICE AREA OF A UTILITY SERVICE PROVIDER: Notice required by §13.257, Water Code: The real property, described in Paragraph 2, that you are about to purchase may be located in a certificated water or sewer service area, which is authorized by law to provide water or sewer service to the properties in the certificated area. If your property is located in a certificated area there may be special costs or charges that you will be required to pay before you can receive water or sewer service. There may be a period required to construct lines or other facilities necessary to provide water or sewer service to your property. You are advised to determine if the property is in a certificated area and contact the utility service provider to determine the cost that you will be required to pay and the period, if any, that is required to provide water or sewer service to your property. The undersigned Buyer hereby acknowledges receipt of the foregoing notice at or before the execution of a binding contract for the purchase of the real property described in Paragraph 2 or at closing of purchase of the real property.

PROPERTY LOCATED IN A CERTIFICATED SERVICE AREA: This subparagraph warns the Buyer that if they are purchasing in such an area there may be a water hookup fee and additional fees required to run water and/or sewer service to the Property.

---

(7) PUBLIC IMPROVEMENT DISTRICTS: If the Property is in a public improvement district, §5.014, Property Code, requires Seller to notify Buyer as follows: As a purchaser of this parcel of real property you are obligated to pay an assessment to a municipality or county for an improvement project undertaken by a public improvement district under Chapter 372, Local Government Code. The assessment may be due annually or in periodic installments. More information concerning the amount of the assessment and the due dates of that assessment may be obtained from the municipality or county levying the assessment. The amount of the assessments is subject to change. Your failure to pay the assessments could result in a lien on and the foreclosure of your property.

PUBLIC IMPROVEMENT DISTRICTS: This subparagraph warns the Buyer that if they are purchasing Property in a Public Improvement District (created by the local government to pay for the initial construction and annual maintenance of an improvement that will only benefit very localized property owners, like sidewalks or putting sewer lines in where there were only septic systems.) It also warns them that if they fail to pay that assessment they could lose the property to foreclosure by that entity.

> **(8) TRANSFER FEES:** If the Property is subject to a private transfer fee obligation, §5.205, Property Code, requires Seller to notify Buyer as follows: The private transfer fee obligation may be governed by Chapter 5, Subchapter G of the Texas Property Code.

TRANSFER FEES: There was a brief period of time when developers figured out a way to have passive income far into the future, by charging a transfer fee every time the property changed hands. In perpetuity. This is, in fact, common in some states. The legislature passed a law outlawing the practice, so the Buyer is being notified that if they are purchasing a property that has such transfer fee language in the deed, it may have been overruled.

> **(9) PROPANE GAS SYSTEM SERVICE AREA:** If the Property is located in a propane gas system service area owned by a distribution system retailer, Seller must give Buyer written notice as required by §141.010, Texas Utilities Code. An addendum containing the notice approved by TREC or required by the parties should be used.

PROPANE GAS SYSTEM SERVICE AREA: Oh, those wily developers. After they were unable to use the transfer fee idea, some developers of large tracts installed a mega-tank for propane within the development, then required the builders who bought lots from them to design the houses they built use propane for heat and hot water. The requirements barred residents from installing their own small propane tank just for their property, so they had to purchase propane from the monopoly established by the developer. This didn't last long, when propane bills for hundreds of dollars per month were brought to legislators by their constituents. So again, laws were passed to prevent this scheme in the future. This subparagraph warns buyers that if they are purchasing in one of the developments that were established in this way, they must be warned with a special addendum, **Addendum for Property Located in a Propane Gas System Service Area**.

> **(10) NOTICE OF WATER LEVEL FLUCTUATIONS:** If the Property adjoins an impoundment of water, including a reservoir or lake, constructed and maintained under Chapter 11, Water Code, that has a storage capacity of at least 5,000 acre-feet at the impoundment's normal operating level, Seller hereby notifies Buyer: "The water level of the impoundment of water adjoining the Property fluctuates for various reasons, including as a result of: (1) an entity lawfully exercising its right to use the water stored in the impoundment; or (2) drought or flood conditions."

NOTICE OF WATER LEVEL FLUCTUATIONS: Yes, we have to warn buyers that if they are purchasing waterfront property, the water level will not stay constant, even in a "constant-level" lake. We can't manufacture water in a drought, nor remove water fast enough in a Texas flood sometimes.

PARAGRAPH 7: PROPERTY CONDITION

7.PROPERTY CONDITION:

A. ACCESS, INSPECTIONS AND UTILITIES: Seller shall permit Buyer and Buyer's agents access to the Property at reasonable times. Buyer may have the Property inspected by inspectors selected by Buyer and licensed by TREC or otherwise permitted by law to make inspections. Any hydrostatic testing must be separately authorized by Seller in writing. Seller at Seller's expense shall immediately cause existing utilities to be turned on and shall keep the utilities on during the time this contract is in effect.

PROPERTY CONDITION: ACCESS, INSPECTIONS AND UTILITIES: The Property Condition paragraph establishes the Buyers' rights to inspect the property, have it inspected by licensed inspectors, and have access for contractors should they need to have bids completed to determine the costs to make repairs revealed in the inspections. Sellers need to be aware that they must have the utilities on for these inspections to take place. Normally, if the house is vacant, the Seller has left the utilities on so that the house can be shown with lights and the temperature can be moderated to tolerable levels for potential buyers while they are initially viewing the home. A Listing Agent might need to remind the Seller to keep those utilities on once there is a signed contract. If the Seller is still occupying the house, this is a good time to point out to them that they need to make sure an inspector will have access to everything he/she needs to see, for example the water heater in the garage shouldn't be blocked off by boxes being packed for the move now that there is a moving date. AC plugs will all be checked, etc. Discourage turning utilities off after the inspections; in summer months temperatures and humidity can reach very high levels, encouraging mold growth, and cabinets can self-destruct when the wood glue comes apart in such conditions. Note: With foreclosed properties, the Seller is a bank, lender, or government entity like HUD. Often they do not keep utilities on for the sales period, since the less they pay out the better and because live water in a house could spring a leak and cause a lot of damage. In the case of no utilities, the Buyer is usually warned in a Special Addendum required by the foreclosing entity (these addenda are all different, not available here, but will be provided by the listing agent for the property) that the responsibility for turning on utilities for inspections is the Buyer's, and the Seller will not be responsible. A few municipalities and utility companies will turn on utilities for just one day at no charge, but most will require that your Buyer client pay any deposits and fulfill any application requirements to turn on the utilities, then order them turned off when no longer needed. In any case, *somebody* is going to have to meet the utility provider at the house to let them inside in case there is a leak in the water or gas. This is for you to work out with the Sellers' agent. Normally it falls to the Buyers' agent, but this is not cast in stone.

Hydrostatic testing is a fairly new inspection process, done when foundation damage is suspected and the house is on an early-era slab (mid-50s to mid-70s). Iron pipes were used in plumbing prior to the advent of PVC in the mid-70s, and iron exposed to water rusts and falls apart. This means that the sewer pipes may now be nonexistent, and the house is sitting on nothing but tunnels in the soil. Hydrostatic testing is a way to test the whole house pipelines using pressure, and damage could occur so it is required that the Seller agree in writing to this test, unlike other inspections. Use the **Addendum for Authorizing Hydrostatic Testing**, to make sure all parties understand who will be responsible for repairs that may be required following such testing prior to purchase.

B. SELLER'S DISCLOSURE NOTICE PURSUANT TO §5.008, TEXAS PROPERTY CODE (Notice): (Check one box only)

__(1) Buyer has received the Notice.

__(2) Buyer has not received the Notice. Within ___days after the effective date of this contract, Seller shall deliver the Notice to Buyer. If Buyer does not receive the Notice, Buyer may terminate this contract at any time prior to the closing and the earnest money will be refunded to Buyer. If Seller delivers the Notice, Buyer may terminate this contract for any reason within 7 days after Buyer receives the Notice or prior to the closing, whichever first occurs, and the earnest money will be refunded to Buyer.

__(3) The Seller is not required to furnish the notice under the Texas Property Code.

SELLER'S DISCLOSURE NOTICE: Big Buyer Out Here!

(1) indicates that the Buyer has received the Sellers Disclosure. *This is the only box you want checked as a Seller's Agent!!!* To understand why, please see (2).

(2) "Buyer has not received the notice..." This selection goes on to set a number of days that the Seller has to provide the Buyer with that notice. Let's say 2 days. Keep reading. If Buyer never receives the Notice, they can back out *at any time* and get their earnest money back [BUYER OUT #5]. Even if the Seller delivers the notice within our (suggested) 2-day time frame, *the contract gives the Buyer the option to back out of the contract for any reason for 7 days after they do receive it* [BUYER OUT #6]. In other words, this is like a free option period. Most local boards have MLS displays in which we can attach the completed Sellers Disclosure document in pdf form to the internet display of the listing so that it is available to any Buyer Agents drafting an offer. In multiple-offer situations when I want my Buyer client's offer to look more appealing than the competition, and the Sellers' agent has *not* made the Sellers Disclosure available to me by attaching it in the MLS, I use checkbox (2) and do not ask for an option period in Paragraph 23, Termination Option. This could make my offer appear stronger, the Seller possibly believing that my client is bound by the contract no matter what, since we didn't ask for an option period. What if you are the Seller's Agent and somebody tries to send you an offer with box (2) checked? Call the other agent, thank them kindly for the offer (always thank them--they have worked for at least 2-3 hours showing your listing and writing that offer, no matter how much it is)

and then let them know that your client can't accept an offer with 7(B)(2) checked. Tell them the Sellers Disclosure is available on the MLS or you can send it to them, but they need to print that out, have their Buyer review it, initial and sign it, then change 7(B) to (1) and re-send the entire offer. At that point you can present it to your Seller client. Of course, you must have cleared all this ahead of time with your client, usually during the listing agreement and again while this is going on.

(3) Seller is not required to furnish the Sellers Disclosure. There are strict limitations to this. According to the Texas Property Code, there are eleven situations of reselling a single-family home that eliminate the requirement for a Sellers Disclosure. The five that a real estate agent might be involved in would be:

1. Foreclosure, owned by a third party lender,

2. Executor/Administrator of an estate,

3. Public official if selling in the course of their job,

4. From one co-owner to another, and

5. A sale of a new home.

An unrepresented Seller must still provide the Sellers Disclosure Notice, an investor who lives in another country and has never been in the house must provide the Sellers Disclosure (and isn't there someone who has been overseeing that property who could provide the information?) There are at least 2 Seller Disclosure forms available, one from TREC and one available through the Texas Association of Realtors for their members. TREC's has the minimum required by law, and the TAR disclosure goes further with more questions about previous conditions. The TAR disclosure is preferred by most REALTORS®

C. SELLER'S DISCLOSURE OF LEAD-BASED PAINT AND LEAD-BASED PAINT HAZARDS is required by Federal law for a residential dwelling constructed prior to 1978.

C. SELLERS' DISCLOSURE OF LEAD-BASED PAINT HAZARDS: This is a separate disclosure that must be provided by the Seller for any Property built prior to 1978, when lead was outlawed in paint. Many brokers have a policy that requires agents to include properties built *in* 1978, just to be safe. It includes a provision for the Buyer to have the property inspected for lead, and to get out and get the earnest money back if lead is found. [BUYER OUT #7] More discussion of this addendum where it appears toward the end of the book.

D. ACCEPTANCE OF PROPERTY CONDITION: "As Is" means the present condition of the Property with any and all defects and without warranty except for the warranties of title and the warranties in this contract. Buyer's agreement to accept the Property As Is under Paragraph 7D(1) or (2) does not preclude Buyer from inspecting the

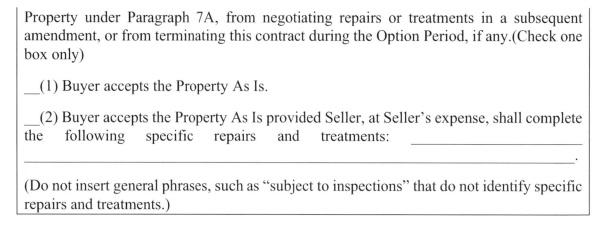

Property under Paragraph 7A, from negotiating repairs or treatments in a subsequent amendment, or from terminating this contract during the Option Period, if any.(Check one box only)

__(1) Buyer accepts the Property As Is.

__(2) Buyer accepts the Property As Is provided Seller, at Seller's expense, shall complete the following specific repairs and treatments: _____
_____ .

(Do not insert general phrases, such as "subject to inspections" that do not identify specific repairs and treatments.)

ACCEPTANCE OF PROPERTY CONDITION: Usually, you will be checking box (1) Buyer accepts the property in its current condition. This does not prevent your Client from asking for repairs in an amendment later, after they have had a chance to have the property inspected. Box (2) duplicates Box 1, then adds "provided Seller, at Seller's expense, shall complete the following specific repairs or treatments:" and has an area to fill those repairs in. If you see something that you would recommend having the seller repair, enter it here. This should only be used if your offering price includes repairs that are obvious. I focus on what I call The Big Four: roof, HVAC, foundation and termites. These will prevent the property from being insured for any Buyer. Including the repair in the offer is saying "OK, we'll give you X amount, but that's WITH a new roof," to make it clear the price offered is contingent on that repair being included. Do not rely on coming back with an amendment later to request obvious repairs, because "as is" means you are accepting all you can see on the property and on the Sellers' Disclosure at the time you make the offer. If you come back later and ask for something that you saw before the offer was made, what the Buyer is saying is, "OK, we now want you to replace the roof, which we knew it needed, for free." It's not fair to a Seller. Bad negotiating. You will cause an adversarial relationship, and what you want is collaboration in completing the transaction. It's not sneaky or smart to spring this on a Seller after they are under contract if you knew about it when you made the offer. It's the sign of a rookie negotiator trying to squeeze out a few more dollars instead of being up front. Listing agents are tired of too many repairs being asked for after contract, many of them unnecessary or just cosmetic, and clearly just a money grab. More and more are advising their seller clients to just say no, unless it's the Big Four or health/safety related and not bringing the property to current codes when it was built to code at its time. If you see it and you want it fixed, enter it in 7D(2).

Additionally, *any* other treatments you are requesting should go here, not in Special Provisions. Treatments would include things like having the septic system pumped out prior to closing and providing appropriate documentation showing completion of that. Please do not request treatments that are not deal-breakers, such as that the Seller have the Property professionally cleaned prior to delivering possession. That is insulting to a Seller, and you do not want to be insulting people in your first impression. Besides, that's an agent's decision to put that in there, not a buyer's. You are not in the decision-making business here. Your job is to inform your client and carry out their instructions. Get control of the property for your Buyer, then ask for changes if necessary. You could be losing the property for your client by advertising that you are going to be difficult to work with.

E. LENDER REQUIRED REPAIRS AND TREATMENTS: Unless otherwise agreed in writing, neither party is obligated to pay for lender-required repairs, which includes treatment for wood destroying insects. If the parties do not agree to pay for the lender required repairs or treatments, this contract will terminate and the earnest money will be refunded to Buyer. If the cost of lender required repairs and treatments exceeds 5% of the Sales Price, Buyer may terminate this contract and the earnest money will be refunded to Buyer.

LENDER REQUIRED REPAIRS AND TREATMENTS: This subparagraph provides for another buyer out [BUYER OUT #8] if required repairs (it would just about have to be one of the Big Four) exceed 5% of the Sales Price. 5% is a pretty big chunk. 5% of a $200,000 house is $10,000. This gives the Buyer the right to say, "Y'know, even if you make the repairs, that is such a big repair that I don't feel good about proceeding." Maybe it's foundation repair and they are rightly worried that cosmetic damage could occur while repairing the foundation, maybe they've just had an opportunity to assess their tolerance to risk that if that much repair is required there may be more deferred maintenance that is unseen at this point. Whatever the reason, they can get out and get their earnest money back. The lender is alerted to these repairs in the appraisal report. The lender doesn't see the property inspection, that's just between the Buyer and the inspector.

F. COMPLETION OF REPAIRS AND TREATMENTS: Unless otherwise agreed in writing: (i) Seller shall complete all agreed repairs and treatments prior to the Closing Date; and (ii) all required permits must be obtained, and repairs and treatments must be performed by persons who are licensed to provide such repairs or treatments or, if no license is required by law, are commercially engaged in the trade of providing such repairs or treatments. At Buyer's election, any transferable warranties received by Seller with respect to the repairs and treatments will be transferred to Buyer at Buyer's expense. If Seller fails to complete any agreed repairs and treatments prior to the Closing Date, Buyer may exercise remedies under Paragraph 15 or extend the Closing Date up to 5 days if necessary for Seller to complete the repairs and treatments.

COMPLETION OF REPAIRS AND TREATMENTS: States that if any repairs are agreed to be completed during the process, the Seller will do so legally, with proper permits and using licensed contractors if the state licenses them in that type of work. *Texas has no license for general contractors or remodelers.* Plumbers, yes, electricians, yes. But not general contractors or remodelers. This requirement can really annoy a Seller who is him/herself an electrician or plumber if they have to hire another licensed plumber to replace a set of washers in a lavatory sink just because they didn't pay attention to it and do it before they put the house on the market or go through the house once again before the inspection to see if anything can be eliminated that would end up on an inspection report. But do remember that the parties can agree in writing that a licensed contractor is not required. This subparagraph further authorizes the Buyer to complete the repairs if the Seller can't/won't (this can become critical if the house can't be insured without the repair, because without an insurance binder the lender won't lend the money), and to even extend the Closing Date by 15 days if they need it to have the work completed.

G. ENVIRONMENTAL MATTERS: Buyer is advised that the presence of wetlands, toxic substances, including asbestos and wastes or other environmental hazards, or the presence of a threatened or endangered species or its habitat may affect Buyer's intended use of the Property. If Buyer is concerned about these matters, an addendum promulgated by TREC or required by the parties should be used.

ENVIRONMENTAL MATTERS: Advises the Buyer that if they are concerned about environmental matters, they also have the right to have the property inspected for those. There is an **ENVIRONMENTAL ASSESSMENT, THREATENED OR ENDANGERED SPECIES AND WETLANDS ADDENDUM** to use for this to establish a specific number of days for those inspections. This addendum provides for 3 more Buyer Outs, one for each condition [BUYER OUTS # 9,10,11] and appears later in this book.

H. RESIDENTIAL SERVICE CONTRACTS: Buyer may purchase a residential service contract from a residential service company licensed by TREC. If Buyer purchases a residential service contract, Seller shall reimburse Buyer at closing for the cost of the residential service contract in an amount not exceeding $_____. Buyer should review any residential service contract for the scope of coverage, exclusions and limitations. The purchase of a residential service contract is optional. Similar coverage may be purchased from various companies authorized to do business in Texas.

RESIDENTIAL SERVICE CONTRACTS: These are often called 'home warranties', but Texas doesn't want us to refer to them as 'warranties' because they are not. They are service contracts because they provide repair/replacement of certain systems and appliances in the house but every instance requires a service call fee, generally $60-80. These service contracts are not required, but we do strongly encourage their use. They can eliminate irate phone calls and small claims suits for minor repairs in the first few months after the sale. It is as if the Seller is saying, "Look, Mr. and Mrs. Buyer, we think everything is in good shape, but just to put your mind at ease we will provide this residential service contract to take care of repairs in the first year."

If the Seller still refuses to go along, just tell them, "This gives them someone else's phone number to call when something breaks." That's usually the end of the reluctance. The amount should be sufficient to cover the best plan offered, otherwise it will not cover the very thing that breaks. That is generally the 'Diamond' plan, the 'Platinum' plan, etc. As of this writing, these cost approximately $500. If the Property has a pool or hot tub, there will be an additional rider to cover those, and larger homes have slightly higher costs. More than likely, the Buyer's Agent will be providing the names of three or more of these companies to their Buyer Client to research and choose one. Then the Buyer's Agent will notify the Title Company of the desired company and plan.

I think it's important to do business with people you know, so I refer companies whose reps' faces I see regularly, either in my office or contributing to the real estate community by sponsoring educational events at their Realtor® association or perhaps serving on boards/committees there. This has come in handy when I had an agent whose client did not add the hot tub rider when it was offered for additional cost at the closing. Guess what broke within a year? I was able to call my local rep for the company to see if they could do anything to help, as this client was very angry and very sure he had never been offered such a rider. And maybe he wasn't, although it's clear on the company's website. My local rep said he would see if there was anything he could do, then called back and said that if our client would pay for the rider, they would make it retroactive 10 months back to the closing and cover the repair. If I had not known the rep, and provided them with 10-20 sales per year, I would not have received this level of service. There are two related businesses that need us more than we need them: title companies and residential service contract companies. They can't really market directly to the public. "Come close your next property with us!" just doesn't provide that urgency to pick up the phone. So the only way they get business is through real estate agents. Let your clients know that although lenders, title companies and residential service contract companies are happy to have their business, *you* are their long-term source for business. Although it is certainly not required, when they use people you recommend you have a better chance of being able to help them down the road if problems occur.

PARAGRAPH 8: BROKERS' FEES

8. BROKERS' FEES: All obligations of the parties for payment of brokers' fees are contained in separate written agreements.

BROKERS' FEES: Simply mentions that all brokers' fees are contained in other agreements, which would be the Listing Agreement and the Broker Rep Agreement. The point to remember is that a broker or broker's agent cannot renegotiate their commission in the contract, as that commission was offered from one broker to another via the MLS. The brokers are not parties to the contract, only the Buyer and Seller are. To change the commission one would need to use the **REGISTRATION AGREEMENT BETWEEN BROKERS** form, available through TAR.

PARAGRAPH 9: CLOSING

9. CLOSING:

A. The closing of the sale will be on or before _____, 20__, or within 7 days after objections made under Paragraph 6D have been cured or waived, whichever date is later (Closing Date). If either party fails to close the sale by the Closing Date, the non-defaulting party may exercise the remedies contained in Paragraph 15.

B. At closing:

(1) Seller shall execute and deliver a general warranty deed conveying title to the Property to Buyer and showing no additional exceptions to those permitted in Paragraph 6 and furnish tax statements or certificates showing no delinquent taxes on the Property.

(2) Buyer shall pay the Sales Price in good funds acceptable to the escrow agent.

(3) Seller and Buyer shall execute and deliver any notices, statements, certificates, affidavits, releases, loan documents and other documents reasonably required for the closing of the sale and the issuance of the Title Policy.

(4) There will be no liens, assessments, or security interests against the Property which will not be satisfied out of the sales proceeds unless securing the payment of any loans assumed by Buyer and assumed loans will not be in default.

(5) If the Property is subject to a residential lease, Seller shall transfer security deposits (as defined under §92.102, Property Code), if any, to Buyer. In such an event, Buyer shall deliver to the tenant a signed statement acknowledging that the Buyer has acquired the Property and is responsible for the return of the security deposit, and specifying the exact dollar amount of the security deposit.

CLOSING: Paragraph 9 specifies the 'on or before' date for the closing and what will take place then, meaning the Seller will provide a general warranty deed free of liens, proof that taxes have been paid, any security deposits held for leases, and Buyer will provide good funds in the amount agreed. The only thing to enter here is the date; if you use a date that is later than you actually intend to close (possibly a good practice, so that you don't have to extend the contract if you don't make the deadline for some reason), you do need to alert the other parties of your intention. The title company and the lender will look at this date and back up from it the time they need to prepare documentation. Then they will file it until that time. So if you intend to close on the 27th and you have entered the 30th here, let both of those entities know in writing and get their confirmation in writing that they are aware of the new target date.

B(1) contains [BUYER OUT #12], in the event the Seller cannot deliver a general warranty deed, but only a special warranty deed. This is not uncommon, since most properties that have ever been foreclosed on were transferred with the more specific special warranty deed. The trustee who delivers the property on behalf of the lender to the new owner is thus not guaranteeing clear title for the entire life of the property, just for the period of time the trustee held it after the bank's foreclosure. But once that chain of title guarantee, or 'warranty' has been broken, most title companies will not revert back to the general warranty as it exposes them to title problems in the future. In some states, there are checkboxes to indicate whether the Seller will be providing a general or a special warranty deed, but not in Texas. If you wanted to make sure as a listing agent that you closed this loophole (if your Seller has a property with a special warranty deed), you could indicate in Special Provisions that the Seller will deliver a special warranty deed and that would override the verbiage in this paragraph. B (2,3,4) are self-explanatory, but if the property is under a current lease the signed statement mentioned here can be completed with the form available from TAR as NOTICE TO TENANT OF CHANGE IN MANAGEMENT AND ACCOUNTABILITY FOR SECURITY DEPOSIT.

PARAGRAPH 10: POSSESSION

10.POSSESSION:

A. Buyer's Possession: Seller shall deliver to Buyer possession of the Property in its present or required condition, ordinary wear and tear excepted: ___upon closing and funding ___ according to a temporary residential lease form promulgated by TREC or other written lease required by the parties. Any possession by Buyer prior to closing or by Seller after closing which is not authorized by a written lease will establish a tenancy at sufferance relationship between the parties. Consult your insurance agent prior to change of ownership and possession because insurance coverage may be limited or terminated. The absence of a written lease or appropriate insurance coverage may expose the parties to economic loss.

B. Leases:

(1)After the Effective Date, Seller may not execute any lease (including but not limited to mineral leases) or convey any interest in the Property without Buyer's written consent.

(2) If the Property is subject to any lease to which Seller is a party, Seller shall deliver to Buyer copies of the lease(s) and any move-in condition form signed by the tenant within 7 days after the Effective Date of the contract.

POSSESSION: Will the possession of the property be delivered at funding? Or will the Seller get a few days to pack their final belongings into a van and watch it drive down the street? Most Sellers obviously prefer the latter if possible. I often put in my agent viewable description in the MLS that "Seller *requests* a 7-day leaseback." Not a deal-breaker if you can't do it, but it would be nice if your Buyer can accommodate it. Use a 100% loan PITI payment and divide it by the number of days in the month to calculate a fair daily rental rate to suggest. Most Buyers, if they are first-time Buyers and leasing their current residence, are happy to oblige, particularly when they receive $400-500 from the Seller at closing for those few days. There are problems to watch out for in this situation. Buyer Reps: make sure you have a substantial deposit in place and complete a thorough walk-through on the day the Seller delivers possession before releasing that deposit. In other words, the Seller will still be occupying the Property on closing day, and a couch can cover up a really big hole in the carpet. Additionally, lots of sheetrock damage can take place when moving large pieces of furniture out of a house, particularly in the stairwell of a 2-story house. So do get that BUYER WALK-THROUGH AND ACCEPTANCE OF CONDITION form (TAR) completed for your file. Seller Reps: Ask the Buyers' Agent for a copy of that form for your file, so that you have a written record of the Buyer's acceptance on the date the Seller delivered possession. Discussion of these temporary leases is in a later section.

PARAGRAPH 11: SPECIAL PROVISIONS

> **11. SPECIAL PROVISIONS:** (Insert only factual statements and business details applicable to the sale. TREC rules prohibit license holders from adding factual statements or business details for which a contract addendum, lease or other form has been promulgated by TREC for mandatory use.)

SPECIAL PROVISIONS: Careful, careful, careful! This is the paragraph where you can get yourself in trouble for the unauthorized practice of law and it's usually because you are just trying to help. You must not enter anything in Special Provisions that would be covered in a TREC promulgated addendum. Here is a list of more common entries:

1. A legal description that would not fit in Paragraph 2.

2. Additional Buyers or Sellers whose names would not fit in Paragraph 1.

3. A deadline for an offer to be considered effective.

This list is not exhaustive, but you get the picture. NOT MUCH. Watching this paragraph's area for entering details shrink over the past versions of the contract has been a clear indication of TREC's view on this. Here are some details that would NOT appear in Special Provisions and need to be covered in a promulgated addendum: personal property conveyed with the real property (there is a NON-REALTY ITEMS ADDENDUM but its use is not recommended as lenders often want the items removed from the sale), Seller or Buyer leases after or before closing (use SELLERS TEMPORARY RESIDENTIAL LEASE or BUYERS TEMPORARY RESIDENTIAL LEASE), that the purchase is contingent on the sale of the Buyer's Property (use ADDENDUM FOR SALE OF OTHER PROPERTY BY BUYER), conveyance of mineral rights (use ADDENDUM FOR RESERVATION OF OIL, GAS, AND OTHER MINERALS), or that the contract is contingent on the lender's approval in the case of a Short Sale (use SHORT SALE ADDENDUM). In addition, here is a list of BAD entries in Special Provisions for which there is no other form:

1. "Time is of the essence". This is a powerful phrase, called a 'term of art' in law. It is an instruction to judges in any future suit based on breach of that condition that they cannot rule according to their subjective opinion of what would be reasonable, it's out of their hands. You would be flat out practicing law without a license to use it.

2. Anything indicating that the purchase is part of a lease-purchase, lease-option or lease-to-own transaction. Texas licensees are NOT allowed to construct these agreements. The reason for this, if you'll remember, is that TREC and the Texas Real Estate License Act were created to protect the consumer, and the consumer is the Buyer. In a Lease Purchase arrangement, the rent is usually above market rate and the Seller deposits the additional money in an escrow account. At the end of the year--presto!--the Seller withdraws the money and credits it to the Tenant-now-Buyer to apply toward the purchase of the Property. So, yes, you could write a one-year lease, and you could write a purchase contract with a one-year close date (but if a title company sees more than 180 days, they're going to start asking questions), but *you cannot tie them together in Special Provisions* nor force the

Seller to escrow that money. An attorney would be required to create a 'middle' document, one that ties the lease and the purchase together and requires specific behavior and accountability of the Seller. If that agreement is not in place, guess what happens? Right! The Seller just uses that money and can't come up with it at the end, or finds some reason to negate the lease and keep the additional money, etc, etc, etc. I am telling you all of this so that you will know what to say when someone asks you if you can help them find a lease-purchase. What they are really saying is, "I don't want to move twice." And Lordy, I know what they mean. But if you can explain what a lease purchase is, and that they would pay $2-300 additional per month, they will likely want to hire you to go ahead and help them find a regular lease property for now. You just stay in touch with them and help them buy in a year, because they are really just saying, "I can't qualify for a loan now but I will be able to in a year."

3. Escalation Clause. This tactic is not technically illegal, but it is skirting so near it and it's so easy to fall into practicing law to write it and try to cover all the variables you should stay away from it. An escalation clause is something that has been written by the Buyer Agent in an offer in which they feel they will have a lot of competition. It says something like, "Seller shall ignore any amount in Paragraph 3C and insert $1000 above any other offer." The agent hasn't made all the other changes that relate to that dollar figure, possibly writing an invalid contract because the math doesn't work. How would the Buyer's Agent force the Seller's Agent to provide proof of the other offer that triggered the increase? And what is the limit of the Buyer's exposure to increases? With TREC, you only get points for coloring INSIDE the lines, so don't get creative here. TREC's view is that the possibility that the Buyer could be treated unfairly is too great. And if the Buyer loses out on the property and wants to sue the Seller to provide the documentation, you could find yourself in the witness box explaining why you didn't think you were practicing law just to advise it, much less write it.

PARAGRAPH 12:

SETTLEMENT AND OTHER EXPENSES

12. SETTLEMENT AND OTHER EXPENSES:

A. The following expenses must be paid at or prior to closing:

(1) Expenses payable by Seller (Seller's Expenses):

(a) Releases of existing liens, including prepayment penalties and recording fees; release of Seller's loan liability; tax statements or certificates; preparation of deed; one-half of escrow fee; and other expenses payable by Seller under this contract.

(b) Seller shall also pay an amount not to exceed $_____ to be applied in the following order: Buyer's Expenses which Buyer is prohibited from paying by FHA, VA, Texas Veterans Land Board or other governmental loan programs, and then to other Buyer's Expenses as allowed by the lender.

(2) Expenses payable by Buyer (Buyer's Expenses): Appraisal fees; loan application fees; origination charges; credit reports; preparation of loan documents; interest on the notes from date of disbursement to one month prior to dates of first monthly payments; recording fees; copies of easements and restrictions; loan title policy with endorsements required by lender; loan-related inspection fees; photos; amortization schedules; one-half of escrow fee; all prepaid items, including required premiums for flood and hazard insurance, reserve deposits for insurance, ad valorem taxes and special governmental assessments; final compliance inspection; courier fee; repair inspection; underwriting fee; wire transfer fee; expenses incident to any loan; Private Mortgage Insurance Premium (PMI), VA Loan Funding Fee, or FHA Mortgage Insurance Premium (MIP) as required by the lender; and other expenses payable by Buyer under this contract.

B. If any expense exceeds an amount expressly stated in this contract for such expense to be paid by a party, that party may terminate this contract unless the other party agrees to pay such excess. Buyer may not pay charges and fees expressly prohibited by FHA, VA, Texas Veterans Land Board or other governmental loan program regulations.

SETTLEMENT AND OTHER EXPENSES: Ah, yes. Paragraph 12. When Listing Agents receive an offer, they look at Paragraph 3C to see the Sales Price amount, then flip-flip-flip to Paragraph 12 before they get excited, to see if the Sellers' net is going to be reduced by paying part of the proceeds back to the Buyer for Buyer Expenses. Paragraph 12 lists all of the possible expenses of a Buyer that can be covered by the Seller, and then at the end adds, "and other expenses payable by Buyer…" to cover anything else not mentioned specifically. Makes you wonder what the point of the list was.

It is not abnormal to have an amount here in the lower price ranges, especially with FHA loans designed for folks who would have a hard time qualifying for a conventional loan. The maximum would be 3% for conventional (owner-occupied), 4% for VA, and 6% for FHA, but in practice most lenders are not going to want there to be more than 3% here for any loan. Their investors in the secondary market do not want to purchase loans with that much money not actually in the property. And don't forget the property has to appraise to cover the full amount, including this part paid toward the buyer's expenses.

Occasionally a Seller has a hard time understanding that this is not money coming out of their pocket. It never goes into their pocket. It comes from the proceeds at closing and is a way for the buyer to structure their loan to cover expenses and closing costs they don't have. You may need to help your Seller (and sometimes the listing agent, unfortunately) see that they are being offered the difference between the Sales Price in 3(C) and what is entered in Paragraph 12. That's the offer.

36

Part B contains some description about charges and fees prohibited by FHA, VA, Texas Vet and other governmental loan programs, but currently there are virtually no expenses that the Buyer is precluded from paying. Please see the full discussion in the Third Party Financing Addendum section.

PARAGRAPH 13: PRORATIONS

13. PRORATIONS: Taxes for the current year, interest, maintenance fees, assessments, dues and rents will be prorated through the Closing Date. The tax proration may be calculated taking into consideration any change in exemptions that will affect the current year's taxes. If taxes for the current year vary from the amount prorated at closing, the parties shall adjust the prorations when tax statements for the current year are available. If taxes are not paid at or prior to closing, Buyer shall pay taxes for the current year.

PRORATIONS: The property taxes, HOA fees, assessments, dues or rents are prorated through Closing Day, with the Seller responsible for that day. The tax proration "may be calculated taking into consideration any change in exemptions that will affect the current year's taxes." These days, the Tax Assessor's office *is* taking advantage of this. Although back in the day the Buyer may have been able to enjoy the lower taxes that include a homestead or senior exemption for the rest of they year, now they are much more meticulous about changing the tax rate midyear for the new owner. Taxes are figured using the previous year's tax amount until the current year's new tax assessed values are certified, around September. If the tax amount varies from the previous year, it is up to the Buyer and Seller to contact each other and settle up. There's just no other way to handle all of the transactions that occur prior to the September-December time frame. So the Seller is going to pay the Buyer at closing for their portion of the year, and the Buyer is going to pay all of the taxes when payable at the end of the year, unless the closing occurs after August and the title company can just go ahead and pay the taxes to the county clerk on behalf of both parties directly. It's good to point out to the Seller that the HUD-1 Settlement Statement will be their only record of paying property taxes for that year; it's even better to send them a copy of their HUD-1 in January to give to their accountant for their income taxes as a deduction after they have packed it away and have no idea where it is. Be a hero. If the Seller has a loan in which the taxes and insurance are escrowed from their monthly payment so that their mortgage company can pay those two bills when due, they may be unhappily surprised about this part. They will be paying those taxes at closing out of their proceeds, and will get the balance sitting in their loan escrow account about 30 days after closing when their lender has settled out their lien release.

PARAGRAPH 14: CASUALTY LOSS

14. CASUALTY LOSS: If any part of the Property is damaged or destroyed by fire or other casualty after the effective date of this contract, Seller shall restore the Property to its previous condition as soon as reasonably possible, but in any event by the Closing Date. If Seller fails to do so due to factors beyond Seller's control, Buyer may (a) terminate this contract and the earnest money will be refunded to Buyer (b) extend the time for performance up to 15 days and the Closing Date will be extended as necessary or (c) accept the Property in its damaged condition with an assignment of insurance proceeds, if permitted by Seller's insurance carrier, and receive credit from Seller at closing in the amount of the deductible under the insurance policy. Seller's obligations under this paragraph are independent of any other obligations of Seller under this contract.

CASUALTY LOSS: If the property is damaged or destroyed by fire or other casualty between the effective contract date and closing, the Seller has a chance to restore the property to its 'previous condition' in time for the closing or the Buyer can terminate and get the earnest money back [BUYER OUT #13]. The Buyer may also choose to give the Seller more time to complete repairs, or accept the property and the insurance proceeds and deductible to complete the repair him/herself.

PARAGRAPH 15: DEFAULT

15. DEFAULT: If Buyer fails to comply with this contract, Buyer will be in default, and Seller may (a) enforce specific performance, seek such other relief as may be provided by law, or both, or (b) terminate this contract and receive the earnest money as liquidated damages, thereby releasing both parties from this contract. If Seller fails to comply with this contract, Seller will be in default and Buyer may (a) enforce specific performance, seek such other relief as may be provided by law, or both, or (b) terminate this contract and receive the earnest money, thereby releasing both parties from this contract.

DEFAULT: This describes how one party defaults on the contract, and what the remedies are for the non-defaulting party. Basically, if the Seller refuses to sell or the Buyer refuses to buy, the other party can sue them for specific performance (to force them to complete what they said they would do in the contract), or terminate the contract and receive the earnest money as liquidated damages. Let's say a Buyer is wanting out and for some reason can't do it in one of the many reasons discussed in this book. The Seller could sue them to compel the Buyer to complete the purchase. More often, the Seller sues for "other relief as may be provided by law". For example, I heard of a case in which a Buyer backed out, breaking the contract, and the seller ultimately sold the house for $40,000 less. The Seller had filed the lawsuit promptly after the first contract fell apart, and then amended the amount to the $40,000 when they closed the second contract, proving that was their loss. The Seller's Broker and Buyer's Broker joined the suit and were paid in addition to that $40,000 difference. With legal fees and court costs, it cost that Buyer $60,000. So do counsel your clients; this is serious and costly and should not be threatened frivolously.

In the opposite case of a Buyer having to sue a Seller to compel the Seller to complete the sale, sometimes a Seller may make some noise about not going through with the sale because they feel they could have sold the house for more, especially if they got a quick offer at list price. Maybe yes, maybe no. Usually, it's just kismet that the right buyer(s) are in the market when their house goes on the market and their real estate agent does a good job of the initial marketing. At any rate, a brief phone call to any attorney will usually settle them down, as this contract is very clear on the issue of default and they will be liable for attorney's fees, court costs, and the earnest money. When this is pointed out, it's usually a quick decision to proceed with the sale.

PARAGRAPH 16. MEDIATION

> **16. MEDIATION:** It is the policy of the State of Texas to encourage resolution of disputes through alternative dispute resolution procedures such as mediation. Any dispute between Seller and Buyer related to this contract which is not resolved through informal discussion will be submitted to a mutually acceptable mediation service or provider. The parties to the mediation shall bear the mediation costs equally. This paragraph does not preclude a party from seeking equitable relief from a court of competent jurisdiction.

MEDIATION: The use of mediation to resolve conflicts down the road has become a standard precursor to filing a lawsuit. It is usually the first question asked by a judge, "Have you completed mediation?" If not, the judge will send the parties off to mediate before litigating. Mediation is only used if the parties cannot resolve their dispute through their Brokers and is not binding like arbitration, meaning if they do not like the result of the mediation process, they are free to go ahead and file suit. Mediation is a good process and it works to benefit both parties. The mediator is basically a disinterested third party, a trained listener and conflict resolver, who is paid their reasonable charge (maybe $2-300) to get the parties together and listen to each side's version of the story and, more importantly, what they want. It's often when hearing what the other side wants that a party says, "Oh, that's not so bad. We can do that." We tend to imagine the worst-case scenario without that simple step. Having a calm third party provide a place to hear the story without the heat of disagreements can make the difference.

PARAGRAPH 17: ATTORNEY'S FEES

> **17. ATTORNEY'S FEES:** A Buyer, Seller, Listing Broker, Other Broker, or escrow agent who prevails in any legal proceeding related to this contract is entitled to recover reasonable attorney's fees and all costs of such proceeding.

ATTORNEY'S FEES: And then if they go on and sue anyway after mediation, the loser has to pay the winner's attorney's fees and court costs.

PARAGRAPH 18: ESCROW

> **18. ESCROW:**

A. ESCROW: The escrow agent is not (i) a party to this contract and does not have liability for the performance or nonperformance of any party to this contract, (ii) liable for interest on the earnest money and (iii) liable for the loss of any earnest money caused by the failure of any financial institution in which the earnest money has been deposited unless the financial institution is acting as escrow agent.

ESCROW: This paragraph describes what 'escrow agent' means, and provides for the process of getting the earnest money from the escrow agent if the transaction fails. Normally, we use title companies as escrow agents in Texas. The same title company who is the escrow agent also handles the settlement, performs the actual closing, and sells the title insurance policy.

The title company is not on your side, not on their side, they are a neutral third party who is going to hold that earnest money in escrow until both sides give them mutual instructions on what to do with it, whether to apply it to the funds used at closing or divide it up in the case of a fail.

B. EXPENSES: At closing, the earnest money must be applied first to any cash down payment, then to Buyer's Expenses and any excess refunded to Buyer. If no closing occurs, escrow agent may: (i) require a written release of liability of the escrow agent from all parties, (ii) require payment of unpaid expenses incurred on behalf of a party, and (iii) only deduct from the earnest money the amount of unpaid expenses incurred on behalf of the party receiving the earnest money.

EXPENSES: This subparagraph explains what will happen to the earnest money at closing, then begins to outline the process and money trail that will happen if the closing doesn't occur. First, the title company will require a written release of liability from all parties before they do anything. Second, they will pay any expenses incurred. These could be invoices for surveying, for subdivision information from an HOA, for septic inspections, etc. But third, they will only deduct those expenses for each party from their rightful portion of the earnest money, not pay every outstanding invoice first and then divide what's left.

C. DEMAND: Upon termination of this contract, either party or the escrow agent may send a release of earnest money to each party and the parties shall execute counterparts of the release and deliver same to the escrow agent. If either party fails to execute the release, either party may make a written demand to the escrow agent for the earnest money. If only one party makes written demand for the earnest money, escrow agent shall promptly provide a copy of the demand to the other party. If escrow agent does not receive written objection to the demand from the other party within 15 days, escrow agent may disburse the earnest money to the party making demand reduced by the amount of unpaid expenses incurred on behalf of the party receiving the earnest money and escrow agent may pay the same to the creditors. If escrow agent complies with the provisions of this paragraph, each party hereby releases escrow agent from all adverse claims related to the disbursal of the earnest money.

DEMAND: The first sentence here starts the how-to of getting the earnest money from the title company. "Execute counterparts" means that the Buyer(s) and Seller(s) can each sign a separate Release of Earnest Money form and the two documents will be viewed the same as one document signed by both parties. This is not allowed on any other document in the contract process, just in case you were wondering. Only here. All the rest of the contract documents require both parties' signatures on the same page. First one of the parties initiates the release of the earnest money by sending a "written demand" to the escrow agent. That is customarily done using the TAR form Release of Earnest Money; interestingly, TREC doesn't have a form for the earnest money release that also releases the title company from any future claims. Even though the contract states the same thing, title companies want to have a separate form with date and signatures specifically for that purpose.

TREC does have a form for terminating the contract, <u>NOTICE OF BUYER'S TERMINATION OF CONTRACT</u>, which allows for specifying the reason for termination.

Once the specific release of earnest money instructions are sent, via TAR form or otherwise, the escrow agent then sends a copy to the other party, and if that escrow agent doesn't receive a response within 15 days, they are authorized to release the earnest money (less expenses) to the demanding party.

Subparagraph D warns of the consequences of stonewalling signing the release, including that the person refusing to sign is liable for not only the earnest money but the costs of suing to get it.

Subparagraph E just says that all notices can be sent via email, fax, mail or hand-delivered to the addresses shown in Paragraph 21 (coming up) and considered as valid as the original.

PARAGRAPH 19: REPRESENTATIONS

> **19. REPRESENTATIONS:** All covenants, representations and warranties in this contract survive closing. If any representation of Seller in this contract is untrue on the Closing Date, Seller will be in default. Unless expressly prohibited by written agreement, Seller may continue to show the Property and receive, negotiate and accept back up offers.

REPRESENTATIONS: Two things: First, if the Seller has misrepresented anything *in the contract* (like liens against the property, claims against title, etc.) he/she will be in default. Note that the property condition as disclosed in the Sellers Disclosure is not strictly covered here as that disclosure is not technically part of the contract. Secondly, 'unless expressly prohibited', the Seller can continue to show the property and receive backup offers. In our MLS system, you have a choice of "P" for Pending and "PB" for Pending Taking Backups. I always choose PB right up until closing. Not that it makes a lot of difference for the general public. Being under contract effectively shuts down showings, because most Realtors® want to show properties that are fully available. But you never know, your listing could be the only perfect house for someone and you don't want to discourage anyone from looking at it if it fits the bill.

PARAGRAPH 20: FEDERAL TAX REQUIREMENTS

20. FEDERAL TAX REQUIREMENTS: If Seller is a "foreign person," as defined by applicable law, or if Seller fails to deliver an affidavit to Buyer that Seller is not a "foreign person," then Buyer shall withhold from the sales proceeds an amount sufficient to comply with applicable tax law and deliver the same to the Internal Revenue Service together with appropriate tax forms. Internal Revenue Service regulations require filing written reports if currency in excess of specified amounts is received in the transaction.

FEDERAL TAX REQUIREMENTS: A "foreign person" means someone who is not part of the US federal tax system and does not have reporting requirements to the IRS, so that it can be determined if they owe taxes on any capital gains from the sale of the property i.e. someone who does not have a Social Security number or a green card. The paragraph then states that the "Buyer shall withhold from sales proceeds an amount sufficient to comply with applicable tax law and deliver the same to the IRS…" Of course, the Buyer is not actually going to do this, the title company/escrow agent is going to do it for them. The law states that this applies to properties sold above $300,000, but in practice the title company will do it for any transaction. I once sold a $6000 lot, and since the owner was Japanese and living in Japan, the title company assumed that she was a foreign person and entered a held out amount of $600 on the HUD-1 statement. I had the Seller contact them and provide her Social Security number, which she did have, and they removed it.

There is also a sentence regarding currency in excess of specified amounts requiring written reports. This is due to Homeland Security requirements for tracking large sums of money to prevent money-laundering by terrorists. The written reports include serial numbers of all of the bills used; this is why title companies never want to receive cash in any amount.

PARAGRAPH 21: NOTICES

21. NOTICES: All notices from one party to the other must be in writing and are effective when mailed to, hand-delivered at, or transmitted by fax or electronic transmission as follows:

To Buyer at:_____ To Seller at:_____

_____ _____

Phone: _____ Phone:_____

Fax: _____ Fax:_____

E-mail:_____ E-mail:_____

NOTICES: This paragraph provides spaces for the Principals' contact information, and will be used primarily by the title company but also for any notices to be received by either party. It is extremely important that this information is filled in because absent an address, the notices will be sent to the Broker's agent for that party. Delivery to the agent (Broker--but you are the agent for the Broker) is the same as delivery to the principal. Don't make yourself or your Broker responsible for delivering timely information!

PARAGRAPH 22: AGREEMENT OF PARTIES

22. AGREEMENT OF PARTIES: This contract contains the entire agreement of the parties and cannot be changed except by their written agreement. Addenda which are a part of this contract are (Check all applicable boxes):

__Third Party Financing Addendum
__Seller Financing Addendum
__Addendum for Property Subject to Mandatory Membership in a Property Owners
     Association
__Buyer's Temporary Residential Lease
__Loan Assumption Addendum
__Addendum for Sale of Other Property by Buyer
__Addendum for Reservation of Oil, Gas and Other Minerals
__Addendum for "Back-Up" Contract
__Addendum for Coastal Area Property
__Addendum for Authorizing Hydrostatic Testing
__Addendum Concerning Right to Terminate Due to Lender's Appraisal
__Environmental Assessment, Threatened or Endangered Species and Wetlands
     Addendum
__Seller's Temporary Residential Lease
__Short Sale Addendum
__Addendum for Property Located Seaward of the Gulf Intracoastal Waterway
__Addendum for Seller's Disclosure of Information on Lead-based Paint and Lead-based
     Paint Hazards as Required by Federal Law
__Addendum for Property in a Propane Gas System Service Area
__Other (list):_____

AGREEMENT OF PARTIES: Frequently-used addenda are easily made a legal part of the contract by checking the appropriate box in this list, and a blank checkbox for "Other" is included as well. This most commonly includes an "Exhibit A" of Field Notes from a survey to convey the property via a metes-and-bounds description if the legal description is currently not specific enough, or a "Special Addendum" provided by a bank or other foreclosing entity that overrides certain parts of our contract. There are links to all of these addenda and some discussion for each, with the most-often-used Third Party Financing Addendum explained paragraph by paragraph following this discussion of the contract.

PARAGRAPH 23: TERMINATION OPTION

> **23. TERMINATION OPTION:** For nominal consideration, the receipt of which is hereby acknowledged by Seller, and Buyer's agreement to pay Seller $_____ (Option Fee) within 3 days after the effective date of this contract, Seller grants Buyer the unrestricted right to terminate this contract by giving notice of termination to Seller within days after the effective date of this contract (Option Period). Notices under this paragraph must be given by 5:00 p.m. (local time where the Property is located) by the date specified. If no dollar amount is stated as the Option Fee or if Buyer fails to pay the Option Fee to Seller within the time prescribed, this paragraph will not be a part of this contract and Buyer shall not have the unrestricted right to terminate this contract. If Buyer gives notice of termination within the time prescribed, the Option Fee will not be refunded; however, any earnest money will be refunded to Buyer. The Option Fee __will __will not be credited to the Sales Price at closing. Time is of the essence for this paragraph and strict compliance with the time for performance is required.

TERMINATION OPTION: Ahhh. Paragraph 23. If the contract overall is your most important tool, your hammer in your toolbox, then this is the hammerhead. Prior to its creation, it was often difficult to get Buyers off the fence. Once you understand what the Termination Option does, it is simple to remind the Buyer that by activating this paragraph they can get control of the property at an agreed-upon price and *then* make up their mind for sure. The cost is very minimal. Buyer's Agents frequently enter as little as $100 for 7-10 days and listing agents frequently accept it. (In the <$500K price range and with no unusual market pressure). As a listing agent, I wish that option money and earnest money were switched, that you had to put up $1000+ for an option, and then $100 earnest money would do. In fact, my standard recommendation to my seller clients is to require $25 per day, offer as many days as you want. That gets people more specific about getting that inspection done quickly and gets your Seller into the meat of the contract sooner, generally. Of course, my recommendation as a Buyer's Agent (other side of the fence) is to ask for 10 days for $100 and see if it goes through. It often does. The option fee is made payable to the Seller, and is cashed. Period. It's not coming back. It is for the purchase of the option. You have an opportunity to specify whether it will or will not apply to the Buyer's proceeds at closing, and normally that is allowed. The option requires that the Property is off the market for that option period--the contract is "Pending taking Backups"--which will effectively stop showings. So this is precious little to compensate the Seller for possibly missing a more qualified or serious Buyer during that period of time. The option allows for the Buyer to terminate the contract and receive their earnest money back *for any reason.* [BUYER OUT #14] They don't even have to have a reasonable reason, just cold feet. This paragraph is the main reason you should walk through the contract with a Buyer long before you actually view houses, to make sure they know that they can make a relatively low-stakes decision when they see something that seems like it might work.

PARAGRAPH 24: CONSULT AN ATTORNEY

24. CONSULT AN ATTORNEY BEFORE SIGNING: TREC rules prohibit real estate license holders from giving legal advice. READ THIS CONTRACT CAREFULLY.

Buyer's Attorney is:_____ Seller's Attorney is:_____

Phone: Fax: E-mail:

EXECUTED the _____ day of _____, 20___ (EFFECTIVE DATE).

(BROKER: FILL IN THE DATE OF FINAL ACCEPTANCE.)

Buyer _____ Seller _____

Buyer _____ Seller _____

CONSULT AN ATTORNEY: Four very important things happen in this paragraph. First, the Buyer and Seller are officially noticed that we are not attorneys, we cannot give legal advice about the contract, how to take title, or anything we think the Buyer or Seller 'should' or 'shouldn't' do beyond the confines of explaining the actual text of the contract and filling in the blanks. If either party does retain an attorney, the paragraph provides an area for attorney's contact information so that they, too, can receive all notices and documents through the contract-to-close period.

EFFECTIVE DATE: Beneath this attorney info area, a block for the Effective Date provides a blank for the last Broker agent to fill in the date of final acceptance, indicated by the signatures of both parties beneath (and both parties' initials at any change made by the other party). The Effective Date will be Day 0 of everything that is counted in numbers of days in the contract. This block starts out with an unfortunate choice of the word "Executed", meaning simply, "Signed". I say unfortunate because it leads everyone to call this an 'executed contract' but at this point it is just an 'effective contract'. It is not legally an 'executed contract' until closing, when all terms have been carried out (Reilly: The Language of Real Estate). Filling in this block is the number one error in contracts at the title company and I have been guilty of this, too. It's easy to do. In the flurry of back-and-forth, agents communicating with each other regarding changes in terms, acceptance of those changes, emails, e-signatures, etc, the agents determine which agent will get the effective contract to the title company to open title, and it's so easy to send it to the title company in the electronic form you have instead of remembering to either enter the date adding a text box in your computer version or print it out, enter the effective date, and *then* get it to title. The best way is to add a "Date Signed" automated date to the last signer's version. Be careful.

BROKER INFORMATION
(Print name(s) only. Do not sign)

Other Broker Firm _____ License No. _____   Listing Broker Firm _____ License No. _____

represents   ☐ Buyer only as Buyer's agent   represents   ☐ Seller and Buyer as an intermediary

              ☐ Seller as Listing Broker's subagent   ☐ Seller only as Seller's agent

Associate's Name _____ License No. _____   Listing Associate's Name _____ License No. _____

Associate's Email Address _____ Phone _____ Listing Associate's Email Address _____ Phone _____

Licensed Supervisor of Associate _____ License No. _____   Licensed Supervisor of Listing Associate _____ License No. _____

Other Broker's Address _____ Phone _____   Listing Broker's Office Address _____ Phone _____

City _____ State _____ Zip _____   City _____ State _____ Zip _____

                                                             Selling Associate's Name _____ License No. _____

                                                             Selling Associate's Email Address _____ Phone _____

                                                             Licensed Supervisor of Selling Associate _____ License No. _____

                                                             Selling Associate's Office Address _____

                                                             City _____ State _____ Zip _____

Listing Broker has agreed to pay Other Broker _____ of the total sales price when the Listing Broker's fee is received. Escrow agent is authorized and directed to pay Other Broker from Listing Broker's fee at closing.

TREC NO. 20-14

46

BROKER INFORMATION

BROKER INFORMATION: The ninth page lists the Broker firms representing the parties, the actual supervising Broker's name for each agent, whether the agents are in separate firms or the same firm, and the contact information for each agent and broker. It also establishes the agency positions of the brokers, whether the Buyer's Broker has a written agency agreement and is thus the agent for the Buyer, or if both agents work for the same broker who is an intermediary for both parties.

Please do a professional job on this page! It is not professional to fill in your own information and leave the listing agent's information blank because you are too lazy to look it up. It is not a good first impression of your professionalism for that other agent, with whom you will be most courteously involved during the negotiations and contract-to-close. You need each other. Show some respect. Okay, off the soapbox. At the bottom of this block, the Buyer's Agency commission is entered, and the Seller's Broker authorizes the escrow agent to pay the Buyer's Broker directly from the total real estate commissions paid at closing. Note that this does not change the commission amount from what was offered in the MLS. That would require a separate agreement between brokers, usually using the TAR form REGISTRATION AGREEMENT BETWEEN BROKERS.

The last page incorporates three receipts. Muy importante!! The Seller or his/her Broker (or that Broker's agent or authorized signer) must sign, acknowledging receipt of the option fee within 3 calendar days of the Effective Date or *the Buyer has no option*, as warned in the Termination Option Paragraph 23. If you are the Buyer's agent and can't get in touch with the Seller's agent, it is not an excuse. Deliver it to the Listing Broker, or perhaps the Broker has authorized someone in their office to sign such documents for them in their absence so that there won't be a problem. If that is still not possible, you should be able to at least reach the Listing Broker or their Listing Agent by phone and get their permission to hand it directly to the Seller and have them sign for receipt. DO NOT DROP IT OFF WITH THE CONTRACT AND EARNEST MONEY AT THE TITLE COMPANY!! The title company is not responsible for receiving it, delivering it, or signing for it. Most title companies know of their liability in this and have stopped the practice of acting as a mailbox for one agent to leave something for another agent to pick up within a specified time, realizing how little control they actually have over anyone else's actions.

The last 2 receipt blocks are completed the title company, acknowledging receipt of the contract, earnest money and any additional earnest money. Finally they include the contact information for the title company and the closing agent assigned. When complete, we call it a "receipted contract" and all parties should replace prior versions with this official receipted one. Once a contract has been receipted, it's done. If you want to make any changes, you must do so on an Amendment, which provides areas for changing prices, loan amounts, closing dates, negotiating repairs, and any other changes to the original receipted contract. Don't forget to provide everyone with the Contract or Amendment once it is complete: the Buyer, the Seller, the other agent, the escrow agent, and the lender.

OPTION FEE RECEIPT

Receipt of $_____ (Option Fee) in the form of _____
is acknowledged.

_____   _____
Seller or Listing Broker   Date

EARNEST MONEY RECEIPT

Receipt of $_____ Earnest Money in the form of _____
is acknowledged.

_____   _____   _____   _____
Escrow Agent   Received by   Email Address   Date/Time

_____   _____
Address   Phone

_____   _____   _____   _____
City   State   Zip   Fax

CONTRACT RECEIPT

Receipt of the Contract is acknowledged.

_____   _____   _____   _____
Escrow Agent   Received by   Email Address   Date

_____   _____
Address   Phone

_____   _____   _____   _____
City   State   Zip   Fax

ADDITIONAL EARNEST MONEY RECEIPT

Receipt of $_____ additional Earnest Money in the form of _____
is acknowledged.

_____   _____   _____   _____
Escrow Agent   Received by   Email Address   Date/Time

_____   _____
Address   Phone

_____   _____   _____   _____
City   State   Zip   Fax

TREC NO. 20-14

RECEIPTS

The tenth and final page of the contract provides receipts to record delivery of the option money, earnest money and additional earnest money, and contact information for the title company/attorney handling the closing.

48

PROMULGATED BY THE TEXAS REAL ESTATE COMMISSION (TREC)

2-12-18

ONE TO FOUR FAMILY RESIDENTIAL CONTRACT (RESALE)

NOTICE: Not For Use For Condominium Transactions

1. PARTIES: The parties to this contract are _____
(Seller) and _____ (Buyer).
Seller agrees to sell and convey to Buyer and Buyer agrees to buy from Seller the Property defined below.

2. PROPERTY: The land, improvements and accessories are collectively referred to as the "Property".

   A. LAND: Lot _____ Block_____, _____
       Addition, City of _____ , County of _____,
       Texas, known as _____
       (address/zip code), or as described on attached exhibit.

   B. IMPROVEMENTS: The house, garage and all other fixtures and improvements attached to the above-described real property, including without limitation, the following **permanently installed and built-in items,** if any: all equipment and appliances, valances, screens, shutters, awnings, wall-to-wall carpeting, mirrors, ceiling fans, attic fans, mail boxes, television antennas, mounts and brackets for televisions and speakers, heating and air-conditioning units, security and fire detection equipment, wiring, plumbing and lighting fixtures, chandeliers, water softener system, kitchen equipment, garage door openers, cleaning equipment, shrubbery, landscaping, outdoor cooking equipment, and all other property owned by Seller and attached to the above described real property.

   C. ACCESSORIES: The following described related accessories, if any: window air conditioning units, stove, fireplace screens, curtains and rods, blinds, window shades, draperies and rods, door keys, mailbox keys, above ground pool, swimming pool equipment and maintenance accessories, artificial fireplace logs, and controls for: (i) garage doors, (ii) entry gates, and (iii) other improvements and accessories.

   D. EXCLUSIONS: The following improvements and accessories will be retained by Seller and must be removed prior to delivery of possession:_____
       _____.

   E. RESERVATIONS: Any reservation for oil, gas, or other minerals, water, timber, or other interests is made in accordance with an attached addendum.

3. SALES PRICE:

   A. Cash portion of Sales Price payable by Buyer at closing .... $_____
   B. Sum of all financing described in the attached: ❑   Third Party Financing Addendum,
       ❑   Loan Assumption Addendum, ❑   Seller Financing Addendum .... $_____
   C. Sales Price (Sum of A and B).. $_____

4. LICENSE HOLDER DISCLOSURE: Texas law requires a real estate license holder who is a party to a transaction or acting on behalf of a spouse, parent, child, business entity in which the license holder owns more than 10%, or a trust for which the license holder acts as a trustee or of which the license holder or the license holder's spouse, parent or child is a beneficiary, to notify the other party in writing before entering into a contract of sale. Disclose if applicable:_____
_____.

5. EARNEST MONEY: Within 3 days after the Effective Date, Buyer must deliver $_____ as earnest money to _____, as escrow agent, at _____ (address). Buyer shall deliver additional earnest money of $_____ to escrow agent within _____ days after the Effective Date of this contract. If Buyer fails to deliver the earnest money within the time required, Seller may terminate this contract or exercise Seller's remedies under Paragraph 15, or both, by providing notice to Buyer before Buyer delivers the earnest money. If the last day to deliver the earnest money falls on a Saturday, Sunday, or legal holiday, the time to deliver the earnest money is extended until the end of the next day that is not a Saturday, Sunday, or legal holiday. **Time is of the essence for this paragraph.**

6. TITLE POLICY AND SURVEY:

   A. TITLE POLICY: Seller shall furnish to Buyer at ❑ Seller's ❑ Buyer's expense an owner policy of title insurance (Title Policy) issued by _____ (Title Company) in the amount of the Sales Price, dated at or after closing, insuring Buyer against loss under the provisions of the Title Policy, subject to the promulgated exclusions (including existing building and zoning ordinances) and the following exceptions:
       (1) Restrictive covenants common to the platted subdivision in which the Property is located.
       (2) The standard printed exception for standby fees, taxes and assessments.

(3) Liens created as part of the financing described in Paragraph 3.

(4) Utility easements created by the dedication deed or plat of the subdivision in which the Property is located.

(5) Reservations or exceptions otherwise permitted by this contract or as may be approved by Buyer in writing.

(6) The standard printed exception as to marital rights.

(7) The standard printed exception as to waters, tidelands, beaches, streams, and related matters.

(8) The standard printed exception as to discrepancies, conflicts, shortages in area or boundary lines, encroachments or protrusions, or overlapping improvements:
❑(i) will not be amended or deleted from the title policy; or
❑(ii) will be amended to read, "shortages in area" at the expense of ❑Buyer ❑Seller.

(9) The exception or exclusion regarding minerals approved by the Texas Department of Insurance.

B. COMMITMENT: Within 20 days after the Title Company receives a copy of this contract, Seller shall furnish to Buyer a commitment for title insurance (Commitment) and, at Buyer's expense, legible copies of restrictive covenants and documents evidencing exceptions in the Commitment (Exception Documents) other than the standard printed exceptions.   Seller authorizes the Title Company to deliver the Commitment and Exception Documents to Buyer at Buyer's address shown in Paragraph 21. If the Commitment and Exception Documents are not delivered to Buyer within the specified time, the time for delivery will be automatically extended up to 15 days or 3 days before the Closing Date, whichever is earlier. If the Commitment and Exception Documents are not delivered within the time required, Buyer may terminate this contract and the earnest money will be refunded to Buyer.

C. SURVEY: The survey must be made by a registered professional land surveyor acceptable to the Title Company and Buyer's lender(s). (Check one box only)
❑(1) Within _____ days after the Effective Date of this contract, Seller shall furnish to Buyer and Title Company Seller's existing survey of the Property and a Residential Real Property Affidavit promulgated by the Texas Department of Insurance (T-47 Affidavit). **If Seller fails to furnish the existing survey or affidavit within the time prescribed, Buyer shall obtain a new survey at Seller's expense no later than 3 days prior to Closing Date.** If the existing survey or affidavit is not acceptable to Title Company or Buyer's lender(s), Buyer shall obtain a new survey at ❑Seller's ❑Buyer's expense no later than 3 days prior to Closing Date.

❑(2) Within _____ days after the Effective Date of this contract, Buyer shall obtain a new survey at Buyer's expense. Buyer is deemed to receive the survey on the date of actual receipt or the date specified in this paragraph, whichever is earlier.

❑(3) Within _____ days after the Effective Date of this contract, Seller, at Seller's expense shall furnish a new survey to Buyer.

D. OBJECTIONS: Buyer may object in writing to defects, exceptions, or encumbrances to title: disclosed on the survey other than items 6A(1) through (7) above; disclosed in the Commitment other than items 6A(1) through (9) above; or which prohibit the following use or activity: _____.
Buyer must object the earlier of (i) the Closing Date or (ii) _____ days after Buyer receives the Commitment, Exception Documents, and the survey. Buyer's failure to object within the time allowed will constitute a waiver of Buyer's right to object; except that the requirements in Schedule C of the Commitment are not waived by Buyer. Provided Seller is not obligated to incur any expense, Seller shall cure any timely objections of Buyer or any third party lender within 15 days after Seller receives the objections (Cure Period) and the Closing Date will be extended as necessary. If objections are not cured within the Cure Period, Buyer may, by delivering notice to Seller within 5 days after the end of the Cure Period: (i) terminate this contract and the earnest money will be refunded to Buyer; or (ii) waive the objections. If Buyer does not terminate within the time required, Buyer shall be deemed to have waived the objections. If the Commitment or Survey is revised or any new Exception Document(s) is delivered, Buyer may object to any new matter revealed in the revised Commitment or Survey or new Exception Document(s) within the same time stated in this paragraph to make objections beginning when the revised Commitment, Survey, or Exception Document(s) is delivered to Buyer.

E. TITLE NOTICES:
(1) ABSTRACT OR TITLE POLICY: Broker advises Buyer to have an abstract of title covering the Property examined by an attorney of Buyer's selection, or Buyer should be furnished with or obtain a Title Policy. If a Title Policy is furnished, the Commitment should be promptly reviewed by an attorney of Buyer's choice due to the time limitations on Buyer's right to object.

(2) MEMBERSHIP IN PROPERTY OWNERS ASSOCIATION(S): The Property ❑is ❑is not

50

subject to mandatory membership in a property owners association(s). If the Property is subject to mandatory membership in a property owners association(s), Seller notifies Buyer under §5.012, Texas Property Code, that, as a purchaser of property in the residential community identified in Paragraph 2A in which the Property is located, you are obligated to be a member of the property owners association(s). Restrictive covenants governing the use and occupancy of the Property and all dedicatory instruments governing the establishment, maintenance, or operation of this residential community have been or will be recorded in the Real Property Records of the county in which the Property is located. Copies of the restrictive covenants and dedicatory instruments may be obtained from the county clerk. **You are obligated to pay assessments to the property owners association(s). The amount of the assessments is subject to change. Your failure to pay the assessments could result in enforcement of the association's lien on and the foreclosure of the Property.**

Section 207.003, Property Code, entitles an owner to receive copies of any document that governs the establishment, maintenance, or operation of a subdivision, including, but not limited to, restrictions, bylaws, rules and regulations, and a resale certificate from a property owners' association. A resale certificate contains information including, but not limited to, statements specifying the amount and frequency of regular assessments and the style and cause number of lawsuits to which the property owners' association is a party, other than lawsuits relating to unpaid ad valorem taxes of an individual member of the association. These documents must be made available to you by the property owners' association or the association's agent on your request.

If Buyer is concerned about these matters, the TREC promulgated Addendum for Property Subject to Mandatory Membership in a Property Owners Association(s) should be used.

(3) STATUTORY TAX DISTRICTS: If the Property is situated in a utility or other statutorily created district providing water, sewer, drainage, or flood control facilities and services, Chapter 49, Texas Water Code, requires Seller to deliver and Buyer to sign the statutory notice relating to the tax rate, bonded indebtedness, or standby fee of the district prior to final execution of this contract.

(4) TIDE WATERS: If the Property abuts the tidally influenced waters of the state, §33.135, Texas Natural Resources Code, requires a notice regarding coastal area property to be included in the contract. An addendum containing the notice promulgated by TREC or required by the parties must be used.

(5) ANNEXATION: If the Property is located outside the limits of a municipality, Seller notifies Buyer under §5.011, Texas Property Code, that the Property may now or later be included in the extraterritorial jurisdiction of a municipality and may now or later be subject to annexation by the municipality. Each municipality maintains a map that depicts its boundaries and extraterritorial jurisdiction. To determine if the Property is located within a municipality's extraterritorial jurisdiction or is likely to be located within a municipality's extraterritorial jurisdiction, contact all municipalities located in the general proximity of the Property for further information.

(6) PROPERTY LOCATED IN A CERTIFICATED SERVICE AREA OF A UTILITY SERVICE PROVIDER: Notice required by §13.257, Water Code: The real property, described in Paragraph 2, that you are about to purchase may be located in a certificated water or sewer service area, which is authorized by law to provide water or sewer service to the properties in the certificated area. If your property is located in a certificated area there may be special costs or charges that you will be required to pay before you can receive water or sewer service. There may be a period required to construct lines or other facilities necessary to provide water or sewer service to your property. You are advised to determine if the property is in a certificated area and contact the utility service provider to determine the cost that you will be required to pay and the period, if any, that is required to provide water or sewer service to your property. The undersigned Buyer hereby acknowledges receipt of the foregoing notice at or before the execution of a binding contract for the purchase of the real property described in Paragraph 2 or at closing of purchase of the real property.

(7) PUBLIC IMPROVEMENT DISTRICTS: If the Property is in a public improvement district, §5.014, Property Code, requires Seller to notify Buyer as follows: As a purchaser of this parcel of real property you are obligated to pay an assessment to a municipality or county for an improvement project undertaken by a public improvement district under Chapter 372, Local Government Code. The assessment may be due annually or in periodic installments. More information concerning the amount of the assessment and the due dates of that assessment may be obtained from the municipality or county levying the assessment. The amount of the assessments is subject to change. Your failure to pay the assessments could result in a lien on and the foreclosure of your property.

(8) TRANSFER FEES: If the Property is subject to a private transfer fee obligation, §5.205, Property Code, requires Seller to notify Buyer as follows: The private transfer fee

obligation may be governed by Chapter 5, Subchapter G of the Texas Property Code.

(9) PROPANE GAS SYSTEM SERVICE AREA: If the Property is located in a propane gas system service area owned by a distribution system retailer, Seller must give Buyer written notice as required by §141.010, Texas Utilities Code. An addendum containing the notice approved by TREC or required by the parties should be used.

(10) NOTICE OF WATER LEVEL FLUCTUATIONS: If the Property adjoins an impoundment of water, including a reservoir or lake, constructed and maintained under Chapter 11, Water Code, that has a storage capacity of at least 5,000 acre-feet at the impoundment's normal operating level, Seller hereby notifies Buyer: "The water level of the impoundment of water adjoining the Property fluctuates for various reasons, including as a result of: (1) an entity lawfully exercising its right to use the water stored in the impoundment; or (2) drought or flood conditions."

7. PROPERTY CONDITION:

A. ACCESS, INSPECTIONS AND UTILITIES: Seller shall permit Buyer and Buyer's agents access to the Property at reasonable times. Buyer may have the Property inspected by inspectors selected by Buyer and licensed by TREC or otherwise permitted by law to make inspections. Any hydrostatic testing must be separately authorized by Seller in writing. Seller at Seller's expense shall immediately cause existing utilities to be turned on and shall keep the utilities on during the time this contract is in effect.

B. SELLER'S DISCLOSURE NOTICE PURSUANT TO §5.008, TEXAS PROPERTY CODE (Notice): (Check one box only)

❑ (1) Buyer has received the Notice.

❑ (2) Buyer has not received the Notice. Within _____ days after the Effective Date of this contract, Seller shall deliver the Notice to Buyer. If Buyer does not receive the Notice, Buyer may terminate this contract at any time prior to the closing and the earnest money will be refunded to Buyer. If Seller delivers the Notice, Buyer may terminate this contract for any reason within 7 days after Buyer receives the Notice or prior to the closing, whichever first occurs, and the earnest money will be refunded to Buyer.

❑ (3) The Seller is not required to furnish the notice under the Texas Property Code.

C. SELLER'S DISCLOSURE OF LEAD-BASED PAINT AND LEAD-BASED PAINT HAZARDS is required by Federal law for a residential dwelling constructed prior to 1978.

D. ACCEPTANCE OF PROPERTY CONDITION: "As Is" means the present condition of the Property with any and all defects and without warranty except for the warranties of title and the warranties in this contract. Buyer's agreement to accept the Property As Is under Paragraph 7D(1) or (2) does not preclude Buyer from inspecting the Property under Paragraph 7A, from negotiating repairs or treatments in a subsequent amendment, or from terminating this contract during the Option Period, if any.
(Check one box only)

❑ (1) Buyer accepts the Property As Is.

❑ (2) Buyer accepts the Property As Is provided Seller, at Seller's expense, shall complete the following specific repairs and treatments: _____
_____.
(Do not insert general phrases, such as "subject to inspections" that do not identify specific repairs and treatments.)

E. LENDER REQUIRED REPAIRS AND TREATMENTS: Unless otherwise agreed in writing, neither party is obligated to pay for lender required repairs, which includes treatment for wood destroying insects. If the parties do not agree to pay for the lender required repairs or treatments, this contract will terminate and the earnest money will be refunded to Buyer. If the cost of lender required repairs and treatments exceeds 5% of the Sales Price, Buyer may terminate this contract and the earnest money will be refunded to Buyer.

F. COMPLETION OF REPAIRS AND TREATMENTS: Unless otherwise agreed in writing: (i) Seller shall complete all agreed repairs and treatments prior to the Closing Date; and (ii) all required permits must be obtained, and repairs and treatments must be performed by persons who are licensed to provide such repairs or treatments or, if no license is required by law, are commercially engaged in the trade of providing such repairs or treatments.   At Buyer's election, any transferable warranties received by Seller with respect to the repairs and treatments will be transferred to Buyer at Buyer's expense. If Seller fails to complete any agreed repairs and treatments prior to the Closing Date, Buyer may exercise remedies under Paragraph 15 or extend the Closing Date up to 5 days if necessary for Seller to complete the repairs and treatments.

G. ENVIRONMENTAL MATTERS: Buyer is advised that the presence of wetlands, toxic substances, including asbestos and wastes or other environmental hazards, or the presence of a threatened or endangered species or its habitat may affect Buyer's intended use of the Property. If Buyer is concerned about these matters, an addendum promulgated by TREC or required by the parties should be used.

Initialed for identification by Buyer_____ _____ and Seller _____ _____   TREC NO. 20-14

H. RESIDENTIAL SERVICE CONTRACTS: Buyer may purchase a residential service contract from a residential service company licensed by TREC. If Buyer purchases a residential service contract, Seller shall reimburse Buyer at closing for the cost of the residential service contract in an amount not exceeding $_____. Buyer should review any residential service contract for the scope of coverage, exclusions and limitations. **The purchase of a residential service contract is optional. Similar coverage may be purchased from various companies authorized to do business in Texas.**

8. BROKERS' FEES: All obligations of the parties for payment of brokers' fees are contained in separate written agreements.

9. CLOSING:

A. The closing of the sale will be on or before _____, 20____, or within 7 days after objections made under Paragraph 6D have been cured or waived, whichever date is later (Closing Date). If either party fails to close the sale by the Closing Date, the non-defaulting party may exercise the remedies contained in Paragraph 15.

B. At closing:

(1) Seller shall execute and deliver a general warranty deed conveying title to the Property to Buyer and showing no additional exceptions to those permitted in Paragraph 6 and furnish tax statements or certificates showing no delinquent taxes on the Property.

(2) Buyer shall pay the Sales Price in good funds acceptable to the escrow agent.

(3) Seller and Buyer shall execute and deliver any notices, statements, certificates, affidavits, releases, loan documents and other documents reasonably required for the closing of the sale and the issuance of the Title Policy.

(4) There will be no liens, assessments, or security interests against the Property which will not be satisfied out of the sales proceeds unless securing the payment of any loans assumed by Buyer and assumed loans will not be in default.

(5) If the Property is subject to a residential lease, Seller shall transfer security deposits (as defined under §92.102, Property Code), if any, to Buyer. In such an event, Buyer shall deliver to the tenant a signed statement acknowledging that the Buyer has acquired the Property and is responsible for the return of the security deposit, and specifying the exact dollar amount of the security deposit.

10. POSSESSION:

A. Buyer's Possession: Seller shall deliver to Buyer possession of the Property in its present or required condition, ordinary wear and tear excepted: ❏upon closing and funding ❏according to a temporary residential lease form promulgated by TREC or other written lease required by the parties. Any possession by Buyer prior to closing or by Seller after closing which is not authorized by a written lease will establish a tenancy at sufferance relationship between the parties. **Consult your insurance agent prior to change of ownership and possession because insurance coverage may be limited or terminated. The absence of a written lease or appropriate insurance coverage may expose the parties to economic loss.**

B. Leases:

(1) After the Effective Date, Seller may not execute any lease (including but not limited to mineral leases) or convey any interest in the Property without Buyer's written consent.

(2) If the Property is subject to any lease to which Seller is a party, Seller shall deliver to Buyer copies of the lease(s) and any move-in condition form signed by the tenant within 7 days after the Effective Date of the contract.

11. SPECIAL PROVISIONS: (Insert only factual statements and business details applicable to the sale. TREC rules prohibit license holders from adding factual statements or business details for which a contract addendum, lease or other form has been promulgated by TREC for mandatory use.)

12. SETTLEMENT AND OTHER EXPENSES:

A. The following expenses must be paid at or prior to closing:

(1) Expenses payable by Seller (Seller's Expenses):

(a) Releases of existing liens, including prepayment penalties and recording fees; release of Seller's loan liability; tax statements or certificates; preparation of deed; one-half of escrow fee; and other expenses payable by Seller under this contract.

(b) Seller shall also pay an amount not to exceed $_____ to be applied in the following order: Buyer's Expenses which Buyer is prohibited from paying by FHA, VA, Texas Veterans Land Board or other governmental loan programs, and then to other Buyer's Expenses as allowed by the lender.

Initialed for identification by Buyer_____ _____ and Seller _____ _____   TREC NO. 20-14

(2) Expenses payable by Buyer (Buyer's Expenses): Appraisal fees; loan application fees; origination charges; credit reports; preparation of loan documents; interest on the notes from date of disbursement to one month prior to dates of first monthly payments; recording fees; copies of easements and restrictions; loan title policy with endorsements required by lender; loan-related inspection fees; photos; amortization schedules; one-half of escrow fee; all prepaid items, including required premiums for flood and hazard insurance, reserve deposits for insurance, ad valorem taxes and special governmental assessments; final compliance inspection; courier fee; repair inspection; underwriting fee; wire transfer fee; expenses incident to any loan; Private Mortgage Insurance Premium (PMI), VA Loan Funding Fee, or FHA Mortgage Insurance Premium (MIP) as required by the lender; and other expenses payable by Buyer under this contract.

B. If any expense exceeds an amount expressly stated in this contract for such expense to be paid by a party, that party may terminate this contract unless the other party agrees to pay such excess. Buyer may not pay charges and fees expressly prohibited by FHA, VA, Texas Veterans Land Board or other governmental loan program regulations.

13. **PRORATIONS:** Taxes for the current year, interest, maintenance fees, assessments, dues and rents will be prorated through the Closing Date. The tax proration may be calculated taking into consideration any change in exemptions that will affect the current year's taxes. If taxes for the current year vary from the amount prorated at closing, the parties shall adjust the prorations when tax statements for the current year are available. If taxes are not paid at or prior to closing, Buyer shall pay taxes for the current year.

14. **CASUALTY LOSS:** If any part of the Property is damaged or destroyed by fire or other casualty after the Effective Date of this contract, Seller shall restore the Property to its previous condition as soon as reasonably possible, but in any event by the Closing Date. If Seller fails to do so due to factors beyond Seller's control, Buyer may (a) terminate this contract and the earnest money will be refunded to Buyer (b) extend the time for performance up to 15 days and the Closing Date will be extended as necessary or (c) accept the Property in its damaged condition with an assignment of insurance proceeds, if permitted by Seller's insurance carrier, and receive credit from Seller at closing in the amount of the deductible under the insurance policy. Seller's obligations under this paragraph are independent of any other obligations of Seller under this contract.

15. **DEFAULT:** If Buyer fails to comply with this contract, Buyer will be in default, and Seller may (a) enforce specific performance, seek such other relief as may be provided by law, or both, or (b) terminate this contract and receive the earnest money as liquidated damages, thereby releasing both parties from this contract. If Seller fails to comply with this contract, Seller will be in default and Buyer may (a) enforce specific performance, seek such other relief as may be provided by law, or both, or (b) terminate this contract and receive the earnest money, thereby releasing both parties from this contract.

16. **MEDIATION:** It is the policy of the State of Texas to encourage resolution of disputes through alternative dispute resolution procedures such as mediation. Any dispute between Seller and Buyer related to this contract which is not resolved through informal discussion will be submitted to a mutually acceptable mediation service or provider. The parties to the mediation shall bear the mediation costs equally. This paragraph does not preclude a party from seeking equitable relief from a court of competent jurisdiction.

17. **ATTORNEY'S FEES:** A Buyer, Seller, Listing Broker, Other Broker, or escrow agent who prevails in any legal proceeding related to this contract is entitled to recover reasonable attorney's fees and all costs of such proceeding.

18. **ESCROW:**
    A. ESCROW: The escrow agent is not (i) a party to this contract and does not have liability for the performance or nonperformance of any party to this contract, (ii) liable for interest on the earnest money and (iii) liable for the loss of any earnest money caused by the failure of any financial institution in which the earnest money has been deposited unless the financial institution is acting as escrow agent.
    B. EXPENSES: At closing, the earnest money must be applied first to any cash down payment, then to Buyer's Expenses and any excess refunded to Buyer. If no closing occurs, escrow agent may: (i) require a written release of liability of the escrow agent from all parties, (ii) require payment of unpaid expenses incurred on behalf of a party, and (iii) only deduct from the earnest money the amount of unpaid expenses incurred on behalf of the party receiving the earnest money.
    C. DEMAND: Upon termination of this contract, either party or the escrow agent may send a release of earnest money to each party and the parties shall execute counterparts of the release and deliver same to the escrow agent. If either party fails to execute the release, either party may make a written demand to the escrow agent for the earnest money. If only one party makes written demand for the earnest money, escrow agent shall promptly

Initialed for identification by Buyer_____ _____ and Seller _____ _____   TREC NO. 20-14

provide a copy of the demand to the other party. If escrow agent does not receive written objection to the demand from the other party within 15 days, escrow agent may disburse the earnest money to the party making demand reduced by the amount of unpaid expenses incurred on behalf of the party receiving the earnest money and escrow agent may pay the same to the creditors. If escrow agent complies with the provisions of this paragraph, each party hereby releases escrow agent from all adverse claims related to the disbursal of the earnest money.

D. DAMAGES: Any party who wrongfully fails or refuses to sign a release acceptable to the escrow agent within 7 days of receipt of the request will be liable to the other party for (i) damages; (ii) the earnest money; (iii) reasonable attorney's fees; and (iv) all costs of suit.

E. NOTICES: Escrow agent's notices will be effective when sent in compliance with Paragraph 21. Notice of objection to the demand will be deemed effective upon receipt by escrow agent.

19. **REPRESENTATIONS:** All covenants, representations and warranties in this contract survive closing. If any representation of Seller in this contract is untrue on the Closing Date, Seller will be in default. Unless expressly prohibited by written agreement, Seller may continue to show the Property and receive, negotiate and accept back up offers.

20. **FEDERAL TAX REQUIREMENTS:** If Seller is a "foreign person," as defined by Internal Revenue Code and its regulations, or if Seller fails to deliver an affidavit or a certificate of non-foreign status to Buyer that Seller is not a "foreign person," then Buyer shall withhold from the sales proceeds an amount sufficient to comply with applicable tax law and deliver the same to the Internal Revenue Service together with appropriate tax forms. Internal Revenue Service regulations require filing written reports if currency in excess of specified amounts is received in the transaction.

21. **NOTICES:** All notices from one party to the other must be in writing and are effective when mailed to, hand-delivered at, or transmitted by fax or electronic transmission as follows:

To Buyer	**To Seller**
at: _____	at: _____
_____	_____
Phone: ( ) _____	Phone: ( ) _____
Fax: ( ) _____	Fax: ( ) _____
E-mail: _____	E-mail: _____

22. **AGREEMENT OF PARTIES:** This contract contains the entire agreement of the parties and cannot be changed except by their written agreement. Addenda which are a part of this contract are (Check all applicable boxes):

❏ Third Party Financing Addendum

❏ Seller Financing Addendum

❏ Addendum for Property Subject to Mandatory Membership in a Property Owners Association

❏ Buyer's Temporary Residential Lease

❏ Loan Assumption Addendum

❏ Addendum for Sale of Other Property by Buyer

❏ Addendum for Reservation of Oil, Gas and Other Minerals

❏ Addendum for "Back-Up" Contract

❏ Addendum for Coastal Area Property

❏ Addendum for Authorizing Hydrostatic Testing

❏ Addendum Concerning Right to Terminate Due to Lender's Appraisal

❏ Environmental Assessment, Threatened or Endangered Species and Wetlands Addendum

❏ Seller's Temporary Residential Lease

❏ Short Sale Addendum

❏ Addendum for Property Located Seaward of the Gulf Intracoastal Waterway

❏ Addendum for Seller's Disclosure of Information on Lead-based Paint and Lead-based Paint Hazards as Required by Federal Law

❏ Addendum for Property in a Propane Gas System Service Area

❏ Other (list): _____
_____
_____
_____
_____

Initialed for identification by Buyer_____ _____ and Seller _____ _____   TREC NO. 20-14

23. **TERMINATION OPTION:** For nominal consideration, the receipt of which is hereby acknowledged by Seller, and Buyer's agreement to pay Seller $_____ (Option Fee) within 3 days after the Effective Date of this contract, Seller grants Buyer the unrestricted right to terminate this contract by giving notice of termination to Seller within _____ days after the Effective Date of this contract (Option Period). Notices under this paragraph must be given by 5:00 p.m. (local time where the Property is located) by the date specified. If no dollar amount is stated as the Option Fee or if Buyer fails to pay the Option Fee to Seller within the time prescribed, this paragraph will not be a part of this contract and Buyer shall not have the unrestricted right to terminate this contract. If Buyer gives notice of termination within the time prescribed, the Option Fee will not be refunded; however, any earnest money will be refunded to Buyer. The Option Fee ❏will ❏will not be credited to the Sales Price at closing. **Time is of the essence for this paragraph and strict compliance with the time for performance is required.**

24. **CONSULT AN ATTORNEY BEFORE SIGNING:** TREC rules prohibit real estate license holders from giving legal advice. READ THIS CONTRACT CAREFULLY.

Buyer's
Attorney is: _____

Seller's
Attorney is: _____

_____

_____

Phone: (____) _____

Phone: (____) _____

Fax: (____) _____

Fax: (____) _____

E-mail: _____

E-mail: _____

**EXECUTED the _____ day of _____, 20_____ (Effective Date).
(BROKER: FILL IN THE DATE OF FINAL ACCEPTANCE.)**

_____
Buyer

_____
Seller

_____
Buyer

_____
Seller

TREC NO. 20-14

BROKER INFORMATION
(Print name(s) only. Do not sign)

Other Broker Firm _____ License No. _____

represents   ☐ Buyer only as Buyer's agent
              ☐ Seller as Listing Broker's subagent

Associate's Name _____ License No. _____

Associate's Email Address _____ Phone _____

Licensed Supervisor of Associate _____ License No. _____

Other Broker's Address _____ Phone _____

City _____ State _____ Zip _____

Listing Broker Firm _____ License No. _____

represents   ☐ Seller and Buyer as an intermediary
              ☐ Seller only as Seller's agent

Listing Associate's Name _____ License No. _____

Listing Associate's Email Address _____ Phone _____

Licensed Supervisor of Listing Associate _____ License No. _____

Listing Broker's Office Address _____ Phone _____

City _____ State _____ Zip _____

Selling Associate's Name _____ License No. _____

Selling Associate's Email Address _____ Phone _____

Licensed Supervisor of Selling Associate _____ License No. _____

Selling Associate's Office Address _____

City _____ State _____ Zip _____

Listing Broker has agreed to pay Other Broker _____ of the total sales price when the Listing Broker's fee is received. Escrow agent is authorized and directed to pay Other Broker from Listing Broker's fee at closing.

TREC NO. 20-14

OPTION FEE RECEIPT

Receipt of $_____ (Option Fee) in the form of _____
is acknowledged.

_____   _____
Seller or Listing Broker   Date

EARNEST MONEY RECEIPT

Receipt of $_____ Earnest Money in the form of _____
is acknowledged.

_____   _____ _____   _____
Escrow Agent   Received by   Email Address   Date/Time

_____   _____
Address   Phone

_____   _____   _____   _____
City   State   Zip   Fax

CONTRACT RECEIPT

Receipt of the Contract is acknowledged.

_____   _____ _____   _____
Escrow Agent   Received by   Email Address   Date

_____   _____
Address   Phone

_____   _____   _____   _____
City   State   Zip   Fax

ADDITIONAL EARNEST MONEY RECEIPT

Receipt of $_____ additional Earnest Money in the form of _____
is acknowledged.

_____   _____ _____   _____
Escrow Agent   Received by   Email Address   Date/Time

_____   _____
Address   Phone

_____   _____   _____   _____
City   State   Zip   Fax

TREC NO. 20-14

58

TREC ADDENDA AND
OTHER CONTRACTS

FIRST THE THIRD PARTY ADDENDUM SINCE IT'S USED MOST OFTEN, THEN ALL OTHER FORMS ARE DISPLAYED ALPHABETICALLY WITH DISCUSSION FOLLOWING EACH.

PROMULGATED BY THE TEXAS REAL ESTATE COMMISSION (TREC)

THIRD PARTY FINANCING ADDENDUM

TO CONTRACT CONCERNING THE PROPERTY AT

EQUAL HOUSING OPPORTUNITY

_____

(Street Address and City)

1. **TYPE OF FINANCING AND DUTY TO APPLY AND OBTAIN APPROVAL:** Buyer shall apply promptly for all financing described below and make every reasonable effort to obtain approval for the financing, including but not limited to furnishing all information and documents required by Buyer's lender. (Check applicable boxes):

❑ A. CONVENTIONAL FINANCING:

  ❑ (1) A first mortgage loan in the principal amount of $_____ (excluding any financed PMI premium), due in full in _____ year(s), with interest not to exceed _____% per annum for the first _____ year(s) of the loan with Origination Charges as shown on Buyer's Loan Estimate for the loan not to exceed _____% of the loan.

  ❑ (2) A second mortgage loan in the principal amount of $_____ (excluding any financed PMI premium), due in full in _____ year(s), with interest not to exceed _____% per annum for the first _____ year(s) of the loan with Origination Charges as shown on Buyer's Loan Estimate for the loan not to exceed _____% of the loan.

❑ B. TEXAS VETERANS LOAN: A loan(s) from the Texas Veterans Land Board of $_____ for a period in the total amount of _____ years at the interest rate established by the Texas Veterans Land Board.

❑ C. FHA INSURED FINANCING: A Section _____ FHA insured loan of not less than $_____(excluding any financed MIP), amortizable monthly for not less than _____ years, with interest not to exceed _____% per annum for the first _____ year(s) of the loan with Origination Charges as shown on Buyer's Loan Estimate for the loan not to exceed _____ % of the loan.

❑ D. VA GUARANTEED FINANCING: A VA guaranteed loan of not less than $_____ (excluding any financed Funding Fee), amortizable monthly for not less than _____ years, with interest not to exceed _____% per annum for the first _____ year(s) of the loan with Origination Charges as shown on Buyer's Loan Estimate for the loan not to exceed _____% of the loan.

❑ E. USDA GUARANTEED FINANCING: A USDA-guaranteed loan of not less than $_____ (excluding any financed Funding Fee), amortizable monthly for not less than _____ years, with interest not to exceed _____% per annum for the first _____ year(s) of the loan with Origination Charges as shown on Buyer's Loan Estimate for the loan not to exceed _____% of the loan.

❑ F. REVERSE MORTGAGE FINANCING: A reverse mortgage loan (also known as a Home Equity Conversion Mortgage loan) in the original principal amount of $_____ (excluding any financed PMI premium or other costs), with interest not to exceed _____% per annum for the first _____ year(s) of the loan with Origination Charges as shown on Buyer's Loan Estimate for the loan not to exceed _____% of the loan. The reverse mortgage loan ❑will ❑ will not be an FHA insured loan.

2. **APPROVAL OF FINANCING**: Approval for the financing described above will be deemed to have been obtained when Buyer Approval and Property Approval are obtained.

A. BUYER APPROVAL *(Check one box only)*:

  ❑ This contract is subject to Buyer obtaining Buyer Approval. If Buyer cannot obtain Buyer Approval, Buyer may give written notice to Seller within _____ days after the effective date of this contract and this contract will terminate and the earnest money will be refunded to Buyer. If Buyer does not terminate the contract under this provision, the contract shall no longer be subject to the Buyer obtaining Buyer Approval. Buyer Approval will be deemed to have been obtained when (i) the terms of the loan(s)

Initialed for identification by Buyer_____ _____ and Seller_____ _____   TREC NO. 40-8

_____
(Address of Property)

described above are available and (ii) lender determines that Buyer has satisfied all of lender's requirements related to Buyer's assets, income and credit history.

☐ This contract is not subject to Buyer obtaining Buyer Approval.

B. **PROPERTY APPROVAL:** If Buyer's lender determines that the Property does not satisfy lender's underwriting requirements for the loan (including but not limited to appraisal, insurability, and lender required repairs) Buyer, not later than 3 days before the Closing Date, may terminate this contract by giving Seller: (i) notice of termination; and (ii) a copy of a written statement from the lender setting forth the reason(s) for lender's determination. If Buyer terminates under this paragraph, the earnest money will be refunded to Buyer. If Buyer does not terminate under this paragraph, Property Approval is deemed to have been obtained.

C. **Time is of the essence for this paragraph and strict compliance with the time for performance is required.**

3. **SECURITY:** Each note for the financing described above must be secured by vendor's and deed of trust liens.

4. **FHA/VA REQUIRED PROVISION:** If the financing described above involves FHA insured or VA financing, it is expressly agreed that, notwithstanding any other provision of this contract, the purchaser (Buyer) shall not be obligated to complete the purchase of the Property described herein or to incur any penalty by forfeiture of earnest money deposits or otherwise: (i) unless the Buyer has been given in accordance with HUD/FHA or VA requirements a written statement issued by the Federal Housing Commissioner, Department of Veterans Affairs, or a Direct Endorsement Lender setting forth the appraised value of the Property of not less than $_____; or (ii) if the contract purchase price or cost exceeds the reasonable value of the Property established by the Department of Veterans Affairs.

A. The Buyer shall have the privilege and option of proceeding with consummation of the contract without regard to the amount of the appraised valuation or the reasonable value established by the Department of Veterans Affairs.

B. If FHA financing is involved, the appraised valuation is arrived at to determine the maximum mortgage the Department of Housing and Urban Development will insure. HUD does not warrant the value or the condition of the Property. The Buyer should satisfy himself/herself that the price and the condition of the Property are acceptable.

C. If VA financing is involved and if Buyer elects to complete the purchase at an amount in excess of the reasonable value established by the VA, Buyer shall pay such excess amount in cash from a source which Buyer agrees to disclose to the VA and which Buyer represents will not be from borrowed funds except as approved by VA. If VA reasonable value of the Property is less than the Sales Price, Seller may reduce the Sales Price to an amount equal to the VA reasonable value and the sale will be closed at the lower Sales Price with proportionate adjustments to the down payment and the loan amount.

5. **AUTHORIZATION TO RELEASE INFORMATION:**
A. Buyer authorizes Buyer's lender to furnish to Seller or Buyer or their representatives information relating to the status of the approval for the financing.
B. Seller and Buyer authorize Buyer's lender, title company, and escrow agent to disclose and furnish a copy of the closing disclosures and settlement statements provided in relation to the closing of this sale to the parties' respective brokers and sales agents provided under Broker Information.

_____   _____
Buyer   Seller

_____   _____
Buyer   Seller

TREC NO. 40-8

THIRD PARTY FINANCING ADDENDUM

A. TYPE OF FINANCING AND DUTY TO APPLY AND OBTAIN APPROVAL:
This addendum describes lender financing, and provides a time limit for the Buyer to complete the application process. That time limit is the most important blank on the addendum, in my opinion, because the Buyer essentially has a huge out here for the duration of that time limit [BUYER OUT #15]. New in 2019: This form now requires a written statement from the lender to the Seller including the reason(s) that the Buyer did not qualify. Hooray!! This is important because the Seller has lost all of that time on the market, during which they might have been able to secure a more credit-worthy Buyer. As a Listing Agent, I want to cut that time as short as possible.

Lenders in the current market are requesting a 30-day closing to prepare the entire loan package but the Buyer's creditworthiness should be able to be established within 2 weeks. The property's appraisal value and insurability, proof that it would support the loan amount as collateral for the loan, do not factor in this time limit. Buyer's agents will blithely enter 30 days in the blank, but that makes a full month that my Seller's property will be essentially off the market, and I'm not willing to recommend that. Period. This is so important that I would even recommend a counteroffer based on this one term alone even if the price, closing date, and all other terms were acceptable. Of course, if I am the Buyer's Agent, I'm going to go for all I can get, and probably see if 30 days will fly (in a balanced or buyer's market), because I know that it is a free option. If the Buyer wants to get out of the contract for any reason, even unrelated to the financing, all they have to provide is their own statement in writing that they can't get financing. That's it. The end. And they get their earnest money back! So beware this blank! What number *should* go in there? The answer is "it depends". If you are a Buyer's agent, you should always <u>ask the lender</u> what to enter for that specific client. If you are a Listing Agent, you should call the lender on the Buyer's Prequalification Letter and <u>ask the lender.</u>

For anything but a cash sale, you will be using the following paragraphs to outline the anticipated financing. Ideally, the Buyer will have already sought the advice of a licensed mortgage loan originator, whom you should contact regarding specific finance terms. Check the appropriate box for A 1-5. Note about box checking: There was a recent court case (ERA Realty Group v. Advocates for Children and Families, Inc.) in which a real estate agency was hired through a buyer/tenant representation agreement to locate and secure an office space lease for an organization. After one year, the organization decided to purchase the office space. In a commercial lease, there is a provision for paying the Tenant Agent additional commission upon renewal of the lease as well as a provision for paying the Tenant Agent a sales commission should the Tenant decide to buy the property in the future. The Tenant Agent had entered the amount they would expect if the property was purchased, but neglected to check the box to activate the clause. The Seller did not want to pay the Tenant Agent for the sales commission and they wound up in court. The judge said that even though an amount was inserted in the blank, he could not be *certain* of the intention of the parties since the box was not checked. *No commission was paid.* Pay attention to checkboxes!!

1. Conventional Financing: Enter the loan amount, the term (probably <u>30</u> years, unless your client has specified that they want a shorter term, like a 15-year mortgage, or if it is a land loan on the Unimproved Property Contract, which is normally 15-20 years). Interest should be quoted at a rate you think your client will be able to get, plus a little pad in case rates drift up between the time you write the offer and the time the loan is approved. Then if it is a fully amortized loan and doesn't balloon sometime before the end, you just re-enter the number of years from the first blank again (as in <u>30</u> years). Adjusted Origination Charges on a conventional loan should be at 3%. Remember, you are trying to get the Seller to sign this thing. You don't want to scare them off with unobtainable loan terms. If your client is putting 20% down, this paragraph is complete and you would not need the second part. If your client is not putting 20% down, there could be a second loan to describe that covers the difference between that 80% loan-to-value (LTV) ratio loan and the down payment, say 10% or 15% (I don't think we are going to see the return of 20% seconds and 0% down conventional loans in the near future). You would fill the blanks for A.(2) with the appropriate amount, number of years, and a slightly higher interest rate (second liens are more risky so lenders charge more interest). The reason for all of this is to avoid PMI (Private Mortgage Insurance) on the entire loan. There is no PMI required for a loan up to 80% LTV, as it is a low risk for the lender: If a borrower defaults on an 80% loan, the lender forecloses, takes the property back, and puts it on the market through a Realtor® at maybe 95% of market, maybe even 90% to get a quick sale, pays their 7-8% costs of sale (real estate commissions and closing costs) and voila! They got the loan repaid. If the loan is for more than 80%, the risk goes up because they don't have that nice 20% cushion, so they require PMI to pick up the difference in the case of a foreclosure. PMI adds a significant amount to the monthly payment for the Buyer, however, easily $100+, depending on the loan amount of course. That is the benefit of conventional loans as opposed to FHA loans, which can't be split into an 80% first with no insurance and a 10,15,or 20% second with mortgage insurance.

2. Texas Veterans Loan: This is a special program for Texas veterans, those who have been residents of Texas for at least one year, or were residents when they entered the service. It does not use their VA eligibility. For home loans, the Buyer applies through a regular lender who participates with Texas Veterans Land Board (TVLB) for a conventional, FHA or VA loan and TVLB purchases the loan on the secondary market as the investor, after it is made. This allows for a mortgage that is usually a little below market rate, and provides additional discounts for disabled vets. This is a wonderful program, and if you are working with a veteran you should always check that the lender is approved for TVLB.

Texas Veterans is not a primary market lender for home mortgages, however, so this paragraph should not be used for a mortgage on an improved property, only land.

For land loans, the loan comes directly from TVLB instead of through a regular lender, and is the best program available for purchasing vacant land. For one thing, it's a 30-year loan. You can't get a 30-year loan for land anywhere else. Most lenders who will loan on vacant land will only do so for 20 years max, usually only 15, and will only go as high as 80% LTV with an interest rate that is generally 3-4 percent more than residences because the risk of default is higher. For the TVLB loan, the property must be at least one acre, the maximum loan amount is currently $110,000. It's at a better interest rate than market rate for land, maybe only 2% more than market for home loans, there is no PMI, and the minimum down payment is only 5%. You can find out more about TVLB loans at their website: http://www.glo.texas.gov/vlb/index.html

3. FHA Insured Financing: "A Section (probably 203b) FHA insured loan…" You must identify which FHA loan you are going for, and the Section 203b is the norm for a house. Another one you might want would be the 203k, which is a loan that includes money to rehab the house after purchase with funds up to $35,000. The additional money for the remodeling is escrowed by the title company and must be used within a tight timeframe. The 203k application is extraordinarily detailed, requiring several bids by contractors who could perform the work and *very* detailed materials lists. So not many lenders would do them. The service to coordinate the loan/rehab and to escrow the funding for that also adds to the overall loan amount. There are now "Streamlined" 203k loans that do not require a consultant, will allow a homeowner to do 'self-help' for some of the work, and are not so detailed in the application process. You can search for one in your area here. They are definitely worth looking for if you have a buyer and a property that fit the scheme, but there are conventional rehab loans as well that may be easier to get approved.

In completing subparagraph 3, follow the same pattern for the Conventional Financing (subparagraph 1) above. The current maximum FHA loan is 96.5%, and although the seller can pay up to all of the Buyer's costs, the Buyer *must* put in 3.5% as pure down payment, not closing costs.

Be careful to enter the sales price, not the loan amount, in Paragraph D on the next page regarding the appraisal. If the property does not appraise for the sales price, the Buyer can terminate the contract and receive their earnest money back [BUYER OUT #16]

4. VA Guaranteed Financing: The VA loan is a true 0% down loan, for owner-occupied properties only. Again, follow the pattern described in the Conventional paragraph above for amounts, years, interest rates, and Origination charges. As in the FHA paragraph, the Buyer is protected by an additional provision Paragraph D on the next page in case the Property does not appraise for the contract price [BUYER OUT #17].

5. USDA Guaranteed Financing: This is a program for rural-area properties and low-to-middle income, but be aware of what areas in your market qualify. Sometimes suburban cities still qualify because their population is low, even though they are really part of a larger metro area. Again, complete in the same process as used in Conventional.

6. Reverse Mortgage Financing: Reverse mortgages to purchase property became available only recently in Texas, although re-fi was available previously. They are for people 62+, and can be an excellent way to purchase a newer home that would require less maintenance. The purchase program is an FHA insured loan. You should go to a class or two about them to learn more!

B. APPROVAL OF FINANCING: Combines buyer's credit approval and appraisal, insurability and lender required repairs in one paragraph.

64

1. Buyer Approval: First, check a box to indicate whether your clients have to get a loan or not. Sometimes, when interest rates are low meaning money is relatively cheap, people get a loan even though they *could* buy for cash. That's the only reason you would be checking the second box. For the first box, the Buyer must obtain a loan to purchase the house.

Next, how many days to fill in that blank? If your buyer is pre-approved, not just pre-qualified, meaning all of their tax returns, pay stubs, bank statements and anything else the lender requires have all been turned in to the lender and verified, then you could put as few as 0 days in this blank and you would be preserving the property approval part but indicating that as far a buyer approval, your client is as good as a cash buyer. Most lenders would tell you even at that stage to enter at least 2-3 days, though, and many will want to reserve 10. Talk to your client's lender directly for guidance on this. In a seller's market, or for a property that is likely to go into multiple offers, you need to prepare to compete against cash, so the fewer days the better.

If your client is only pre-qualified (meaning the lender has just verified their credit score and maybe employment but not all the financial docs), again ask the lender, but a listing agent is going to question more than 10-15 days to complete that process. Again, the fewer days the better for the Seller, the more the better for the Buyer. Depends what side you're on.

If the Buyer is not approved in the number of days specified, send written notice to the Seller via the listing agent along with a Release of Earnest Money and the earnest money will be returned to the Buyer [BUYER OUT #18]

2. Property Approval: Specifies requirements for property approval: appraisal, insurability, and lender required repairs (resulting from appraiser's notes). There is no time limit on this part, it runs until closing.

If either of these approvals are not met, written notice must be provided in order to receive earnest money. [BUYER OUT #19]

If conventional financing or cash is used, and the Buyer client wants to be protected in case the property doesn't appraise, you must use the ADDENDUM CONCERNING RIGHT TO TERMINATE DUE TO LENDER'S APPRAISAL. This addendum also covers placing a cap on the Buyer's offer above list price in a highly competitive market. It is considered later in this series.

3. This is also one of the six places in our contract where the phrase "time is of the essence" appears. This is a hugely important phrase to TREC. It means that it doesn't matter if both parties agree otherwise orally, like to extend the date a couple of days. If you pass the date without amending it in writing, your client has breached the contract and has no recourse.

C. Security: The loan will be secured, or collateralized, with a lien on the property.

D. FHA/VA Required Provision: Makes the requirement for appraisal absolute. The Buyer can't ask to add something in Special Provisions offering to pay the difference between appraised value and sales price in additional funds, because of that word "notwithstanding". That word means that no matter what anything else in the contract says, this clause trumps it. So, although with a conventional loan your Buyer might offer to cover the difference between sales price and appraised value, it can't be done with FHA or VA.

E. Authorization to Release Information: (1) authorizes the lender to tell the agents the status of the loan. (2) Authorizes the lender and title company to send you a copy of the Closing Disclosure, or settlement statement. This changed with TRID rules, so that now we must be separately authorized.

ADDENDUM CONCERNING RIGHT TO TERMINATE
DUE TO LENDER'S APPRAISAL
*Use only if the Third Party Financing Addendum is attached to the contract and
the transaction does not involve FHA insured or VA guaranteed financing*

CONCERNING THE PROPERTY AT:_____

(Street Address and City)

The financing described in the Third Party Financing Addendum attached to the contract for the sale of the above-referenced Property does not involve FHA or VA financing. *(Check one box only)*

❑ (1) **WAIVER.** Buyer waives Buyer's right to terminate the contract under Paragraph 2B of the Third Party Financing Addendum if Property Approval is not obtained because the opinion of value in the appraisal does not satisfy lender's underwriting requirements.

If the lender reduces the amount of the loan due to the opinion of value, the cash portion of Sales Price is increased by the amount the loan is reduced due to the appraisal.

❑ (2) **PARTIAL WAIVER.** Buyer waives Buyer's right to terminate the contract under Paragraph 2B of the Third Party Financing Addendum if:

(i) Property Approval is not obtained because the opinion of value in the appraisal does not satisfy lender's underwriting requirements; and

(ii) the opinion of value is $_____ or more.

If the lender reduces the amount of the loan due to the opinion of value, the cash portion of Sales Price is increased by the amount the loan is reduced due to the appraisal.

❑ (3) **ADDITIONAL RIGHT TO TERMINATE.** In addition to Buyer's right to terminate under Paragraph 2B of the Third Party Financing Addendum, Buyer may terminate the contract within _____ days after the Effective Date if:

(i) the appraised value, according to the appraisal obtained by Buyer's lender, is less than $_____; and

(ii) Buyer delivers a copy of the appraisal to the Seller.

If Buyer terminates under this paragraph, the earnest money will be refunded to Buyer.

_____   _____
Buyer   Seller

_____   _____
Buyer   Seller

TREC NO. 49-1

ADDENDUM CONCERNING RIGHT TO TERMINATE
DUE TO LENDER'S APPRAISAL

Sometimes, when a conventional loan is being used and the Buyer is paying a substantial down payment, 20-50%, the lower appraisal may not make the loan disapproved and the Buyer could be forced to pay the difference. Additionally, in a highly competitive sellers' market, Buyers may be willing to offer more than what the property appraisal limit to secure the Property.

This addendum resolves three scenarios involving appraisals. The first two are regarding what will happen if the property doesn't appraise for the sales price. Paragraph (1) states that the Buyer will proceed without regard to the appraisal amount, Paragraph (2) is for the same scenario but puts a limit on how <u>far</u> above sales price the Buyer would pay the difference, and Paragraph (3) establishes the Buyer's right to terminate if the appraisal does not match the sales price.

It's important to remember that if FHA or VA financing is being used, this addendum has no power, since the wording in the Third Party Financing Addendum states that "notwithstanding any other provision of this contract" meaning no matter what you put in this addendum it can't be enforced.

**EQUAL HOUSING
OPPORTUNITY**

ADDENDUM FOR
"BACK-UP" CONTRACT

TO CONTRACT CONCERNING THE PROPERTY AT

_____

(Address of Property)

A. The contract to which this Addendum is attached (the Back-Up Contract) is binding upon execution by the parties, and the earnest money and any Option Fee must be paid as provided in the Back-Up Contract. The Back-Up Contract is contingent upon the termination of a previous contract (the First Contract) dated _____, 20_____, for the sale of Property. Except as provided by this Addendum, neither party is required to perform under the Back-Up Contract while it is contingent upon the termination of the First Contract.

B. If the First Contract does not terminate on or before _____, 20_____, the Back-Up Contract terminates and the earnest money will be refunded to Buyer. Seller must notify Buyer immediately of the termination of the First Contract. For purposes of performance, the effective date of the Back-Up Contract changes to the date Buyer receives notice of termination of the First Contract (Amended Effective Date).

C. An amendment or modification of the First Contract will not terminate the First Contract.

D. If Buyer has the unrestricted right to terminate the Back-Up Contract, the time for giving notice of termination begins on the effective date of the Back-Up Contract, continues after the Amended Effective Date and ends upon the expiration of Buyer's unrestricted right to terminate the Back-Up Contract.

E. For purposes of this Addendum, time is of the essence. Strict compliance with the times for performance stated herein is required.

_____   _____
Buyer   Seller

_____   _____
Buyer   Seller

TREC No. 11-7

ADDENDUM FOR "BACK-UP" CONTRACT: When a Buyer client tells you, "We just can't make a decision without sleeping on it. We're just not that kind of people," then they call you the next day to say they decided that yes, you were right, it is the only house on the market with their three must-haves so they are now ready to make an offer. If you check the MLS and find that the house is now "Active Contingent", meaning someone talked the Seller into accepting an offer contingent on the sale of *their* home, a Back-Up offer is quite effective. The Buyer must make it a good enough price to encourage the Seller to accept it and force the First Position Buyer to choose between waiving the contingency and letting the Seller get out of the contract to accept your offer. But what if you check the MLS and it's Pending Taking Backups? Somebody else saw it the day before, realized what it was, and got it under contract, and it's *not* contingent. Secretly, you think, "Ha, ha, told you so!" But then you realize that instead of beginning work on a transaction, you are still in the research and driving around phase. Not so funny.

Then the client asks you about making a Backup offer. This is almost as good as a contingent contract in front of you if the timing is right. You make sure the Buyers understand that a Backup offer functions just like a contract that is in first position--earnest money, title commitment, loan approval process, etc--and they decide that yes, they are willing to go that route. Offering a Back-up is tricky. If you do it within the first 10 days or so, when the first position Buyer is in their option period, it may cause the Seller to mistreat the first position Buyer if that Buyer ask for repairs to be completed as a result of their inspection findings. The Seller may just say "No," to any requests and this may drive off the first position Buyer so your Back-up Buyer moves into first position. If it's much beyond 10 days, I would contact the listing agent and inquire how sure he/she is that the first position contract is going to make it through loan approval, etc. If you tie your Buyer up in a Back-up Contract, their tendency is to quit shopping and hope. The other point to make to your Buyer when placing a Back-up offer is that they are not in a great negotiation position. That is, they need to make their price offered better than the first position contract, in order to incentivize the Seller's ill treatment of the first position Buyer. With our termination option properly used, you should not find yourself in a position of writing a Back-up offer on a property you saw as active and just couldn't get the Buyers off the fence. It only costs a small amount, often as little as $100, to get the property under the Buyer's control, *then* they can make a more thorough decision. But some people are just stubborn about "sleeping on it". You can just see their Mom sitting on their shoulder, whispering, "Don't do it! Don't make a decision this big without sleeping on it!" Or you may find something that has been Pending through driving by and inquiring, and it turns out to be perfect.

This Addendum starts out noting that the Earnest money and any Option Fee must be paid. It further states that the Back-Up Contract is contingent on the termination of a previous contract, identifies the First Contract by its closing date, which you can get from the date pending in the MLS, or call up the listing agent and ask. Paragraph B sets a time limit for automatic withdrawal of this offer, usually a day or two beyond what you think the option period is. If the First Contract survives the option period, your chances of moving into First Position drop significantly. However, with the lenders these days disapproving people right up to closing when they re-verify credit or employment and something has changed, it could happen. Depends how crazy your Buyer is for this Property. The amendment then

70

outlines the process for moving into first position. The Seller must notify your Buyer immediately of the termination of the First Contract, ideally through the use of the TAR-1913 form SELLER'S NOTICE TO BUYER OF REMOVAL OF CONTINGENCY UNDER ADDENDUM FOR BACK-UP CONTRACT which is a brief form and is used to note the change in the effective date of the offer when it becomes an effective contract. Back to the Addendum for Back-Up, Paragraph D also legally changes the Effective Date as originally written to the date the Back-Up contract moves into First Position, starting the Option period over as well. "Time is of the essence", as you can imagine, for all of these critical points to take place.

Hot Market Revision: As of 2018, many of our Texas market are in an extraordinarily long sellers market, and multiple offers are common at more affordable price points. I have had listings in which we received 23 offers, picked one, 22 agents were told theirs was not picked, and no one brought a backup offer. Then the contract fell apart because there was an unknown (to both me and the buyer's agent) decision maker when Daddy came to town. I put the property back on the market the following weekend. 16 offers, one was chosen, 15 were told no, no one brought a backup offer. That contract was terminated on the second day because the buyers "decided they wanted something newer" in spite of my best efforts to ensure the buyers had actually seen the property. I put the property back on the market and finally got a contract that closed, but this episode shows the lack of expertise and willingness to persevere of many agents.

26% of houses go from pending back to active across the US! I have succeeded in about a quarter of my transactions from second place, so this doesn't surprise me. You must get better at writing backups, people! The secret is to offer a limited amount for earnest and option fee and then Additional Earnest Money can be offered upon "Amended Effective Date" by entering that information in Special Provisions. Yes, I know I've warned you off of Special Provisions so keep it short and sweet and refer to that specific term, as that is a recognized indication that your client has moved into first place.

ADDENDUM FOR AUTHORIZING HYDROSTATIC TESTING

EQUAL HOUSING
OPPORTUNITY

CONCERNING THE PROPERTY AT:_____

(Street Address and City)

Consult a licensed plumber about the risks associated with hydrostatic testing before signing this form.

A. **AUTHORIZATION:** Seller authorizes Buyer, at Buyer's expense, to engage a licensed plumber to perform a hydrostatic plumbing test on the Property.

B. **ALLOCATION OF RISK**:

   ❏ (1) Seller shall be liable for damages caused by the hydrostatic plumbing test.

   ❏ (2) Buyer shall be liable for damages caused by the hydrostatic plumbing test.

   ❏ (3) Buyer shall be liable for damages caused by the hydrostatic plumbing test in an amount not to exceed $_____.

_____   _____
Buyer   Seller

_____   _____
Buyer   Seller

TREC NO. 48-0

ADDENDUM FOR AUTHORIZING HYDROSTATIC TESTING: In older slab foundations, pre-70s, the plumbing beneath the slab was iron pipes. Iron pipes and water are natural enemies, so the iron pipe has lost and could be completely rusted away, causing significant plumbing issues. They can be repaired by replumbing that system. Hydrostatic testing involves sealing up the exit plumbing and filling the drains with water to see if the level goes down. It is not a high pressure test, but in cases where the plumbing appliances need to be removed (like a toilet) they may not go right back to the way they were following the test and require additional cost to fix leaks caused by the test itself. This addendum addresses not only the permission, but clarifies who will be responsible for the costs to return the system to functional if necessary.

PROMULGATED BY THE TEXAS REAL ESTATE COMMISSION (TREC)   12-05-11

EQUAL HOUSING
OPPORTUNITY

ADDENDUM FOR
COASTAL AREA PROPERTY
(SECTION 33.135, TEXAS NATURAL RESOURCES CODE)

TO CONTRACT CONCERNING THE PROPERTY AT

_____
(Address of Property)

NOTICE REGARDING COASTAL AREA PROPERTY

1. The real property described in and subject to this contract adjoins and shares a common boundary with the tidally influenced submerged lands of the state. The boundary is subject to change and can be determined accurately only by a survey on the ground made by a licensed state land surveyor in accordance with the original grant from the sovereign. The owner of the property described in this contract may gain or lose portions of the tract because of changes in the boundary.

2. The seller, transferor, or grantor has no knowledge of any prior fill as it relates to the property described in and subject to this contract except:_____
_____
_____.

3. State law prohibits the use, encumbrance, construction, or placing of any structure in, on, or over state-owned submerged lands below the applicable tide line, without proper permission.

4. The purchaser or grantee is hereby advised to seek the advice of an attorney or other qualified person as to the legal nature and effect of the facts set forth in this notice on the property described in and subject to this contract. Information regarding the location of the applicable tide line as to the property described in and subject to this contract may be obtained from the surveying division of the General Land Office in Austin.

_____   _____
Buyer   Seller

_____   _____
Buyer   Seller

TREC No. 33-2

ADDENDUM FOR COASTAL AREA PROPERTY: Notifies the Buyer that the Property adjoins a tidally influenced area and thus its boundary is subject to change, provides for Seller's disclosure of knowledge of landfills, warns of the illegality of placing a structure beyond the tide line without permission, and reminds the Buyer that they are advised to seek the advice of an attorney.

PROMULGATED BY THE TEXAS REAL ESTATE COMMISSION (TREC)   2-10-2014

EQUAL HOUSING OPPORTUNITY

ADDENDUM FOR PROPERTY IN A PROPANE GAS SYSTEM SERVICE AREA
(Section 141.010, Utilities Code)

CONCERNING THE PROPERTY AT _____
(Street Address and City)

NOTICE

The above referenced real property that you are about to purchase may be located in a propane gas system service area, which is authorized by law to provide propane gas service to the properties in the area pursuant to Chapter 141, Utilities Code. If your property is located in a propane gas system service area, there may be special costs or charges that you will be required to pay before you can receive propane gas service. There may be a period required to construct lines or other facilities necessary to provide propane gas service to your property. You are advised to determine if the property is in a propane gas system service area and contact the distribution system retailer to determine the cost that you will be required to pay and the period, if any, that is required to provide propane gas service to your property.

Buyer hereby acknowledges receipt of this notice at or before execution of a binding contract for the purchase of the above referenced real property or at the closing of the real property.

Section 141.010(a), Utilities Code, requires this notice to include a copy of the notice the distribution system retailer is required to record in the real property records. A copy of the recorded notice is attached.

NOTE: Seller can obtain a copy of the required recorded notice from the county clerk's office where the property is located or from the distribution system retailer.

_____   Date   _____   Date
Buyer   Seller

_____   Date   _____   Date
Buyer   Seller

TREC NO. 47-0

ADDENDUM FOR PROPERTY IN A PROPANE GAS SYSTEM SERVICE AREA:

This addendum completes the requirement that a Buyer be notified that the property is in a subdivision in which they must purchase their propane from only one vendor. Advise them to verify costs to see if they are competitive with other non-captive serviced areas!

EQUAL HOUSING
OPPORTUNITY

ADDENDUM FOR
PROPERTY LOCATED SEAWARD OF THE
GULF INTRACOASTAL WATERWAY
(SECTION 61.025, TEXAS NATURAL RESOURCES CODE)

TO CONTRACT CONCERNING THE PROPERTY AT

_____
(Address of Property)

DISCLOSURE NOTICE CONCERNING LEGAL AND ECONOMIC RISKS OF PURCHASING COASTAL REAL PROPERTY NEAR A BEACH

WARNING: THE FOLLOWING NOTICE OF POTENTIAL RISKS OF ECONOMIC LOSS TO YOU AS THE PURCHASER OF COASTAL REAL PROPERTY IS REQUIRED BY STATE LAW.

- READ THIS NOTICE CAREFULLY. DO NOT SIGN THIS CONTRACT UNTIL YOU FULLY UNDERSTAND THE RISKS YOU ARE ASSUMING.

- BY PURCHASING THIS PROPERTY, YOU MAY BE ASSUMING ECONOMIC RISKS OVER AND ABOVE THE RISKS INVOLVED IN PURCHASING INLAND REAL PROPERTY.

- IF YOU OWN A STRUCTURE LOCATED ON COASTAL REAL PROPERTY NEAR A GULF COAST BEACH, IT MAY COME TO BE LOCATED ON THE PUBLIC BEACH BECAUSE OF COASTAL EROSION AND STORM EVENTS.

- AS THE OWNER OF A STRUCTURE LOCATED ON THE PUBLIC BEACH, YOU COULD BE SUED BY THE STATE OF TEXAS AND ORDERED TO REMOVE THE STRUCTURE.

- THE COSTS OF REMOVING A STRUCTURE FROM THE PUBLIC BEACH AND ANY OTHER ECONOMIC LOSS INCURRED BECAUSE OF A REMOVAL ORDER WOULD BE SOLELY YOUR RESPONSIBILITY.

The real property described in this contract is located seaward of the Gulf Intracoastal Waterway to its southernmost point and then seaward of the longitudinal line also known as 97 degrees, 12', 19" which runs southerly to the international boundary from the intersection of the centerline of the Gulf Intracoastal Waterway and the Brownsville Ship Channel. If the property is in close proximity to a beach fronting the Gulf of Mexico, the purchaser is hereby advised that the public has acquired a right of use or easement to or over the area of any public beach by prescription, dedication, or presumption, or has retained a right by virtue of continuous right in the public since time immemorial, as recognized in law and custom.

The extreme seaward boundary of natural vegetation that spreads continuously inland customarily marks the landward boundary of the public easement. If there is no clearly marked natural vegetation line, the landward boundary of the easement is as provided by Sections 61.016 and 61.017, Natural Resources Code.

Much of the Gulf of Mexico coastline is eroding at rates of more than five feet per year. Erosion rates for all Texas Gulf property subject to the open beaches act are available from the Texas General Land Office.

State law prohibits any obstruction, barrier, restraint, or interference with the use of the public easement, including the placement of structures seaward of the landward boundary of the easement. OWNERS OF STRUCTURES ERECTED SEAWARD OF THE VEGETATION LINE (OR OTHER APPLICABLE EASEMENT BOUNDARY) OR THAT BECOME SEAWARD OF THE VEGETATION LINE AS A RESULT OF PROCESSES SUCH AS SHORELINE EROSION ARE SUBJECT TO A LAWSUIT BY THE STATE OF TEXAS TO REMOVE THE STRUCTURES.

The purchaser is hereby notified that the purchaser should: (1) determine the rate of shoreline erosion in the vicinity of the real property; and (2) seek the advice of an attorney or other qualified person before executing this contract or instrument of conveyance as to the relevance of these statutes and facts to the value of the property the purchaser is hereby purchasing or contracting to purchase.

_____   _____
Buyer   Seller

_____   _____
Buyer   Seller

TREC No. 34-4

ADDENDUM FOR PROPERTY LOCATED SEAWARD OF THE GULF INTRACOASTAL WATERWAY: The coastline of Texas is protected by barrier islands. Between those islands and the mainland lies the Laguna Madre, also known as the Intracoastal Waterway. This addendum applies to those islands, and notifies the Buyer that they may not place a structure beyond the vegetation line (dunes) or it will be subject to removal at Owner's cost by the state, and that the Buyer should find out about erosion in the area.

EQUAL HOUSING OPPORTUNITY

ADDENDUM FOR PROPERTY SUBJECT TO MANDATORY MEMBERSHIP IN A PROPERTY OWNERS ASSOCIATION
(NOT FOR USE WITH CONDOMINIUMS)
ADDENDUM TO CONTRACT CONCERNING THE PROPERTY AT

_____

(Street Address and City)

_____

(Name of Property Owners Association, (Association) and Phone Number)

A. SUBDIVISION INFORMATION: "Subdivision Information" means: (i) a current copy of the restrictions applying to the subdivision and bylaws and rules of the Association, and (ii) a resale certificate, all of which are described by Section 207.003 of the Texas Property Code.

(Check only one box):

❑ 1. Within _____ days after the effective date of the contract, Seller shall obtain, pay for, and deliver the Subdivision Information to the Buyer. If Seller delivers the Subdivision Information, Buyer may terminate the contract within 3 days after Buyer receives the Subdivision Information or prior to closing, whichever occurs first, and the earnest money will be refunded to Buyer. If Buyer does not receive the Subdivision Information, Buyer, as Buyer's sole remedy, may terminate the contract at any time prior to closing and the earnest money will be refunded to Buyer.

❑ 2. Within _____ days after the effective date of the contract, Buyer shall obtain, pay for, and deliver a copy of the Subdivision Information to the Seller.   If Buyer obtains the Subdivision Information within the time required, Buyer may terminate the contract within 3 days after Buyer receives the Subdivision Information or prior to closing, whichever occurs first, and the earnest money will be refunded to Buyer.   If Buyer, due to factors beyond Buyer's control, is not able to obtain the Subdivision Information within the time required, Buyer may, as Buyer's sole remedy, terminate the contract within 3 days after the time required or prior to closing, whichever occurs first, and the earnest money will be refunded to Buyer.

❑ 3. Buyer has received and approved the Subdivision Information before signing the contract. Buyer ❑ does ❑ does not require an updated resale certificate. If Buyer requires an updated resale certificate, Seller, at Buyer's expense, shall deliver it to Buyer within 10 days after receiving payment for the updated resale certificate from Buyer. Buyer may terminate this contract and the earnest money will be refunded to Buyer if Seller fails to deliver the updated resale certificate within the time required.

❑ 4. Buyer does not require delivery of the Subdivision Information.

The title company or its agent is authorized to act on behalf of the parties to obtain the Subdivision Information ONLY upon receipt of the required fee for the Subdivision Information from the party obligated to pay.

B. MATERIAL CHANGES. If Seller becomes aware of any material changes in the Subdivision Information, Seller shall promptly give notice to Buyer. Buyer may terminate the contract prior to closing by giving written notice to Seller if: (i) any of the Subdivision Information provided was not true; or (ii) any material adverse change in the Subdivision Information occurs prior to closing, and the earnest money will be refunded to Buyer.

C FEES: Except as provided by Paragraphs A, D and E, Buyer shall pay any and all Association fees or other charges associated with the transfer of the Property not to exceed $_____ and Seller shall pay any excess.

D. DEPOSITS FOR RESERVES: Buyer shall pay any deposits for reserves required at closing by the Association.

E. AUTHORIZATION: Seller authorizes the Association to release and provide the Subdivision Information and any updated resale certificate if requested by the Buyer, the Title Company, or any broker to this sale. If Buyer does not require the Subdivision Information or an updated resale certificate, and the Title Company requires information from the Association (such as the status of dues, special assessments, violations of covenants and restrictions, and a waiver of any right of first refusal), ❑ Buyer ❑ Seller shall pay the Title Company the cost of obtaining the information prior to the Title Company ordering the information.

NOTICE TO BUYER REGARDING REPAIRS BY THE ASSOCIATION: The Association may have the sole responsibility to make certain repairs to the Property. If you are concerned about the condition of any part of the Property which the Association is required to repair, you should not sign the contract unless you are satisfied that the Association will make the desired repairs.

_____   _____
Buyer   Seller

_____   _____
Buyer   Seller

TREC NO. 36-8

ADDENDUM FOR PROPERTY SUBJECT TO MANDATORY MEMBERSHIP IN A PROPERTY OWNERS ASSOCIATION: This addendum contains one of the biggest loopholes for the Buyer, and many agents have no idea. Often Property Owner Associations are called Home Owner Associations, and so we shorten that to HOA. I'm going to use POA, the legal term, to match up with the addendum, but they mean the same thing.

First off, **Subdivision Information** is defined, and includes the restrictions of the community, the bylaws, and a resale certificate. This information must be delivered by the POA and there is a cost involved to the Seller, anywhere from $150 to as much as $650 or more. Even if the Seller is an active member of the POA and offers to provide the most recent set of restrictions and bylaws, the POA will not provide the resale certificate without the full fee. It's not fair, but they don't have to be. The Property cannot legally be transferred without the resale certificate. That resale certificate contains general contact information for the POA as well as any special assessments current or looming, lawsuits pending, unpermitted construction, etc. This is important information, and the Texas Property Code ensures that a Buyer is apprised of what he/she is getting into. The tricky part is this: The Seller's agent might not recommend incurring this expense for the Seller until he/she has some certainty that the transaction will close. It would be nice to wait until after the option period is over, at least. However, early timing is crucial. It is likely that these documents have not been ordered from the POA prior to a contract being made, as there is a cost and the information is only good for 180 days. The Addendum states that if the Buyer never receives the information, they can terminate the contract at any time and get their earnest money back [BUYER OUT #20]. No problem, that just makes sense. But it goes further to say that whenever the Seller *does* deliver the information (or the title company delivers it for them), the Buyer has 3 days to terminate the contract *for any reason*. In other words, a reason need not even be related to the restrictions or indebtedness of the POA [BUYER OUT #21]. This is not a negotiable blank in the TREC contract, it's 3 days; but if it appears that it will take longer to provide the documentation, the Seller and Buyer could agree to a different number of days with an addendum to effect that change. Add to that the days for the POA to provide the information to the title company. It can take anywhere from 3 days to 15 days to get the documents from the POA. The POA is not limited in the time they can take to provide it. Some POAs are managed by a larger company that handles this process, but some are just groups of neighbors that handle the business of the POA as volunteers. You can see that as a Seller, it would be much better for the Buyer to be able to check box A(3), indicating that the Buyer has already received and approved the documents, just like the Sellers Disclosure in Paragraph 7 of the contract. As a Listing Agent, a good practice would be to encourage ordering the POA documents and resale certificate during the listing period. It is an expense for the Seller, but it's far better than handing over a free option period. Remember, the POA has to update this information upon request for up to 180 days from when they first issue it. Box A(4), removing all requirement for subdivision info can't be used if there is a need for a resale certificate, and there usually is. The only time you would use A(4) would be if the Buyer were already a member of the HOA, i.e. buying another house in their current subdivision.

The bolded paragraph in the middle of the page states that the title company will only order the subdivision information upon receipt of payment for it. That would indicate that they would need to wait for specific instructions from whomever that was, but in practice title companies are pretty much disregarding this step and will go ahead and order, often taking payment at closing with no further said. So be careful about ordering it yourself, it may have already been done, and you will end up rebating it back to your client instead of them being charged twice for it.

B. Material Changes provides yet another Buyer Out [BUYER OUT #22] in the case of a rule change or other change in the HOA's fiscal status [BUYER OUT #23] occurs between contract and close.

C. Fees, the Buyer and Seller can negotiate how to split those costs for the POA info. Some people say it should be split 50/50, some say that it's the Seller's cost to sell the property. It's negotiable, but pay attention to it to either limit the Buyer's exposure or get back half of what the Seller paid, depending on your side.

D. Deposits for Reserves requires the Buyer to pay any deposits required by the POA.

E. Authorization authorizes the buyer, title company, or brokers to order and receive the POA information on the Seller's behalf. It also allows for a choice of which party will pay for updated information if necessary.

Notice to Buyer Regarding Repairs By The Association: a notice to the Buyer to make sure they are satisfied with the likelihood that the POA will complete any repairs to the property that they are responsible for (usually structural and exterior), not to rely on the Seller. Before they sign the contract.

EQUAL HOUSING OPPORTUNITY

ADDENDUM FOR
RELEASE OF LIABILITY ON ASSUMED LOAN
AND/OR RESTORATION OF SELLER'S VA ENTITLEMENT

TO CONTRACT CONCERNING THE PROPERTY AT

_____

(Address of Property)

❑ **A. RELEASE OF SELLER'S LIABILITY ON LOAN TO BE ASSUMED:**

Within _____ days after the effective date of this contract Seller and Buyer shall apply for release of Seller's liability from (a) any conventional lender, (b) VA and any lender whose loan has been guaranteed by VA, or (c) FHA and any lender whose loan has been insured by FHA. Seller and Buyer shall furnish all required information and documents. If any release of liability has not been approved by the Closing Date: (check one box only)

❑ (1) This contract will terminate and the earnest money will be refunded to Buyer.

❑ (2) Failure to obtain release approval will not delay closing.

❑ **B. RESTORATION OF SELLER'S ENTITLEMENT FOR VA LOAN:**

Within _____ days after the effective date of this contract Seller and Buyer shall apply for restoration of Seller's VA entitlement and shall furnish all information and documents required by VA. If restoration has not been approved by the Closing Date: (check one box only)

❑ (1) This contract will terminate and the earnest money will be refunded to Buyer.

❑ (2) Failure to obtain restoration approval will not delay closing.

NOTICE: VA will not restore Seller's VA entitlement unless Buyer: (a) is a veteran, (b) has sufficient unused VA entitlement and (c) is otherwise qualified. If Seller desires restoration of VA entitlement, paragraphs A and B should be used.

Seller shall pay the cost of securing the release and restoration.

Seller's deed will contain any loan assumption clause required by FHA, VA or any lender.

_____   _____
Buyer   Seller

_____   _____
Buyer   Seller

TREC No. 12-3

ADDENDUM FOR RELEASE OF LIABILITY ON ASSUMED LOAN: should be used with any loan assumption, which we will get back into whenever interest rates return to the more normal level around 8%. At that time, there will be homes with FHA and VA loans that were made at the 4% interest rate, that will be very attractive to your buyer. This addendum establishes what will be done if the lender will not release the Seller from further liability on an assumed loan, providing the Buyer an Out if that does not occur within a specified timeframe [BUYER OUT #24]. Paragraph B is also used in the case of an assumed VA loan, and establishes what will be done if the Seller cannot have his/her VA loan entitlement restored within a certain timeframe, again providing for the Buyer to get out and receive the earnest money back [BUYER OUT #25]. Paired with the Loan Assumption Addendum.

EQUAL HOUSING OPPORTUNITY

ADDENDUM FOR RESERVATION OF OIL, GAS, AND OTHER MINERALS

ADDENDUM TO CONTRACT CONCERNING THE PROPERTY AT

_____

(Street Address and City)

NOTICE: For use ONLY if Seller reserves all or a portion of the Mineral Estate.

A. "Mineral Estate" means all oil, gas, and other minerals in and under and that may be produced from the Property, any royalty under any existing or future mineral lease covering any part of the Property, executive rights (including the right to sign a mineral lease covering any part of the Property), implied rights of ingress and egress, exploration and development rights, production and drilling rights, mineral lease payments, and all related rights and benefits. The Mineral Estate does NOT include water, sand, gravel, limestone, building stone, caliche, surface shale, near-surface lignite, and iron, but DOES include the reasonable use of these surface materials for mining, drilling, exploring, operating, developing, or removing the oil, gas, and other minerals from the Property.

B. *Subject to Section C below,* the Mineral Estate owned by Seller, if any, will be conveyed unless reserved as follows (check one box only):

☐ (1) Seller reserves all of the Mineral Estate owned by Seller.

☐ (2) Seller reserves an undivided _____ interest in the Mineral Estate owned by Seller. *NOTE: If Seller does not own all of the Mineral Estate, Seller reserves only this percentage or fraction of Seller's interest.*

C. Seller ☐ does ☐ does *not* reserve and retain implied rights of ingress and egress and of reasonable use of the Property (including surface materials) for mining, drilling, exploring, operating, developing, or removing the oil, gas, and other minerals. *NOTE: Surface rights that may be held by other owners of the Mineral Estate who are not parties to this transaction (including existing mineral lessees) will NOT be affected by Seller's election. Seller's failure to complete Section C will be deemed an election to convey all surface rights described herein.*

D. If Seller does not reserve all of Seller's interest in the Mineral Estate, Seller shall, within 7 days after the Effective Date, provide Buyer with the contact information of any existing mineral lessee known to Seller.

IMPORTANT NOTICE: The Mineral Estate affects important rights, the full extent of which may be unknown to Seller. A full examination of the title to the Property completed by an attorney with expertise in this area is the only proper means for determining title to the Mineral Estate with certainty. In addition, attempts to convey or reserve certain interest out of the Mineral Estate separately from other rights and benefits owned by Seller may have unintended consequences. Precise contract language is essential to preventing disagreements between present and future owners of the Mineral Estate. If Seller or Buyer has any questions about their respective rights and interests in the Mineral Estate and how such rights and interests may be affected by this contract, they are strongly encouraged to consult an attorney with expertise in this area.

CONSULT AN ATTORNEY BEFORE SIGNING: TREC rules prohibit real estate licensees from giving legal advice. READ THIS FORM CAREFULLY.

_____   _____
Buyer   Seller

_____   _____
Buyer   Seller

TREC NO. 44-2

ADDENDUM FOR RESERVATION OF OIL, GAS AND OTHER MINERALS: This addendum came about when the Barnett Shale field was being leased out for natural gas extraction. This shale lies underneath an area of Fort Worth that is now covered with subdivisions. The shale has always been there, of course, but only within the past few years has it become economically feasible to extract its natural gas, because of the "fracturing" or "fracking" process of pushing water and chemicals into the shale to push out the gas, combined with the advent of horizontal drilling. There was a point at which petroleum landmen were going through those little subdivisions and leasing up the mineral rights from homeowners, and the homeowners would start getting lease payments, some $2-300, even as much as $800 per month. When they went to sell the properties, the Sellers wanted to continue to receive the lease payments. And what do you think the Buyers wanted? To get the lease payments. So a lot of arguments ensued, and real estate agents were trying to parse out the mineral rights in Special Provisions. Definitely practicing law. The Farm and Ranch Contract does address the mineral rights, but not the Residential. TREC put a stop to this law-practicing, which effectively stopped the real estate transactions in those areas of Fort Worth where the Sellers wanted to hang on to their mineral rights. No matter what type of land it is, Sellers seem to want this, but it makes the land much less valuable to a Buyer if someone else retains the surface rights to come onto their property and drill or even just explore. With a small residential property, that wouldn't be likely, but still. And of course as I said before, the Buyers want the added bonus of the lease payments, too. I may have avoided higher math, but I do know that two people cannot have the same thing so this must be negotiated on this addendum, and it should be used if addressing mineral rights that will not simply transfer as part of the deed. If that is the case, no addendum is necessary, as it is understood that a property includes surface, subsurface and air rights *unless* they are separately transferred.

EQUAL HOUSING
OPPORTUNITY

PROMULGATED BY THE TEXAS REAL ESTATE COMMISSION (TREC)

ADDENDUM FOR
SALE OF OTHER PROPERTY BY BUYER

TO CONTRACT CONCERNING THE PROPERTY AT

_____

_____
(Address of Property)

A. The contract is contingent upon Buyer's **receipt of the proceeds** from the sale of Buyer's property at_____
(Address) on or before _____, 20_____ (the Contingency). If the Contingency is not satisfied or waived by Buyer by the above date, the contract will terminate automatically and the earnest money will be refunded to Buyer.

NOTICE: The date inserted in this Paragraph should be no later than the Closing Date specified in Paragraph 9 of the contract.

B. If Seller accepts a written offer to sell the Property, Seller shall notify Buyer (1) of such acceptance **AND** (2) that Seller requires Buyer to waive the Contingency. Buyer must waive the Contingency on or before the _____ day after Seller's notice to Buyer; otherwise the contract will terminate automatically and the earnest money will be refunded to Buyer.

C. Buyer may waive the Contingency only by notifying Seller of the waiver and depositing $_____ with escrow agent as additional earnest money. All notices and waivers must be in writing and are effective when delivered in accordance with the contract.

D. If Buyer waives the Contingency and fails to close and fund solely due to Buyer's non-receipt of proceeds from Buyer's property described in Paragraph A above, Buyer will be in default. If such default occurs, Seller may exercise the remedies specified in Paragraph 15 of the contract.

E. For purposes of this Addendum time is of the essence; strict compliance with the times for performance stated herein is required.

_____   _____
Buyer   Seller

_____   _____
Buyer   Seller

This form has been approved by the Texas Real Estate Commission for use with similarly approved or promulgated contract forms. Such approval relates to this form only. TREC forms are intended for use only by trained real estate licensees. No representation is made as to the legal validity or adequacy of any provision in any specific transactions. It is not suitable for complex transactions. Texas Real Estate Commission, P.O. Box 12188, Austin, TX 78711-2188, 512-936-3000 (http://www.trec.texas.gov) TREC No. 10-6. This form replaces TREC No. 10-5.

TREC No. 10-6

ADDENDUM FOR SALE OF OTHER PROPERTY BY BUYER: This is the "Contingency Addendum", for use when your Buyer client still has a house to sell and must do so to have the money/credit to purchase the subject property. Frankly, I don't know why anyone would accept a contingent offer. If I were the Seller, I would say, "Go, sell your house. If we're still here when you get that done, come back. We'll talk." But people do; maybe they have had the property on the market for a long time and a bird in the hand is worth two in the bush. The opportunity usually presents itself to a Buyer's Agent when working with folks early on; sometimes they have not even admitted that they must sell their other house before they can purchase the one you are showing them that is... just...perfect. Of course, you let them know that it's not a very strong offer but they insist. Usually, I offer to present a contingent offer in person. A Buyer's Agent can ask the Listing Agent for this opportunity any time, and unless the Seller has specifically forbidden it, the Listing Agent should allow it and set it up. You go in, pitch your offer to the Seller(s) and Listing Agent, then leave and allow them to discuss it. I always say, "I'll be right outside in my car in case you have any questions" assuming a quick response.

What I tell Buyers who want to make a contingent offer is this: You need to know that you are using up all of your negotiation currency on the contingency, so you can't also offer a lowball price. If you want me to pitch this offer for you in the best light, the absolute best situation is if I can say, "My clients are making this great offer, they do have a house to sell but it is under contract, scheduled to close in ___ weeks. Here is their contract, their Buyer's prequalification letter and any other documentation your agent could want me to provide." *Second* best would be, "My clients are making this great offer, they do have a house to sell but it is on the market at a great price. Here is a market analysis so that you can see it is the best price in the neighborhood and why I estimate it will take 60 days to sell and close. I invite you and your agent to view the property and analyze the sale probability." *Worst* would be, "My clients are making this great offer, they do have a house to sell and it's not even on the market yet." So if it is number three, we're probably not writing an offer just yet, but the Buyers are now super-motivated to get staged, photographed, and on the market at a very realistic price.

In the first paragraph, the contract is made contingent upon receipt of the proceeds from the sale of the Buyer's property, and the Buyer's Agent fills in the Buyer's property address and the closing date. If this contract doesn't close, the contract on the replacement house automatically terminates and earnest money goes to Buyer. [BUYER OUT #26] Paragraph B says that if the Seller accepts another *written* offer (this would be a Backup Offer), the Buyer must either waive the contingency (stay in contract without it), or release the Seller from the contract and take their earnest money back. [BUYER OUT #27] There is a blank provided for the Seller to limit the time for this decision to be made. I recommend keeping it very short, no more than 2 days. Why would they need more time? They couldn't buy it without selling theirs, what rabbit are they going to pull out of a hat? Unless they have a contract now and feel SOOO confident about it closing that they would risk losing their earnest money. This doesn't make me or TREC feel confident, though. So in paragraph C, TREC is demanding that if the Buyer does waive the contingency, we should get more earnest money. I recommend a *lot* more if you are the Seller's agent. What, you couldn't buy it without selling yours last week, but now you can? We want more skin in the game. At least my Seller will be compensated in money for having their property off the market, possibly losing a real Buyer. Paragraph E contains another instance of 'time is of the essence', so TREC is saying that the close date and time for waiving the contingency will not be viewed as flexible in any way by a court.

ADDENDUM FOR SELLER'S DISCLOSURE OF INFORMATION ON LEAD-BASED PAINT AND LEAD-BASED PAINT HAZARDS AS REQUIRED BY FEDERAL LAW

CONCERNING THE PROPERTY AT _____
(Street Address and City)

A. LEAD WARNING STATEMENT: "Every purchaser of any interest in residential real property on which a residential dwelling was built prior to 1978 is notified that such property may present exposure to lead from lead-based paint that may place young children at risk of developing lead poisoning. Lead poisoning in young children may produce permanent neurological damage, including learning disabilities, reduced intelligence quotient, behavioral problems, and impaired memory. Lead poisoning also poses a particular risk to pregnant women. The seller of any interest in residential real property is required to provide the buyer with any information on lead-based paint hazards from risk assessments or inspections in the seller's possession and notify the buyer of any known lead-based paint hazards. A risk assessment or inspection for possible lead-paint hazards is recommended prior to purchase."
NOTICE: Inspector must be properly certified as required by federal law.

B. SELLER'S DISCLOSURE:
   1. PRESENCE OF LEAD-BASED PAINT AND/OR LEAD-BASED PAINT HAZARDS (check one box only):
     ☐(a) Known lead-based paint and/or lead-based paint hazards are present in the Property (explain): _____
     _____ .
     ☐(b) Seller has no actual knowledge of lead-based paint and/or lead-based paint hazards in the Property.
   2. RECORDS AND REPORTS AVAILABLE TO SELLER (check one box only):
     ☐(a) Seller has provided the purchaser with all available records and reports pertaining to lead-based paint and/or lead-based paint hazards in the Property (list documents):_____
     _____ .
     ☐(b) Seller has no reports or records pertaining to lead-based paint and/or lead-based paint hazards in the Property.

C. BUYER'S RIGHTS (check one box only):
   ☐1. Buyer waives the opportunity to conduct a risk assessment or inspection of the Property for the presence of lead-based paint or lead-based paint hazards.
   ☐2. Within ten days after the effective date of this contract, Buyer may have the Property inspected by inspectors selected by Buyer. If lead-based paint or lead-based paint hazards are present, Buyer may terminate this contract by giving Seller written notice within 14 days after the effective date of this contract, and the earnest money will be refunded to Buyer.

D. BUYER'S ACKNOWLEDGMENT (check applicable boxes):
   ☐1. Buyer has received copies of all information listed above.
   ☐2. Buyer has received the pamphlet *Protect Your Family from Lead in Your Home*.

E. BROKERS' ACKNOWLEDGMENT: Brokers have informed Seller of Seller's obligations under 42 U.S.C. 4852d to: (a) provide Buyer with the federally approved pamphlet on lead poisoning prevention; (b) complete this addendum; (c) disclose any known lead-based paint and/or lead-based paint hazards in the Property; (d) deliver all records and reports to Buyer pertaining to lead-based paint and/or lead-based paint hazards in the Property; (e) provide Buyer a period of up to 10 days to have the Property inspected; and (f) retain a completed copy of this addendum for at least 3 years following the sale. Brokers are aware of their responsibility to ensure compliance.

F. CERTIFICATION OF ACCURACY: The following persons have reviewed the information above and certify, to the best of their knowledge, that the information they have provided is true and accurate.

_____	_____	_____	_____
Buyer	Date	Seller	Date
_____	_____	_____	_____
Buyer	Date	Seller	Date
_____	_____	_____	_____
Other Broker	Date	Listing Broker	Date

The form of this addendum has been approved by the Texas Real Estate Commission for use only with similarly approved or promulgated forms of contracts. Such approval relates to this contract form only. TREC forms are intended for use only by trained real estate licensees. No representation is made as to the legal validity or adequacy of any provision in any specific transactions. It is not suitable for complex transactions. Texas Real Estate Commission, P.O. Box 12188, Austin, TX 78711-2188, 512-936-3000 (http://www.trec.texas.gov)

TREC NO. OP-L

ADDENDUM FOR SELLERS DISCLOSURE OF INFORMATION ON LEAD-BASED PAINT: Applies to properties built prior to 1978, when lead was an ingredient in paint. Most brokers will also want this form in their files for properties built during that year, since that paint was probably still on the market for a while. This is an *extremely* important form. It is the Seller's responsibility to disclose any information they have regarding lead-based paint, and even to disclose that they do NOT have such information. According to the Centers for Disease Control and Prevention, we still have over a quarter-million children per year in the US alone diagnosed with lead poisoning, which can cause neurological damage resulting in decreased IQ, behavioral problems and other learning disabilities. The further we get from getting lead out of paint and gasoline in 1978, the higher the overall IQ of the children tested (25 IQ points now--it's not your imagination that your kids are smarter than you). It is believed that much of the offending lead is now found in soil, a result of auto emissions over the years that lead was an allowed additive in gasoline, as well as exterior paint leaching down to the ground. That theory is supported by the fact that in Japan, where it is common practice to remove street shoes before entering the home, the incidence of lead poisoning is far lower.

Contractors who remodel homes built before 1978 must now have at least one worker on site at all times who has attended an EPA-sponsored course in the proper handling of old lead paint in remodeling, which includes capturing lead paint that is removed or even just sawn through, shielding other areas from contamination by the lead dust, wetting the dust for removal, etc. Penalties for not having a certified worker on site or for not following the EPA's guidelines can be as much as $17,000 for a first offense. http://www.epa.gov/compliance/resources/policies/civil/tsca/1018erpp-1207.pdf

More importantly for you, though, is the fact that the EPA audits Brokers' files for this form *and its completeness* for up to 4 years from the closing date, and the fine for the lack of a completely filled out form signed by all parties (which includes the Brokers or their agents) can be as much as $11,000 and would NOT be covered by E&O or liability insurance. So you can see why your Broker is such a stickler for this form. It provides for the Seller to disclose whether he/she has *actual knowledge* of lead-based paint used in/on the Property, to include copies of any reports of that lead, for the Buyer to either take a 10-day opportunity to have a professional inspection completed and terminate the contract if any is found [BUYER OUT TAGGED EARLIER] or to waive that opportunity, and for the Buyer to state whether he/she received the pamphlet *Protect Your Family from Lead in Your Home*. This pamphlet is critical. It is a 16-page government pamphlet that is available to you in Zipforms if you have that software (if you are a Realtor®, you do). My recommendation to you is to provide that pamphlet to the Buyer's agent via email if you are the Listing agent, so that you have written proof that you provided it. If you are a Buyer's agent, similarly emailing it to your client provides that written proof. That email (and all others) should be part of your file upon closing. Both brokers or their agents must also sign this form, indicating that they know of their responsibility to have the form completed by both parties and to retain the form in their files.

EQUAL HOUSING
OPPORTUNITY

AMENDMENT
TO CONTRACT CONCERNING THE PROPERTY AT

_____

(Street Address and City)

Seller and Buyer amend the contract as follows: (check each applicable box)

☐(1) The Sales Price in Paragraph 3 of the contract is:

A. Cash portion of Sales Price payable by Buyer at closing ....$_____

B. Sum of financing described in the contract..$_____

C. Sales Price (Sum of A and B) ....$_____

☐(2) In addition to any repairs and treatments otherwise required by the contract, Seller, at Seller's expense, shall complete the following repairs and treatments:

☐(3) The date in Paragraph 9 of the contract is changed to _____, 20_____.

☐(4) The amount in Paragraph 12A(1)(b) of the contract is changed to $ _____.

☐(5) The cost of lender required repairs and treatment, as itemized on the attached list, will be paid as follows: $ _____ by Seller; $ _____ by Buyer.

☐(6) Buyer has paid Seller an additional Option Fee of $ _____ for an extension of the unrestricted right to terminate the contract on or before _____ , 20_____. This additional Option Fee ☐ will ☐ will not be credited to the Sales Price.

☐(7) Buyer waives the unrestricted right to terminate the contract for which the Option Fee was paid.

☐(8) The date for Buyer to give written notice to Seller that Buyer cannot obtain Credit Approval as set forth in the Third Party Financing Condition Addendum for Credit Approval is changed to _____, 20_____.

☐(9) **Other Modifications**: (Insert only factual statements and business details applicable to this sale.)

EXECUTED the _____day of _____, 20_____ . (BROKER: FILL IN THE DATE OF FINAL ACCEPTANCE.)

_____   _____
Buyer   Seller

_____   _____
Buyer   Seller

TREC NO. 39-7

AMENDMENT provides a formal way to make 8 of the most often-used changes in the contract, and a box for "Other Modifications" if the change needed does not conform to those first 8. This form must be used unless an attorney has drafted another amendment. You can add as many amendments to the contract as become necessary during the contract-to-close process. It's pretty self-explanatory, except a question that often comes up is how much to offer to extend the option period. TREC is very clear that if no additional money is offered, there is no option. Since our standard deed uses 'ten dollars and other good and valuable consideration,' they obviously think that is a sufficient place-holder.

BUYER'S TEMPORARY RESIDENTIAL LEASE

1. PARTIES: The parties to this Lease are_____
(Landlord) and _____(Tenant).

2. LEASE: Landlord leases to Tenant the Property described in the Contract between Landlord as Seller and Tenant as Buyer known as _____(address).
_____

3. TERM: The term of this Lease commences _____ and terminates as specified in Paragraph 18.

4. RENTAL: Rental will be $_____ per day. Upon commencement of this Lease, Tenant shall pay to Landlord the full amount of rental of $ _____ for the anticipated term of the Lease (commencement date to the Closing Date specified in Paragraph 9 of the Contract). If the actual term of this Lease differs from the anticipated term, any additional rent or reimbursement will be paid at closing. No portion of the rental will be applied to payment of any items covered by the Contract.

5. DEPOSIT: Tenant has paid to Landlord $_____ as a deposit to secure performance of this Lease by Tenant. If this Lease is terminated before the Closing Date, Landlord may use the deposit to satisfy Tenant's obligations under this Lease. Landlord shall refund to Tenant any unused portion of the deposit together with an itemized list of all deductions from the deposit within 30 days after Tenant (a) surrenders possession of the Property and (b) provides Landlord written notice of Tenant's forwarding address. If this Lease is terminated by the closing and funding of the sale of the Property, the deposit will be refunded to Tenant at closing and funding.
NOTICE: The deposit must be in addition to the earnest money under the Contract.

6. UTILITIES: Tenant shall pay all utility connections, deposits and charges except _____
_____, which Landlord shall pay.

7. USE OF PROPERTY: Tenant may use the Property only for residential purposes. Tenant may not assign this Lease or sublet any part of the Property.

8. PETS: Tenant may not keep pets on the Property except _____.

9. CONDITION OF PROPERTY: Tenant accepts the Property in its present condition and state of repair, but Landlord shall make all repairs and improvements required by the Contract. If this Lease is terminated prior to closing, Tenant shall surrender possession of the Property to Landlord in its present condition, as improved by Landlord, except normal wear and tear and any casualty loss.

10. ALTERATIONS: Tenant may not: (a) make any holes or drive nails into the woodwork, floors, walls or ceilings (b) alter, paint or decorate the Property or (c) install improvements or fixtures without the prior written consent of Landlord. Any improvements or fixtures placed on the Property during the Lease become a part of the Property.

11. SPECIAL PROVISIONS:

12. INSPECTIONS: Landlord may enter at reasonable times to inspect, replace, repair or complete the improvements. Tenant shall provide Landlord door keys and access codes to allow access to the Property during the term of the Lease.

13. LAWS: Tenant shall comply with all applicable laws, restrictions, ordinances, rules and regulations with respect to the Property.

14. REPAIRS AND MAINTENANCE: Except as otherwise provided in this Lease, Tenant shall bear all expense of repairing, replacing and maintaining the Property, including but not limited to the yard, trees, shrubs, and all equipment and appliances, unless otherwise required by the Texas Property Code. Tenant shall promptly repair at Tenant's expense any damage to the Property caused directly or indirectly by any act or omission of the Tenant or any person other than the Landlord, Landlord's agents or invitees.

Initialed for identification by Landlord _____ and Tenant_____   TREC NO. 16-5

15.INDEMNITY: Tenant indemnifies Landlord from the claims of all third parties for injury or damage to the person or property of such third party arising from the use or occupancy of the Property by Tenant. This indemnification includes attorney's fees, costs and expenses incurred by Landlord.

16.INSURANCE: Landlord and Tenant shall each maintain such insurance on the contents and Property as each party may deem appropriate during the term of this Lease. <u>NOTE</u>: CONSULT YOUR INSURANCE AGENT; POSSESSION OF THE PROPERTY BY BUYER AS TENANT MAY CHANGE INSURANCE POLICY COVERAGE.

17.DEFAULT: If Tenant fails to perform or observe any provision of this Lease and fails, within 24 hours after notice by Landlord, to commence and diligently pursue to remedy such failure, Tenant will be in default.

18.TERMINATION: This Lease terminates upon (a) closing and funding of the sale under the Contract, (b) termination of the Contract prior to closing, (c) Tenant's default under this Lease, or (d) Tenant's default under the Contract, whichever occurs first. Upon termination other than by closing and funding of the sale, Tenant shall surrender possession of the property.

19.HOLDING OVER: Any possession by Tenant after termination creates a tenancy at sufferance and will not operate to renew or extend this Lease. Tenant shall pay $_____ per day during the period of any possession after termination as damages, in addition to any other remedies to which Landlord is entitled.

20.ATTORNEY'S FEES: The prevailing party in any legal proceeding brought under or with respect to this Lease is entitled to recover from the non-prevailing party all costs of such proceeding and reasonable attorney's fees.

21.SMOKE ALARMS: The Texas Property Code requires Landlord to install smoke alarms in certain locations within the Property at Landlord's expense. <u>Tenant expressly waives Landlord's duty to inspect and repair smoke alarms.</u>

22.SECURITY DEVICES: The requirements of the Texas Property Code relating to security devices do not apply to a residential lease for a term of 90 days or less.

23.CONSULT YOUR ATTORNEY: Real estate licensees cannot give legal advice. This Lease is intended to be legally binding. READ IT CAREFULLY. If you do not understand the effect of this Lease, consult your attorney BEFORE signing.

24.NOTICES: All notices from one party to the other must be in writing and are effective when mailed to, hand-delivered at, or transmitted by facsimile or electronic transmission as follows:

To Landlord: _____   **To Tenant:** _____

_____   _____

_____   _____

_____   _____

Telephone: (___) _____   Telephone: (___) _____

Facsimile: (___) _____   Facsimile: (___) _____

E-mail: _____   E-mail: _____

_____   _____
Landlord   Tenant

_____   _____
Landlord   Tenant

TREC NO. 16-5

BUYER'S TEMPORARY RESIDENTIAL LEASE: Good for 90 days only, these are very short forms--only 2 pages. They are not meant to cover everything a regular 14-page lease covers, since the parties are known to each other and the main point is to establish liability in case of loss (fire, someone being injured) or damage (moving out can mess up sheetrock in a stairway). The Buyer's lease starts on a date prior to closing and ends on closing day, when they become the owner. The Seller's lease starts on closing day and ends on an agreed date afterward.

In practice, I am very opposed to allowing a Buyer to move into a house before closing. I had to do it once but it was my Seller's decision in spite of my advice. It was a serviceman and his family, set to close on Friday but got pushed to Monday, so the Buyer would be staying in a hotel over the weekend with their five kids. I told the Seller it wasn't our fault that they chose to have five kids, but the Buyer was a Marine, the Seller was a Marine, and he said let them move in.

That was the single instance I have of Buyer temporary leasing, but I have heard of several others resulting in disputes over Buyers deciding they did not want to purchase the property after all, Buyers who only needed to put their possessions into the garage overnight who were discovered moved in and cooking supper by the Seller's agent. Even if that worked out alright and they weren't breaking in, what happens if something happens to their possessions in that garage? The Seller could be liable for it (and their homeowner's insurance would likely deny the claim). Lots of problems can come up when a Buyer is allowed to take possession early. And what if the contract falls apart and you have to evict the not-buyers?

EQUAL HOUSING
OPPORTUNITY

ENVIRONMENTAL ASSESSMENT, THREATENED OR ENDANGERED SPECIES, AND WETLANDS ADDENDUM

TO CONTRACT CONCERNING THE PROPERTY AT

_____

(Address of Property)

❑ A. ENVIRONMENTAL ASSESSMENT: Buyer, at Buyer's expense, may obtain an environmental assessment report prepared by an environmental specialist.

❑ B. THREATENED OR ENDANGERED SPECIES: Buyer, at Buyer's expense, may obtain a report from a natural resources professional to determine if there are any threatened or endangered species or their habitats as defined by the Texas Parks and Wildlife Department or the U.S. Fish and Wildlife Service.

❑ C. WETLANDS: Buyer, at Buyer's expense, may obtain a report from an environmental specialist to determine if there are wetlands, as defined by federal or state law or regulation.

Within _____ days after the effective date of the contract, Buyer may terminate the contract by furnishing Seller a copy of any report noted above that adversely affects the use of the Property and a notice of termination of the contract. Upon termination, the earnest money will be refunded to Buyer.

_____   _____
Buyer   Seller

_____   _____
Buyer   Seller

TREC No. 28-2

ENVIRONMENTAL, THREATENED OR ENDANGERED SPECIES AND WETLANDS ADDENDUM: Notifies the Buyer that he/she is free to obtain special inspections for these any of these three conditions, and allows a separate negotiated number of days for those inspections to occur. There could be several ways these conditions could impact the Buyer's use of the property. For example, in my area there are areas designated for nesting of the golden-cheeked warbler, and no timber cutting, brush burning, etc, can occur during those months when the birds would be active. That would be bad to find out if you had planned to clear and break ground on your new home at that time. The Buyer may terminate the contract by providing adverse findings and get their earnest money back. BUYER OUTS TAGGED EARLIER.

EQUAL HOUSING OPPORTUNITY

LOAN ASSUMPTION ADDENDUM
TO CONTRACT CONCERNING THE PROPERTY AT

_____

(Address of Property)

A. CREDIT DOCUMENTATION. To establish Buyer's creditworthiness, Buyer shall deliver to Seller within_____days after the effective date of this contract ❑ credit report ❑ verification of employment, including salary ❑ verification of funds on deposit in financial institutions ❑ current financial statement and ❑_____.
Buyer hereby authorizes any credit reporting agency to furnish copies of Buyer's credit reports to Seller at Buyer's sole expense.

B. CREDIT APPROVAL. If the credit documentation described in Paragraph A is not delivered within the specified time, Seller may terminate this contract by notice to Buyer within 7 days after expiration of the time for delivery, and the earnest money will be paid to Seller. If the credit documentation is timely delivered, and Seller determines in Seller's sole discretion that Buyer's credit is unacceptable, Seller may terminate this contract by notice to Buyer within 7 days after expiration of the time for delivery and the earnest money will be refunded to Buyer. If Seller does not terminate this contract within the time specified, Seller will be deemed to have approved Buyer's creditworthiness.

C. ASSUMPTION. Buyer's assumption of an existing note includes all obligations imposed by the deed of trust securing the note.
❑ (1) The unpaid principal balance of a first lien promissory note payable to_____
_____which unpaid balance at closing will be $ _____.
The total current monthly payment including principal, interest and any reserve deposits is $ _____. Buyer's initial payment will be the first payment due after closing.

❑ (2) The unpaid principal balance of a second lien promissory note payable to _____
_____which unpaid balance at closing will be $ _____.
The total current monthly payment including principal, interest and any reserve deposits is $ _____. Buyer's initial payment will be the first payment due after closing.

If the unpaid principal balance of any assumed loan as of the Closing Date varies from the loan balance stated above, the ❑ cash payable at closing ❑ Sales Price will be adjusted by the amount of any variance. If the total principal balance of all assumed loans varies in an amount greater than $500 at closing, either party may terminate this contract and the earnest money will be refunded to Buyer unless the other party elects to pay the excess of the variance.

D. LOAN ASSUMPTION TERMS. Buyer may terminate this contract and the earnest money will be refunded to Buyer if the noteholder requires:
(1) payment of an assumption fee in excess of $ _____in C(1) or $ _____in C(2) and Seller declines to pay such excess, or
(2) an increase in the interest rate to more than _____% in C(1) or_____% in C(2), or
(3) any other modification of the loan documents.

E. CONSENT BY NOTEHOLDER. If the noteholder fails to consent to the assumption of the loan, either Seller or Buyer may terminate this contract by notice to the other party and the earnest money will be refunded to the Buyer.

F. SELLER'S LIENS. Unless Seller is released from liability on any assumed note, a vendor's lien and deed of trust to secure assumption will be required. The vendor's lien will automatically be released on delivery of an executed release by noteholder.

Initialed for identification by Buyer_____ and Seller_____   TREC NO. 41-2

_____
(Address of Property)

G. TAX AND INSURANCE ESCROW. If noteholder maintains an escrow account for ad valorem taxes, casualty insurance premiums or mortgage insurance premiums, Seller shall transfer the escrow account to Buyer without any deficiency. Buyer shall reimburse Seller for the amount in the transferred accounts.

NOTICE TO BUYER: If you are concerned about the possibility of future adjustments, monthly payments, interest rates or other terms, do not sign the contract without examining the notes and deeds of trust.

NOTICE TO SELLER: Your liability to pay the notes assumed by Buyer will continue unless you obtain a release of liability from the noteholders. If you are concerned about future liability, you should use the TREC Release of Liability Addendum.

_____   _____
Buyer   Seller

_____   _____
Buyer   Seller

A. Credit Documentation: This addendum lays out the requirements for the Buyer to provide their credit information to the Seller for approval, including a time frame for providing that information. The time frame should be very minimal; in fact, I would not recommend to my Seller client that they accept any offer without already having the credit info as part of the offer. When we do get back to selling houses with assumable loans (when interest rates go back up), if you have a Buyer client who is interested in one of those properties with those great 4% interest assumable loans, they'd better have their credit info ready and updated weekly. If the property were put under contract without the credit info, and the Buyer did not provide it within this timeframe, this has one of only THREE Seller Outs in the whole contract series. The Seller, who took their house off the market to wait for the credit info, can terminate the contract and keep the earnest money!

B. Credit Approval: The Buyer gets out with their Earnest Money if their credit is not satisfactory to the Seller [BUYER OUT #28].

C. Assumption: The existing loan is described, and how adjustments will be handled if the terms described in the contract are not accurate (they won't be, but they'll be close).

D. Loan Assumption Terms: define any assumption fee and/or allowed increase in interest rate. These would be available in the original loan documents, and there probablh aren't either, as they are not allowed in FHA or VA loans. The Buyer gets out if they don't like those terms [BUYER OUT #29].

E. Consent by Noteholder: Finally, the original Noteholder (Third Party Lender) must consent to the assumption or either party can terminate [BUYER OUT #30].

F. Seller's Liens and **G. Tax and Insurance Escrow** describe how the lien and escrow account will be handled.

Notice to Buyer instructs the Buyer to examine the loan docs before signing the contract.

Notice to Seller warns the Seller that they will stay on the hook for the loan balance unless they actually get a release from the lender. Using the RELEASE OF LIABILITY ADDENDUM (described earlier here) will assure that the contract is contingent on getting that release.

APPROVED BY THE TEXAS REAL ESTATE COMMISSION (TREC)
FOR VOLUNTARY USE

10-10-11

NON-REALTY ITEMS ADDENDUM

TO CONTRACT CONCERNING THE PROPERTY AT

_____
(Address of Property)

A. For an additional sum of $_____and other and good valuable consideration, Seller shall convey to Buyer at closing the following personal property (specify each item carefully, include description, model numbers, serial numbers, location, and other information):

_____

_____

_____

_____

_____

_____

_____

_____

_____

_____

_____

B. Seller represents and warrants that Seller owns the personal property described in Paragraph A free and clear of all encumbrances.

C. Seller does not warrant or guarantee the condition or future performance of the personal property conveyed by this document.

_____   _____
Buyer   Seller

_____   _____
Buyer   Seller

TREC NO. OP-M

NON-REALTY ITEMS ADDENDUM: Only necessary when transferring personal property, like furniture, appliances not built-in, etc. Be sure to use this instead of entering the information in Special Provisions, however, be warned that lenders usually kick this back and want the personal property removed from the contract altogether. They don't want to be amortizing that refrigerator for 30 years. Encourage the parties to strike a deal on these items in a separate transaction between themselves; this keeps the Buyer from asking the poor seller to just give them stuff without paying for it. Best to just handle the real estate.

EQUAL HOUSING
OPPORTUNITY

SELLER FINANCING ADDENDUM
TO CONTRACT CONCERNING THE PROPERTY AT

_____

(Address of Property)

A. CREDIT DOCUMENTATION. To establish Buyer's creditworthiness, Buyer shall deliver to Seller within_____days after the effective date of this contract, ❏ credit report ❏ verification of employment, including salary ❏ verification of funds on deposit in financial institutions ❏ current financial statement and ❏ _____
_____. Buyer hereby authorizes any credit reporting agency to furnish copies of Buyer's credit reports to Seller at Buyer's sole expense.

B. BUYER'S CREDIT APPROVAL. If the credit documentation described in Paragraph A is not delivered within the specified time, Seller may terminate this contract by notice to Buyer within 7 days after expiration of the time for delivery, and the earnest money will be paid to Seller. If the credit documentation is timely delivered, and Seller determines in Seller's sole discretion that Buyer's credit is unacceptable, Seller may terminate this contract by notice to Buyer within 7 days after expiration of the time for delivery and the earnest money will be refunded to Buyer. If Seller does not terminate this contract, Seller will be deemed to have approved Buyer's creditworthiness.

C. PROMISSORY NOTE. The promissory note in the amount of $_____(Note), included in Paragraph 3B of the contract payable by Buyer to the order of Seller will bear interest at the rate of _____% per annum and be payable at the place designated by Seller. Buyer may prepay the Note in whole or in part at any time without penalty. Any prepayments are to be applied to the payment of the installments of principal last maturing and interest will immediately cease on the prepaid principal.   The Note will contain a provision for payment of a late fee of 5% of any installment not paid within 10 days of the due date. Matured unpaid amounts will bear interest at the rate of 1½% per month or at the highest lawful rate, whichever is less. The Note will be payable as follows:

❏ (1) In one payment due _____ after the date of the Note
  with interest payable ❏ at maturity ❏ monthly ❏ quarterly. (check one box only)

❏ (2) In monthly installments of $ _____ ❏ including interest ❏plus interest (check
  one box only) beginning _____ after the date of the Note and continuing
  monthly thereafter for_____ months when the balance of the Note will be due and
  payable.

❏ (3) Interest only in monthly installments for the first _____ month(s) and thereafter in
  installments of $_____ ❏ including interest ❏ plus interest (check one box
  only) beginning _____ after the date of the Note and continuing monthly
  thereafter for_____ months when the balance of the Note will be due and payable.

D. DEED OF TRUST. The deed of trust securing the Note will provide for the following:

(1) PROPERTY TRANSFERS: (check one box only)

❏ (a) Consent Not Required: The Property may be sold, conveyed or leased without the
  consent of Seller, provided any subsequent buyer assumes the Note.

❏ (b) Consent Required: If all or any part of the Property is sold, conveyed, leased for a
  period longer than 3 years, leased with an option to purchase, or otherwise sold
  (including any contract for deed), without Seller's prior written consent, which consent
  may be withheld in Seller's sole discretion, Seller may declare the balance of the Note

Initialed for identification by Buyer_____ and Seller_____   TREC NO. 26-7

_____
(Address of Property)

under threat or order of condemnation, any deed solely between buyers, or the passage of title by reason of the death of a buyer or by operation of law will not entitle Seller to exercise the remedies provided in this paragraph.

NOTE: _Under (a) or (b), Buyer's liability to pay the Note will continue unless Buyer obtains a release of liability from Seller._

(2) TAX AND INSURANCE ESCROW: (check one box only)

❑ (a) Escrow Not Required: Buyer shall furnish Seller, before each year's ad valorem taxes become delinquent, evidence that all ad valorem taxes on the Property have been paid. Buyer shall annually furnish Seller evidence of paid-up casualty insurance naming Seller as a mortgagee loss payee.

❑ (b) Escrow Required: With each installment Buyer shall deposit in escrow with Seller a pro rata part of the estimated annual ad valorem taxes and casualty insurance premiums for the Property. Buyer shall pay any deficiency within 30 days after notice from Seller. Buyer's failure to pay the deficiency will be a default under the deed of trust. Buyer is not required to deposit any escrow payments for taxes and insurance that are deposited with a superior lienholder. The casualty insurance must name Seller as a mortgagee loss payee.

(3) PRIOR LIENS: Any default under any lien superior to the lien securing the Note will be a default under the deed of trust securing the Note.

_____   _____
Buyer   Seller

_____   _____
Buyer   Seller

SELLER FINANCING ADDENDUM: Similar to the Loan Assumption Addendum, Paragraph A provides the credit documentation requirements for the Buyer along with a timeline for providing that credit info. Paragraph B contains #2 of 3 Seller Outs in the entire contract series, in the case that the Buyer has just ignored the timeline and not provided the credit info. In that case the Seller can terminate the contract and keep the earnest money.

The paragraph goes on to state that of course, as the lender, 'Seller can determine in his/her sole discretion that Buyer's credit is unacceptable.' But the earnest money is still, of course, returned to the Buyer [BUYER OUT #31].

Paragraph C establishes the terms of the loan to be created with the Promissory Note, and Paragraph D does the same for the Deed of Trust (mortgage), both of which must be prepared by an attorney of the Seller's choice; this can be done by an attorney at the title company.

EQUAL HOUSING OPPORTUNITY

APPROVED BY THE TEXAS REAL ESTATE COMMISSION (TREC)

SELLER'S DISCLOSURE OF PROPERTY CONDITION

CONCERNING THE PROPERTY AT＿＿＿＿＿＿＿＿＿＿＿＿＿＿＿＿＿＿＿＿＿＿＿＿＿

(Street Address and City)

THIS NOTICE IS A DISCLOSURE OF SELLER'S KNOWLEDGE OF THE CONDITION OF THE PROPERTY AS OF THE DATE SIGNED BY SELLER AND IS NOT A SUBSTITUTE FOR ANY INSPECTIONS OR WARRANTIES THE PURCHASER MAY WISH TO OBTAIN. IT IS NOT A WARRANTY OF ANY KIND BY SELLER OR SELLER'S AGENTS.

Seller ☐ is ☐ is not occupying the Property. If unoccupied, how long since Seller has occupied the Property? ＿＿＿＿＿＿

1. The Property has the items checked below [Write Yes (Y), No (N), or Unknown (U)]:

_____ Range	_____ Oven	_____ Microwave
_____ Dishwasher	_____ Trash Compactor	_____ Disposal
_____ Washer/Dryer Hookups	_____ Window Screens	_____ Rain Gutters
_____ Security System	_____ Fire Detection Equipment	_____ Intercom System
	_____ Smoke Detector	
	_____ Smoke Detector-Hearing Impaired	
	_____ Carbon Monoxide Alarm	
	_____ Emergency Escape Ladder(s)	
_____ TV Antenna	_____ Cable TV Wiring	_____ Satellite Dish
_____ Ceiling Fan(s)	_____ Attic Fan(s)	_____ Exhaust Fan(s)
_____ Central A/C	_____ Central Heating	_____ Wall/Window Air Conditioning
_____ Plumbing System	_____ Septic System	_____ Public Sewer System
_____ Patio/Decking	_____ Outdoor Grill	_____ Fences
_____ Pool	_____ Sauna	_____ Spa _____ Hot Tub
_____ Pool Equipment	_____ Pool Heater	_____ Automatic Lawn Sprinkler System
_____ Fireplace(s) & Chimney (Wood burning)		_____ Fireplace(s) & Chimney (Mock)
_____ Natural Gas Lines		_____ Gas Fixtures
_____ Liquid Propane Gas	_____ LP Community (Captive)	_____ LP on Property

Garage: _____ Attached   _____ Not Attached   _____ Carport

Garage Door Opener(s):   _____ Electronic   _____ Control(s)

Water Heater: _____ Gas   _____ Electric

Water Supply: _____ City   _____ Well   _____ MUD   _____ Co-op

Roof Type: ＿＿＿＿＿＿＿＿＿＿＿＿＿＿＿ Age: ＿＿＿＿＿＿＿＿ (approx.)

Are you (Seller) aware of any of the above items that are not in working condition, that have known defects, or that are in need of repair? ☐ Yes ☐ No ☐ Unknown. If yes, then describe. (Attach additional sheets if necessary): ＿＿＿＿＿＿

＿＿＿＿＿＿＿＿＿＿＿＿＿＿＿＿＿＿＿＿＿＿＿＿＿＿＿＿＿＿＿＿＿＿＿＿＿＿

＿＿＿＿＿＿＿＿＿＿＿＿＿＿＿＿＿＿＿＿＿＿＿＿＿＿＿＿＿＿＿＿＿＿＿＿＿＿

＿＿＿＿＿＿＿＿＿＿＿＿＿＿＿＿＿＿＿＿＿＿＿＿＿＿＿＿＿＿＿＿＿＿＿＿＿＿

2. Does the property have working smoke detectors installed in accordance with the smoke detector requirements of Chapter 766, Health and Safety Code? ☐ Yes ☐ No ☐ Unknown. If the answer to this question is no or unknown, explain (Attach additional sheets if necessary): _____

_____

_____

_____

* Chapter 766 of the Health and Safety Code requires one-family or two-family dwellings to have working smoke detectors installed in accordance with the requirements of the building code in effect in the area in which the dwelling is located, including performance, location, and power source requirements. If you do not know the building code requirements in effect in your area, you may check unknown above or contact your local building official for more information. A buyer may require a seller to install smoke detectors for the hearing impaired if: (1) the buyer or a member of the buyer's family who will reside in the dwelling is hearing impaired; (2) the buyer gives the seller written evidence of the hearing impairment from a licensed physician; and (3) within 10 days after the effective date, the buyer makes a written request for the seller to install smoke detectors for the hearing impaired and specifies the locations for the installation. The parties may agree who will bear the cost of installing the smoke detectors and which brand of smoke detectors to install.

3. Are you (Seller) aware of any known defects/malfunctions in any of the following? Write Yes (Y) if you are aware, write No (N) if you are not aware.

_____ Interior Walls	_____ Ceilings	_____ Floors
_____ Exterior Walls	_____ Doors	_____ Windows
_____ Roof	_____ Foundation/Slab(s)	_____ Sidewalks
_____ Walls/Fences	_____ Driveways	_____ Intercom System
_____ Plumbing/Sewers/Septics	_____ Electrical Systems	_____ Lighting Fixtures

_____ Other Structural Components (Describe): _____

_____

_____

If the answer to any of the above is yes, explain. (Attach additional sheets if necessary): _____

_____

_____

4. Are you (Seller) aware of any of the following conditions? Write Yes (Y) if you are aware, write No (N) if you are not aware.

_____ Active Termites (includes wood destroying insects)	_____ Previous Structural or Roof Repair
_____ Termite or Wood Rot Damage Needing Repair	_____ Hazardous or Toxic Waste
_____ Previous Termite Damage	_____ Asbestos Components
_____ Previous Termite Treatment	_____ Urea-formaldehyde Insulation
_____ Previous Flooding	_____ Radon Gas
_____ Improper Drainage	_____ Lead Based Paint
_____ Water Penetration	_____ Aluminum Wiring
_____ Located in 100-Year Floodplain	_____ Previous Fires
_____ Present Flood Insurance Coverage	_____ Unplatted Easements
_____ Landfill, Settling, Soil Movement, Fault Lines	_____ Subsurface Structure or Pits
_____ Single Blockable Main Drain in Pool/Hot Tub/Spa*	_____ Previous Use of Premises for Manufacture of Methamphetamine

If the answer to any of the above is yes, explain. (Attach additional sheets if necessary): _____

_____

_____

* A single blockable main drain may cause a suction entrapment hazard for an individual.

TREC No. OP-H

SELLERS DISCLOSURE: Although not technically a part of the contract, and not turned in to the title company or recorded, the Seller's Disclosure is mandatory for all but five instances in the sale of a single family residence: A foreclosure, a sale by an executor/administrator of an estate, a government employee in the course of their job, from one co-owner to another, and in the sale of a new home. Note that an unrepresented Seller must still provide a Seller's Disclosure, as does an investor who has never even seen the Property. If the latter were the case, there would be someone who managed the Property for the Seller who could fill out a disclosure to be attached to the Seller's Disclosure.

There are several forms available. The TREC Seller's Disclosure shown above provides the minimum for legal compliance. TAR has an expanded version that most agents use, and your local board may have developed one for use in your area, but you may choose from any of them, since the TREC one is not promulgated. The agent must not *ever* fill in anything on the Seller's Disclosure, nor even give instruction on its content beyond checking to make sure it's complete. These disclosures are self-explanatory, and it is the *Seller's* Disclosure. This document is often at the heart of lawsuits between Buyers and Sellers, when Buyers sue Sellers for not disclosing a defect that they can prove the Seller must have known about. Your Broker does not want to assume unnecessary liability because you were being helpful filling out the form. If a client asks you if something should go on the Seller's Disclosure, perhaps because they are concerned with portraying the condition of the Property in its best light, you should encourage them to "Disclose, disclose, disclose!" Everything they disclose at this point they can't be sued for later. That usually puts them in the right frame of mind. This is not a marketing piece. Encourage the Seller to put him/herself in the Buyer's place. If you received a Seller's Disclosure with the bare minimums indicated, and lots of 'unknowns' where there really shouldn't be, what would you think about proceeding with the purchase of the Property? Pretty wary, right? Conversely, if you received a Seller's Disclosure with extreme detail, like, "Well, it did have a foundation issue but we had it repaired by so-and-so foundation repair company, and will transfer the warranty to the Buyer at closing," or even, "We had a leak at the flashing of the chimney 2 years ago which was repaired on this date and no indication of leak has occurred since then," how would you feel about the purchase now? Much better, right? The Buyer deserves to know what they are getting into, and the Seller's Disclosure is meant to provide them with that knowledge. If you, the Listing Agent, can see something that would affect the function of the property (a "material fact" in law is anything that would cause a prudent Buyer to decide to purchase or not to purchase a property) that the Seller refuses to put on the Sellers Disclosure, you should refuse the listing (after discussion with your broker, of course). Again, the Seller's Disclosure is not a recorded document, only Paragraph 7 of the contract indicates that the Buyer has received and approved it, so it is not provided to the title company or lender.

EQUAL HOUSING OPPORTUNITY

SELLER'S TEMPORARY RESIDENTIAL LEASE

1. **PARTIES:** The parties to this Lease are_____
   (Landlord) and _____(Tenant).

2. **LEASE:** Landlord leases to Tenant the Property described in the Contract between Landlord as Buyer and Tenant as Seller known as _____
   _____(address).

3. **TERM:** The term of this Lease commences on the date the sale covered by the Contract is closed and funded and terminates _____, unless terminated earlier by reason of other provisions.

4. **RENTAL:** Tenant shall pay to Landlord as rental $_____ per day (excluding the day of closing and funding) with the full amount of rental for the term of the Lease to be paid at the time of funding of the sale. Tenant will not be entitled to a refund of rental if this Lease terminates early due to Tenant's default or voluntary surrender of the Property.

5. **DEPOSIT:** Tenant shall pay to Landlord at the time of funding of the sale $_____ as a deposit to secure performance of this Lease by Tenant. Landlord may use the deposit to satisfy Tenant's obligations under this Lease. Landlord shall refund any unused portion of the deposit to Tenant with an itemized list of all deductions from the deposit within 30 days after Tenant (a) surrenders possession of the Property and (b) provides Landlord written notice of Tenant's forwarding address.

6. **UTILITIES:** Tenant shall pay all utility charges except _____ which Landlord shall pay.

7. **USE OF PROPERTY:** Tenant may use the Property only for residential purposes. Tenant may not assign this Lease or sublet any part of the Property.

8. **PETS:** Tenant may not keep pets on the Property except _____.

9. **CONDITION OF PROPERTY:** Tenant accepts the Property in its present condition and state of repair at the commencement of the Lease. Upon termination, Tenant shall surrender the Property to Landlord in the condition required under the Contract, except normal wear and tear and any casualty loss.

10. **ALTERATIONS:** Tenant may not alter the Property or install improvements or fixtures without the prior written consent of the Landlord. Any improvements or fixtures placed on the Property during the Lease become the Property of Landlord.

11. **SPECIAL PROVISIONS:**

12. **INSPECTIONS:** Landlord may enter at reasonable times to inspect the Property. Tenant shall provide Landlord door keys and access codes to allow access to the Property during the term of Lease.

13. **LAWS:** Tenant shall comply with all applicable laws, restrictions, ordinances, rules and regulations with respect to the Property.

14. **REPAIRS AND MAINTENANCE:** Except as otherwise provided in this Lease, Tenant shall bear all expense of repairing and maintaining the Property, including but not limited to the yard, trees and shrubs, unless otherwise required by the Texas Property Code. Tenant shall promptly repair at Tenant's expense any damage to the Property caused directly or indirectly by any act or omission of the Tenant or any person other than the Landlord, Landlord's agents or invitees.

Initialed for identification by Landlord _____ and Tenant_____   TREC NO. 15-5

15. INDEMNITY: Tenant indemnifies Landlord from the claims of all third parties for injury or damage to the person or property of such third party arising from the use or occupancy of the Property by Tenant. This indemnification includes attorney's fees, costs and expenses incurred by Landlord.

16. INSURANCE: Landlord and Tenant shall each maintain such insurance on the contents and Property as each party may deem appropriate during the term of this Lease. NOTE: CONSULT YOUR INSURANCE AGENT; POSSESSION OF THE PROPERTY BY SELLER AS TENANT MAY CHANGE INSURANCE POLICY COVERAGE.

17. DEFAULT: If Tenant fails to perform or observe any provision of this Lease and fails, within 24 hours after notice by Landlord, to commence and diligently pursue to remedy such failure, Tenant will be in default.

18. TERMINATION: This Lease terminates upon expiration of the term specified in Paragraph 3 or upon Tenant's default under this Lease.

19. HOLDING OVER: Tenant shall surrender possession of the Property upon termination of this Lease. Any possession by Tenant after termination creates a tenancy at sufferance and will not operate to renew or extend this Lease. Tenant shall pay $_____ per day during the period of any possession after termination as damages, in addition to any other remedies to which Landlord is entitled.

20. ATTORNEY'S FEES: The prevailing party in any legal proceeding brought under or with respect to this Lease is entitled to recover from the non-prevailing party all costs of such proceeding and reasonable attorney's fees.

21. SMOKE ALARMS: The Texas Property Code requires Landlord to install smoke alarms in certain locations within the Property at Landlord's expense. <u>Tenant expressly waives Landlord's duty to inspect and repair smoke alarms</u>.

22. SECURITY DEVICES: The requirements of the Texas Property Code relating to security devices do not apply to a residential lease for a term of 90 days or less.

23. CONSULT YOUR ATTORNEY: Real estate licensees cannot give legal advice. This Lease is intended to be legally binding. READ IT CAREFULLY. If you do not understand the effect of this Lease, consult your attorney BEFORE signing.

24. NOTICES: All notices from one party to the other must be in writing and are effective when mailed to, hand-delivered at, or transmitted by facsimile or electronic transmission as follows:

To Landlord: _____   **To Tenant:** _____

_____   _____

_____   _____

_____   _____

Telephone: ( ) _____   Telephone: ( ) _____

Facsimile: ( ) _____   Facsimile: ( ) _____

E-mail: _____   E-mail: _____

_____   _____
Landlord   Tenant

_____   _____
Landlord   Tenant

TREC NO. 15-5

SELLERS TEMPORARY RESIDENTIAL LEASE Will the Seller get a few days to pack their final belongings into a van and watch it drive down the street? Most Sellers obviously would prefer this if possible. In fact, it is customary in other states that the seller have a time after closing to vacate the house. It's a week in Colorado, as much as a month in Michigan. What we ask sellers to do, vacate their property before going to closing, is *hard!* I often put in my agent viewable description in the MLS that "Seller *requests* a 7-day leaseback." Not a deal-breaker if you can't do it, but it would be nice if your Buyer can accommodate it. Use a 100% loan PITI payment and divide it by the number of days in the month to calculate a fair daily rental rate to suggest. Most Buyers, if they are first-time Buyers and thus leasing their current residence, are happy to oblige, particularly when they receive $400-500 from the Seller at closing for a few days. There are problems to watch out for in this situation. Buyer Reps: make sure you have a substantial deposit in place and complete a thorough walk-through on the day the Seller delivers possession before releasing that deposit. In other words, the Seller will still be occupying the Property on closing day, and a couch can cover up a really big hole in the carpet. Additionally, lots of sheetrock damage can take place when moving large pieces of furniture out of a house, particularly in the stairwell of a 2-story house. So do get that Buyer Walk-Through and Acceptance of Property Condition form (TAR) completed for your file. I also recommend a significant increase in holdover rent, to make sure the Seller knows that they do have to get out when they said or it will hurt. Seller Reps: Ask the Buyers' Agent for a copy of that walk-through form for your file, so that you have a written record of the Buyer's acceptance on the date the Seller delivered possession.

EQUAL HOUSING
OPPORTUNITY

SHORT SALE ADDENDUM

ADDENDUM TO CONTRACT CONCERNING THE PROPERTY AT

_____

(Street Address and City)

A. This contract involves a "short sale" of the Property. As used in this Addendum, "short sale" means that:

   (1) Seller's net proceeds at closing will be insufficient to pay the balance of Seller's mortgage loan; and

   (2) Seller requires:
       (a) the consent of the lienholder to sell the Property pursuant to this contract; and
       (b) the lienholder's agreement to:
           (i) accept Seller's net proceeds in full satisfaction of Seller's liability under the mortgage loan; and
           (ii) provide Seller an executed release of lien against the Property in a recordable format.

B. As used in this Addendum, "Seller's net proceeds" means the Sales Price less Seller's Expenses under Paragraph 12 of the contract and Seller's obligation to pay any brokerage fees.

C. The contract to which this Addendum is attached is binding upon execution by the parties and the earnest money and the Option Fee must be paid as provided in the contract. The contract is contingent on the satisfaction of Seller's requirements under Paragraph A(2) of this Addendum (Lienholder's Consent and Agreement). Seller shall apply promptly for and make every reasonable effort to obtain Lienholder's Consent and Agreement, and shall furnish all information and documents required by the lienholder. Except as provided by this Addendum, neither party is required to perform under the contract while it is contingent upon obtaining Lienholder's Consent and Agreement.

D. If Seller does not notify Buyer that Seller has obtained Lienholder's Consent and Agreement on or before _____, this contract terminates and the earnest money will be refunded to Buyer. Seller must notify Buyer immediately if Lienholder's Consent and Agreement is obtained. For purposes of performance, the effective date of the contract changes to the date Seller provides Buyer notice of the Lienholder's Consent and Agreement (Amended Effective Date).

E. This contract will terminate and the earnest money will be refunded to Buyer if the Lienholder refuses or withdraws its Consent and Agreement prior to closing and funding. Seller shall promptly notify Buyer of any lienholder's refusal to provide or withdrawal of a Lienholder's Consent and Agreement.

F. If Buyer has the unrestricted right to terminate this contract, the time for giving notice of termination begins on the effective date of the contract, continues after the Amended Effective Date and ends upon the expiration of Buyer's unrestricted right to terminate the contract under Paragraph 23.

G. For the purposes of this Addendum, time is of the essence. Strict compliance with the times for performance stated in this Addendum is required.

H. Seller authorizes any lienholder to furnish to Buyer or Buyer's representatives information relating to the status of the request for a Lienholder's Consent and Agreement.

I. If there is more than one lienholder or loan secured by the Property, this Addendum applies to each lienholder.

_____   _____
Buyer   Seller

_____   _____
Buyer   Seller

TREC NO. 45-1

SHORT SALE ADDENDUM: Defines "short sale" as one which provides proceeds which are 'short' of what is owed on the Property, establishes the requirement that the lender approve the sale, allows for a negotiated period of time for that lender approval as a 'fuse' for automatically negating the offer [BUYER OUT #32], and amends the Effective Date to reflect the date that lender approval is made. It also establishes the release of lien for the Seller as a condition of the sale, which requires the lender to forgo any further attempts to secure the difference between the amount owed and the sale proceeds from the Seller, such as suing the Seller for the difference or sending the Seller an IRS Form 1099 for the difference so that the Seller has to pay taxes on it as though they received it as income. Once again, 'time is of the essence' in this addendum.

TREC
TEXAS REAL ESTATE COMMISSION

EQUAL HOUSING
OPPORTUNITY

SUBDIVISION INFORMATION, INCLUDING
RESALE CERTIFICATE FOR PROPERTY SUBJECT TO
MANDATORY MEMBERSHIP IN A PROPERTY OWNERS' ASSOCIATION
(Chapter 207, Texas Property Code)

Resale Certificate concerning the Property (including any common areas assigned to the Property) located at _____(Street Address), City of _____, County of _____, Texas, prepared by the property owners' association (Association).

A. The Property ☐is ☐ is not subject to a right of first refusal (other than a right of first refusal prohibited by statute) or other restraint contained in the restrictions or restrictive covenants that restricts the owner's right to transfer the owner's property.

B. The current regular assessment for the Property is $_____ per _____.

C. A special assessment for the Property due after this resale certificate is delivered is $_____
payable as follows_____
for the following purpose:_____.

D. The total of all amounts due and unpaid to the Association that are attributable to the Property is
$ _____ .

E. The capital expenditures approved by the Association for its current fiscal year are
$ _____.

F. The amount of reserves for capital expenditures is $_____.

G. Unsatisfied judgments against the Association total $_____.

H. Other than lawsuits relating to unpaid ad valorem taxes of an individual member of the association, there ☐ are ☐ are not any suits pending in which the Association is a party. The style and cause number of each pending suit is: _____.

I. The Association's board ☐has actual knowledge ☐has no actual knowledge of conditions on the Property in violation of the restrictions applying to the subdivision or the bylaws or rules of the Association. Known violations are: _____.

J. The Association ☐has ☐has not received notice from any governmental authority regarding health or building code violations with respect to the Property or any common areas or common facilities owned or leased by the Association. A summary or copy of each notice is attached.

K. The amount of any administrative transfer fee charged by the Association for a change of ownership of property in the subdivision is $_____. Describe all fees associated with the transfer of ownership (include a description of each fee, to whom each fee is payable and the amount of each fee)._____
_____
_____

TREC NO. 37-5

111

L. The Association's managing agent is_____
                                              (Name of Agent)

_____
                                      (Mailing Address)

_____   _____
        (Telephone Number)   (Fax Number)

_____
(E-mail Address)

M. The restrictions ❑ do ❑ do not allow foreclosure of the Association's lien on the Property for failure to pay assessments.
   REQUIRED ATTACHMENTS:

   1. Restrictions   5. Current Operating Budget

   2. Rules   6. Certificate of Insurance concerning Property and Liability Insurance for Common Areas and Facilities

   3. Bylaws

   4. Current Balance Sheet   7. Any Governmental Notices of Health or Housing Code Violations

NOTICE: This Subdivision Information may change at any time.

_____
                             Name of Association

By: _____

Print Name: _____

Title: _____

Date:_____

Mailing Address: _____

E-mail: _____

TREC NO. 37-5

112

SUBDIVISION INFORMATION INCLUDING RESALE CERTIFICATE FOR PROPERTY SUBJECT TO MANDATORY MEMBERSHIP IN A PROPERTY OWNERS' ASSOCIATION

This form or one substantially like it is completed by the HOA. It's a good idea to review what is (and what is not) contained in the information that will be supplied to your Buyer client. There is discussion of red flags you should look for on behalf of your particular client in the section on AMENDMENT FOR PROPERTY LOCATED IN A MANDATORY PROPERTY OWNERS ASSOCIATION. That amendment is requesting the info, this one shows you what will be received. Page 1 references many of the fiscal aspects of the association, any lawsuits pending, and specifies the dollar amount of anything that must be paid in the transfer of the property. Page 2 provides contact information and requires the attachments that make HOA doc files so huge: Restrictions, Rules and Bylaws (check for rules that might make the subdivision unacceptable to your client), a current balance sheet and budget, and certificate of insurance. Note that the budget may be in month 11 of the year, so it could be a good idea to ask for meeting minutes to see if anything out of the ordinary has been discussed for the next year.

OTHER FORMS AND CONTRACT NOTES

TAR FORMS: All of the previously discussed forms in this ebook, with the exception of the TAR Sellers Disclosure and Release of Earnest Money, are available on the TREC website. Realtors® can access these forms and many others through the Texas Association of Realtors® gateway to Zipforms, a benefit of membership only available to real estate licensees. There are many additional forms there for use in transactions that make things clearer, smoother, and reduce misunderstandings that can result in legal issues. If you are a Texas Realtor®, please see two of my favorites:

TAR-1506 General Information and Notice to Buyers and Sellers: Provides definitions and information about so many of the terms used in our practice, and a place for the Buyer to initial and sign acknowledging their receipt of that information.

TAR-1928 For Your Protection: Get a Home Inspection: Outlines what an inspection does and provides a signature line to prove that the agent has given the Buyer the form in case the Buyer waives their right to an inspection and it turns out to have been a bad idea.

And finally, TREC has promulgated contract forms for five other types of Property sales beyond the ONE TO FOUR FAMILY RESIDENTIAL CONTRACT (Resale). They follow the basic pattern of the 1-4 Family with distinct differences required for the other property types, and may be accessed online through the TREC website http://www.trec.state.tx.us/formslawscontracts/forms/forms-contracts.asp and are included following this page.

RESIDENTIAL CONDOMINIUM CONTRACT (RESALE) Property description is different, with unit and building number instead of lot and block, and information on the addendum for property located in a POA is included in the contract instead of a separate addendum.

FARM AND RANCH CONTRACT Property description is different, not set up for lot & block type, and allowing for inclusion of accessories and improvements associated with agricultural property. Timber and water rights can be included or excluded. Roll-back taxes are addressed in case the property comes out of agricultural tax exemption. Provides a place for listing property on last page.

NEW HOME CONTRACT (Completed Construction) Eliminates requirement for sellers disclosure, specs insulation.

NEW HOME CONTRACT (Incomplete Construction) Eliminates requirement for sellers disclosure, specifies insulation values and outlines change order time frames and costs, specifies completion date.

UNIMPROVED PROPERTY CONTRACT Property description eliminates lot and block format, addresses roll-back taxes and eliminates sellers disclosure requirement.

AND, AT THE END OF IT ALL, THE TERMINATION FORM, OR NOTICE OF BUYER'S TERMINATION OF CONTRACT.

RESIDENTIAL CONDOMINIUM CONTRACT (RESALE)

1. PARTIES: The parties to this contract are _____ (Seller) and
_____ (Buyer). Seller agrees to
sell and convey to Buyer and Buyer agrees to buy from Seller the Property defined below.

2. PROPERTY AND CONDOMINIUM DOCUMENTS:
A. The Condominium Unit, improvements and accessories described below are collectively
referred to as the "Property".
   (1) CONDOMINIUM UNIT: Unit _____, in Building _____,
   of _____, a condominium project, located at
   _____
   _____ (address/zip code), City of _____, County of _____,
   Texas, described in the Condominium Declaration and Plat and any amendments thereto
   of record in said County; together with such Unit's undivided interest in the Common
   Elements designated by the Declaration, including those areas reserved as Limited
   Common Elements appurtenant to the Unit and such other rights to use the Common
   Elements which have been specifically assigned to the Unit in any other manner. Parking
   areas assigned to the Unit are:_____.
   (2) IMPROVEMENTS: All fixtures and improvements attached to the above described real
   property including without limitation, the following **permanently installed and built-in
   items**, if any: all equipment and appliances, valances, screens, shutters,
   awnings, wall-to-wall carpeting, mirrors, ceiling fans, attic fans, mail boxes, television
   antennas, mounts and brackets for televisions and speakers, heating and air conditioning
   units, security and fire detection equipment, wiring, plumbing and lighting fixtures,
   chandeliers, shrubbery, landscaping, outdoor cooking equipment, and all other property
   owned by Seller and attached to the above described Condominium Unit.
   (3) ACCESSORIES: The following described related accessories, if any: window air
   conditioning units, stove, fireplace screens, curtains and rods, blinds, window shades,
   draperies and rods, door keys, mailbox keys, above ground pool, swimming pool
   equipment and maintenance accessories, artificial fireplace logs, and controls for:
   (i) garage doors, (ii) entry gates, and (iii) other improvements and accessories.
   (4) EXCLUSIONS: The following improvements and accessories will be retained by Seller and
   must be removed prior to delivery of possession:_____.
B. The Declaration, Bylaws and any Rules of the Association are called "Documents". (Check
one box only):
❑ (1) Buyer has received a copy of the Documents. Buyer is advised to read the Documents
   before signing the contract.
❑ (2) Buyer has not received a copy of the Documents. Seller, at Seller's expense, shall deliver
   the Documents to Buyer within _____ days after the Effective Date of the contract. Buyer
   may cancel the contract before the sixth day after Buyer receives the Documents by hand
   -delivering or mailing written notice of cancellation to Seller by certified United States
   mail, return receipt requested. If Buyer cancels the contract pursuant to this paragraph,
   the contract will terminate and the earnest money will be refunded to Buyer.
C. The Resale Certificate from the condominium owners association (the Association) is called
the "Certificate". The Certificate must be in a form promulgated by TREC or required by the
parties. The Certificate must have been prepared, at Seller's expense, no more than 3
months before the date it is delivered to Buyer and must contain at a minimum the
information required by Section 82.157, Texas Property Code.
(Check one box only):
❑ (1) Buyer has received the Certificate.
❑ (2) Buyer has not received the Certificate. Seller shall deliver the Certificate to Buyer within
   _____ days after the Effective Date of the contract. Buyer may cancel the contract
   before the sixth day after the date Buyer receives the Certificate by hand-delivering or
   mailing written notice of cancellation to Seller by certified United States mail, return
   receipt requested. If Buyer cancels the contract pursuant to this paragraph, the contract
   will terminate and the earnest money will be refunded to Buyer.
❑ (3) Buyer has received Seller's affidavit that Seller requested information from the
   Association concerning its financial condition as required by the Texas Property Code, and
   that the Association did not provide a Certificate or information required in the
   Certificate. Buyer and Seller agree to waive the requirement to furnish the Certificate.
D. If the Documents reveal that the Property is subject to a right of refusal under which the
Association or a member of the Association may purchase the Property, the Effective Date
shall be amended to the date that Buyer receives a copy of the Association's certification
that: (i) Seller has complied with the requirements under the right of refusal; and (ii) all
persons who may exercise the right of refusal have not exercised or have waived the right to
buy the Property. If Buyer does not receive the Association's certification within
_____ days after the Effective Date or if the right of refusal is exercised, this contract shall
terminate and the earnest money shall be refunded to Buyer.

Initialed for identification by Buyer_____ _____ and Seller _____ _____   TREC NO. 30-13

3. SALES PRICE:
  A. Cash portion of Sales Price payable by Buyer at closing ....$_____
  B. Sum of all financing described in the attached: ❏ Third Party Financing Addendum,
    ❏ Loan Assumption Addendum, ❏ Seller Financing Addendum ....$_____
  C. Sales Price (Sum of A and B) ....$_____

4. LICENSE HOLDER DISCLOSURE: Texas law requires a real estate license holder who is a party to a transaction or acting on behalf of a spouse, parent, child, business entity in which the license holder owns more than 10%, or a trust for which the license holder acts as trustee or of which the license holder or the license holder's spouse, parent or child is a beneficiary, to notify the other party in writing before entering into a contract of sale. Disclose if applicable:___
_____.

5. EARNEST MONEY: Within 3 days after the Effective Date, Buyer must deliver $_____ as earnest money to _____,
as escrow agent, at _____
(address). Buyer shall deliver additional earnest money of $_____ to escrow agent within _____ days after the Effective Date of this contract. If Buyer fails to deliver the earnest money within the time required, Seller may terminate this contract or exercise Seller's remedies under Paragraph 15, or both, by providing notice to Buyer before Buyer delivers the earnest money. If the last day to deliver the earnest money falls on a Saturday, Sunday, or legal holiday, the time to deliver the earnest money is extended until the end of the next day that is not a Saturday, Sunday, or legal holiday. **Time is of the essence for this paragraph.**

6. TITLE POLICY:
  A. TITLE POLICY: Seller shall furnish to Buyer at ❏Seller's ❏Buyer's expense an owner policy of title insurance (Title Policy) issued by _____(Title Company) in the amount of the Sales Price, dated at or after closing, insuring Buyer against loss under the provisions of the Title Policy, subject to the promulgated exclusions (including existing building and zoning ordinances) and the following exceptions:
    (1) Restrictive covenants common to the platted subdivision in which the Property is located.
    (2) The standard printed exception for standby fees, taxes and assessments.
    (3) Liens created as part of the financing described in Paragraph 3.
    (4) Terms and provisions of the Documents including the assessments and platted easements.
    (5) Reservations or exceptions otherwise permitted by this contract or as may be approved by Buyer in writing.
    (6) The standard printed exception as to marital rights.
    (7) The standard printed exception as to waters, tidelands, beaches, streams, and related matters.
    (8) The standard printed exception as to discrepancies, conflicts, shortages in area or boundary lines, encroachments or protrusions, or overlapping improvements.
    (9) The exception or exclusion regarding minerals approved by the Texas Department of Insurance.
  B. COMMITMENT: Within 20 days after the Title Company receives a copy of this contract, Seller shall furnish to Buyer a commitment for title insurance (Commitment) and, at Buyer's expense, legible copies of restrictive covenants and documents evidencing exceptions in the Commitment (Exception Documents) other than the standard printed exceptions. Seller authorizes the Title Company to deliver the Commitment and Exception Documents to Buyer at Buyer's address shown in Paragraph 21. If the Commitment and Exception Documents are not delivered to Buyer within the specified time, the time for delivery will be automatically extended up to 15 days or 3 days before the Closing Date, whichever is earlier. If the Commitment and Exception Documents are not delivered within the time required, Buyer may terminate this contract and the earnest money will be refunded to Buyer.
  C. OBJECTIONS: Buyer may object in writing to defects, exceptions, or encumbrances to title: disclosed in the Commitment other than items 6A(1) through (9) above; or which prohibit the following use or activity: _____
_____.
Buyer must object the earlier of (i) the Closing Date or (ii) _____ days after Buyer receives the Commitment and Exception Documents. Buyer's failure to object within the time allowed will constitute a waiver of Buyer's right to object; except that the requirements in Schedule C of the Commitment are not waived by Buyer. Provided Seller is not obligated to incur any expense, Seller shall cure any timely objections of Buyer or any third party lender within 15 days after Seller receives the objections (Cure Period) and the Closing Date will be extended as necessary. If objections are not cured within the Cure Period, Buyer may, by delivering notice to Seller within 5 days after the end of the Cure Period: (i) terminate this contract and the earnest money will be refunded to Buyer; or (ii) waive the objections. If Buyer does not terminate within the time required, Buyer shall be deemed to have waived the objections. If the Commitment or Survey is revised or any new Exception Document(s) is delivered, Buyer may object to any new matter revealed in the revised Commitment or Survey or new Exception Document(s) within the same time stated in this paragraph to make objections beginning when the revised Commitment, Survey, or Exception Document(s) is delivered to Buyer.

Initialed for identification by Buyer_____ _____ and Seller _____ _____   TREC NO. 30-13

D. TITLE NOTICES:

(1) ABSTRACT OR TITLE POLICY: Broker advises Buyer to have an abstract of title covering the Property examined by an attorney of Buyer's selection, or Buyer should be furnished with or obtain a Title Policy. If a Title Policy is furnished, the Commitment should be promptly reviewed by an attorney of Buyer's choice due to the time limitations on Buyer's right to object.

(2) STATUTORY TAX DISTRICTS: If the Property is situated in a utility or other statutorily created district providing water, sewer, drainage, or flood control facilities and services, Chapter 49, Texas Water Code, requires Seller to deliver and Buyer to sign the statutory notice relating to the tax rate, bonded indebtedness, or standby fee of the district prior to final execution of this contract.

(3) TIDE WATERS: If the Property abuts the tidally influenced waters of the state, §33.135, Texas Natural Resources Code, requires a notice regarding coastal area property to be included in the contract. An addendum containing the notice promulgated by TREC or required by the parties must be used.

(4) ANNEXATION: If the Property is located outside the limits of a municipality, Seller notifies Buyer under §5.011, Texas Property Code, that the Property may now or later be included in the extraterritorial jurisdiction of a municipality and may now or later be subject to annexation by the municipality. Each municipality maintains a map that depicts its boundaries and extraterritorial jurisdiction. To determine if the Property is located within a municipality's extraterritorial jurisdiction or is likely to be located within a municipality's extraterritorial jurisdiction, contact all municipalities located in the general proximity of the Property for further information.

(5) PROPERTY LOCATED IN A CERTIFICATED SERVICE AREA OF A UTILITY SERVICE PROVIDER: Notice required by §13.257, Water Code: The real property, described in Paragraph 2, that you are about to purchase may be located in a certificated water or sewer service area, which is authorized by law to provide water or sewer service to the properties in the certificated area. If your property is located in a certificated area there may be special costs or charges that you will be required to pay before you can receive water or sewer service. There may be a period required to construct lines or other facilities necessary to provide water or sewer service to your property. You are advised to determine if the property is in a certificated area and contact the utility service provider to determine the cost that you will be required to pay and the period, if any, that is required to provide water or sewer service to your property. The undersigned Buyer hereby acknowledges receipt of the foregoing notice at or before the execution of a binding contract for the purchase of the real property described in Paragraph 2 or at closing of purchase of the real property.

(6) TRANSFER FEES: If the Property is subject to a private transfer fee obligation, §5.205, Property Code, requires Seller to notify Buyer as follows: The private transfer fee obligation may be governed by Chapter 5, Subchapter G of the Texas Property Code.

(7) PROPANE GAS SYSTEM SERVICE AREA: If the Property is located in a propane gas system service area owned by a distribution system retailer, Seller must give Buyer written notice as required by §141.010, Texas Utilities Code. An addendum containing the notice approved by TREC or required by the parties should be used.

(8) NOTICE OF WATER LEVEL FLUCTUATIONS: If the Property adjoins an impoundment of water, including a reservoir or lake, constructed and maintained under Chapter 11, Water Code, that has a storage capacity of at least 5,000 acre-feet at the impoundment's normal operating level, Seller hereby notifies Buyer: "The water level of the impoundment of water adjoining the Property fluctuates for various reasons, including as a result of: (1) an entity lawfully exercising its right to use the water stored in the impoundment; or (2) drought or flood conditions."

7. **PROPERTY CONDITION:**

A. ACCESS, INSPECTIONS AND UTILITIES: Seller shall permit Buyer and Buyer's agents access to the Property at reasonable times. Buyer may have the Property inspected by inspectors selected by Buyer and licensed by TREC or otherwise permitted by law to make inspections. Any hydrostatic testing must be separately authorized by Seller in writing. Seller at Seller's expense shall immediately cause existing utilities to be turned on and shall keep the utilities on during the time this contract is in effect .

B. SELLER'S DISCLOSURE NOTICE PURSUANT TO §5.008, TEXAS PROPERTY CODE (Notice): (Check one box only)

❑ (1) Buyer has received the Notice.

❑ (2) Buyer has not received the Notice. Within _____ days after the Effective Date of this contract, Seller shall deliver the Notice to Buyer. If Buyer does not receive the Notice, Buyer may terminate this contract at any time prior to the closing and the earnest money will be refunded to Buyer. If Seller delivers the Notice, Buyer may terminate this contract for any reason within 7 days after Buyer receives the Notice or prior to the closing, whichever first occurs, and the earnest money will be refunded to Buyer.

❑ (3) The Texas Property Code does not require this Seller to furnish the Notice.

C. SELLER'S DISCLOSURE OF LEAD-BASED PAINT AND LEAD-BASED PAINT HAZARDS is required by Federal law for a residential dwelling constructed prior to 1978.

D. ACCEPTANCE OF PROPERTY CONDITION: "As Is" means the present condition of the Property with any and all defects and without warranty except for the warranties of title and the warranties in this contract. Buyer's agreement to accept the Property As Is under Paragraph 7D(1) or (2) does not preclude Buyer from inspecting the Property under Paragraph 7A, from

negotiating repairs or treatments in a subsequent amendment, or from terminating this contract during the Option Period, if any.
(Check one box only)
❏ (1) Buyer accepts the Property As Is.
❏ (2) Buyer accepts the Property As Is provided Seller, at Seller's expense, shall complete the following specific repairs and treatments:_____
_____.
(Do not insert general phrases, such as "subject to inspections," that do not identify specific repairs and treatments.)

   E. LENDER REQUIRED REPAIRS AND TREATMENTS: Unless otherwise agreed in writing, neither party is obligated to pay for lender required repairs, which includes treatment for wood destroying insects. If the parties do not agree to pay for the lender required repairs or treatments, this contract will terminate and the earnest money will be refunded to Buyer. If the cost of lender required repairs and treatments exceeds 5% of the Sales Price, Buyer may terminate this contract and the earnest money will be refunded to Buyer.

   F. COMPLETION OF REPAIRS AND TREATMENTS: Unless otherwise agreed in writing: (i) Seller shall complete all agreed repairs and treatments prior to the Closing Date; and (ii) all required permits must be obtained, and repairs and treatments must be performed by persons who are licensed to provide such repairs or treatments or, if no license is required by law, are commercially engaged in the trade of providing such repairs or treatments. At Buyer's election, any transferable warranties received by Seller with respect to the repairs and treatments will be transferred to Buyer at Buyer's expense. If Seller fails to complete any agreed repairs and treatments prior to the Closing Date, Buyer may exercise remedies under Paragraph 15 or extend the Closing Date up to 5 days if necessary for Seller to complete repairs and treatments.

   G. ENVIRONMENTAL MATTERS: Buyer is advised that the presence of wetlands, toxic substances, including asbestos and wastes or other environmental hazards or the presence of a threatened or endangered species or its habitat may affect Buyer's intended use of the Property. If Buyer is concerned about these matters, an addendum promulgated by TREC or required by the parties should be used.

   H. RESIDENTIAL SERVICE CONTRACTS: Buyer may purchase a residential service contract from a residential service company licensed by TREC. If Buyer purchases a residential service contract, Seller shall reimburse Buyer at closing for the cost of the residential service contract in an amount not exceeding $_____. Buyer should review any residential service contract for the scope of coverage, exclusions and limitations. **The purchase of a residential service contract is optional. Similar coverage may be purchased from various companies authorized to do business in Texas.**

8. BROKERS' FEES: All obligations of the parties for payment of brokers' fees are contained in separate written agreements.

9. CLOSING:
   A. The closing of the sale will be on or before _____, 20____, or within 7 days after objections to matters disclosed in the Commitment have been cured, whichever date is later (Closing Date). If either party fails to close the sale by the Closing Date, the non-defaulting party may exercise the remedies contained in Paragraph 15.
   B. At closing:
     (1) Seller shall execute and deliver a general warranty deed conveying title to the Property to Buyer and showing no additional exceptions to those permitted in Paragraph 6 and furnish tax statements or certificates showing no delinquent taxes on the Property.
     (2) Buyer shall pay the Sales Price in good funds acceptable to the escrow agent.
     (3) Seller and Buyer shall execute and deliver any notices, statements, certificates, affidavits, releases, loan documents and other documents reasonably required for the closing of the sale and the issuance of the Title Policy.
     (4) There will be no liens, assessments, or security interests against the Property which will not be satisfied out of the sales proceeds unless securing the payment of any loans assumed by Buyer and assumed loans will not be in default.
     (5) If the Property is subject to a residential lease, Seller shall transfer security deposits (as defined under §92.102, Property Code), if any, to Buyer. In such an event, Buyer shall deliver to the tenant a signed statement acknowledging that the Buyer has acquired the Property and is responsible for the return of the security deposit, and specifying the exact dollar amount of the security deposit.

10. POSSESSION:
   A. Buyers Possession: Seller shall deliver to Buyer possession of the Property in its present or required condition, ordinary wear and tear excepted: ❏ upon closing and funding ❏ according to a temporary residential lease form promulgated by TREC or other written lease required by the parties. Any possession by Buyer prior to closing or by Seller after closing which is not authorized by a written lease will establish a tenancy at sufferance relationship between the parties. **Consult your insurance agent prior to change of ownership and possession because insurance coverage may be limited or terminated. The absence of a written lease or appropriate insurance coverage may expose the parties to economic loss.**
   B. Leases:
     (1) After the Effective Date, Seller may not execute any lease (including but not limited to mineral leases) or convey any interest in the Property without Buyer's written consent.
     (2) If the Property is subject to any lease to which Seller is a party, Seller shall deliver to Buyer copies of the lease(s) and any move-in condition form signed by the tenant within 7 days after the Effective Date of the contract.

Initialed for identification by Buyer_____ _____ and Seller _____ _____   TREC NO. 30-13

negotiating repairs or treatments in a subsequent amendment, or from terminating this contract during the Option Period, if any.
(Check one box only)
❏ (1) Buyer accepts the Property As Is.
❏ (2) Buyer accepts the Property As Is provided Seller, at Seller's expense, shall complete the following specific repairs and treatments:_____.

_____
(Do not insert general phrases, such as "subject to inspections," that do not identify specific repairs and treatments.)

E. LENDER REQUIRED REPAIRS AND TREATMENTS: Unless otherwise agreed in writing, neither party is obligated to pay for lender required repairs, which includes treatment for wood destroying insects. If the parties do not agree to pay for the lender required repairs or treatments, this contract will terminate and the earnest money will be refunded to Buyer. If the cost of lender required repairs and treatments exceeds 5% of the Sales Price, Buyer may terminate this contract and the earnest money will be refunded to Buyer.

F. COMPLETION OF REPAIRS AND TREATMENTS: Unless otherwise agreed in writing: (i) Seller shall complete all agreed repairs and treatments prior to the Closing Date; and (ii) all required permits must be obtained, and repairs and treatments must be performed by persons who are licensed to provide such repairs or treatments or, if no license is required by law, are commercially engaged in the trade of providing such repairs or treatments. At Buyer's election, any transferable warranties received by Seller with respect to the repairs and treatments will be transferred to Buyer at Buyer's expense. If Seller fails to complete any agreed repairs and treatments prior to the Closing Date, Buyer may exercise remedies under Paragraph 15 or extend the Closing Date up to 5 days if necessary for Seller to complete repairs and treatments.

G. ENVIRONMENTAL MATTERS: Buyer is advised that the presence of wetlands, toxic substances, including asbestos and wastes or other environmental hazards or the presence of a threatened or endangered species or its habitat may affect Buyer's intended use of the Property. If Buyer is concerned about these matters, an addendum promulgated by TREC or required by the parties should be used.

H. RESIDENTIAL SERVICE CONTRACTS: Buyer may purchase a residential service contract from a residential service company licensed by TREC. If Buyer purchases a residential service contract, Seller shall reimburse Buyer at closing for the cost of the residential service contract in an amount not exceeding $_____. Buyer should review any residential service contract for the scope of coverage, exclusions and limitations. **The purchase of a residential service contract is optional. Similar coverage may be purchased from various companies authorized to do business in Texas.**

8.BROKERS' FEES: All obligations of the parties for payment of brokers' fees are contained in separate written agreements.

9.CLOSING:
A. The closing of the sale will be on or before _____, 20____, or within 7 days after objections to matters disclosed in the Commitment have been cured, whichever date is later (Closing Date). If either party fails to close the sale by the Closing Date, the non-defaulting party may exercise the remedies contained in Paragraph 15.
B. At closing:
   (1) Seller shall execute and deliver a general warranty deed conveying title to the Property to Buyer and showing no additional exceptions to those permitted in Paragraph 6 and furnish tax statements or certificates showing no delinquent taxes on the Property.
   (2) Buyer shall pay the Sales Price in good funds acceptable to the escrow agent.
   (3) Seller and Buyer shall execute and deliver any notices, statements, certificates, affidavits, releases, loan documents and other documents reasonably required for the closing of the sale and the issuance of the Title Policy.
   (4) There will be no liens, assessments, or security interests against the Property which will not be satisfied out of the sales proceeds unless securing the payment of any loans assumed by Buyer and assumed loans will not be in default.
   (5) If the Property is subject to a residential lease, Seller shall transfer security deposits (as defined under §92.102, Property Code), if any, to Buyer. In such an event, Buyer shall deliver to the tenant a signed statement acknowledging that the Buyer has acquired the Property and is responsible for the return of the security deposit, and specifying the exact dollar amount of the security deposit.

10.POSSESSION:
A. Buyers Possession: Seller shall deliver to Buyer possession of the Property in its present or required condition, ordinary wear and tear excepted: ❏ upon closing and funding ❏ according to a temporary residential lease form promulgated by TREC or other written lease required by the parties. Any possession by Buyer prior to closing or by Seller after closing which is not authorized by a written lease will establish a tenancy at sufferance relationship between the parties. **Consult your insurance agent prior to change of ownership and possession because insurance coverage may be limited or terminated. The absence of a written lease or appropriate insurance coverage may expose the parties to economic loss.**
B. Leases:
   (1) After the Effective Date, Seller may not execute any lease (including but not limited to mineral leases) or convey any interest in the Property without Buyer's written consent.
   (2) If the Property is subject to any lease to which Seller is a party, Seller shall deliver to Buyer copies of the lease(s) and any move-in condition form signed by the tenant within 7 days after the Effective Date of the contract.

Initialed for identification by Buyer_____ _____ and Seller _____ _____   TREC NO. 30-13

11. SPECIAL PROVISIONS: (Insert only factual statements and business details applicable to the sale. TREC rules prohibit license holders from adding factual statements or business details for which a contract addendum, lease or other form has been promulgated by TREC for mandatory use.)

12. SETTLEMENT AND OTHER EXPENSES:

A. The following expenses must be paid at or prior to closing:

(1) Expenses payable by Seller (Seller's Expenses):

(a) Releases of existing liens, including prepayment penalties and recording fees; lender, FHA, or VA completion requirements; tax statements or certificates; preparation of deed; one-half of escrow fee; and other expenses payable by Seller under this contract.

(b) Seller shall also pay an amount not to exceed $_____ to be applied in the following order: Buyer's Expenses which Buyer is prohibited from paying by FHA, VA, Texas Veterans Land Board or other governmental loan programs, and then to other Buyer's Expenses as allowed by the lender.

(2) Expenses payable by Buyer (Buyer's Expenses): Appraisal fees; loan application fees; origination charges; credit reports; preparation of loan documents; interest on the notes from date of disbursement to one month prior to dates of first monthly payments; recording fees; copies of easements and restrictions; loan title policy with endorsements required by lender; loan-related inspection fees; photos; amortization schedules; one-half of escrow fee; all prepaid items, including required premiums for flood and hazard insurance, reserve deposits for insurance, ad valorem taxes and special governmental assessments; final compliance inspection; courier fee; repair inspection; underwriting fee; wire transfer fee; expenses incident to any loan; Private Mortgage Insurance Premium (PMI), VA Loan Funding Fee, or FHA Mortgage Insurance Premium (MIP) as required by the lender; and other expenses payable by Buyer under this contract.

(3) Except as provided by 12(A)(4) below, Buyer shall pay any and all Association fees or other charges resulting from the transfer of the Property not to exceed $_____ and Seller shall pay any excess.

(4) Buyer shall pay any deposits for reserves required at closing by the Association.

B. If any expense exceeds an amount expressly stated in this contract for such expense to be paid by a party, that party may terminate this contract unless the other party agrees to pay such excess. Buyer may not pay charges and fees expressly prohibited by FHA, VA, Texas Veterans Land Board or other governmental loan program regulations.

13. PRORATIONS: Taxes for the current year, interest, maintenance fees, regular condominium assessments, dues and rents will be prorated through the Closing Date. The tax proration may be calculated taking into consideration any change in exemptions that will affect the current year's taxes. If taxes for the current year vary from the amount prorated at closing, the parties shall adjust the prorations when tax statements for the current year are available. If taxes are not paid at or prior to closing, Buyer shall pay taxes for the current year. Cash reserves from regular condominium assessments for deferred maintenance or capital improvements established by the Association will not be credited to Seller. Any special condominium assessment due and unpaid at closing will be the obligation of Seller.

14. CASUALTY LOSS: If any part of the Unit which Seller is solely obligated to maintain and repair under the terms of the Declaration is damaged or destroyed by fire or other casualty, Seller shall restore the same to its previous condition as soon as reasonably possible, but in any event by the Closing Date. If Seller fails to do so due to factors beyond Seller's control, Buyer may (a) terminate this contract and the earnest money will be refunded to Buyer, (b) extend the time for performance up to 15 days and the Closing Date will be extended as necessary or (c) accept the Property in its damaged condition with an assignment of insurance proceeds, if permitted by Seller's insurance carrier, and receive credit from Seller at closing in the amount of the deductible under the insurance policy. If any part of the Common Elements or Limited Common Elements appurtenant to the Unit is damaged or destroyed by fire or other casualty loss, Buyer will have 7 days from receipt of notice of such casualty loss within which to notify Seller in writing that the contract will be terminated unless Buyer receives written confirmation from the Association that the damaged condition will be restored to its previous condition within a reasonable time at no cost to Buyer. Unless Buyer gives such notice within such time, Buyer will be deemed to have accepted the Property without confirmation of such restoration. Seller will have 7 days from the date of receipt of Buyer's notice within which to cause to be delivered to Buyer such confirmation. If written confirmation is not delivered to Buyer as required above, Buyer may terminate this contract and the earnest money will be refunded to Buyer. Seller's obligations under this paragraph are independent of any other obligations of Seller under this contract.

Initialed for identification by Buyer_____ _____ and Seller _____ _____   TREC NO. 30-13

15. DEFAULT: If Buyer fails to comply with this contract, Buyer will be in default, and Seller may (a) enforce specific performance, seek such other relief as may be provided by law, or both, or (b) terminate this contract and receive the earnest money as liquidated damages, thereby releasing both parties from this contract. If Seller fails to comply with this contract for any other reason, Seller will be in default and Buyer may (a) enforce specific performance, seek such other relief as may be provided by law, or both, or (b) terminate this contract and receive the earnest money, thereby releasing both parties from this contract.

16. MEDIATION: It is the policy of the State of Texas to encourage resolution of disputes through alternative dispute resolution procedures such as mediation. Any dispute between Seller and Buyer related to this contract which is not resolved through informal discussion will be submitted to a mutually acceptable mediation service or provider. The parties to the mediation shall bear the mediation costs equally. This paragraph does not preclude a party from seeking equitable relief from a court of competent jurisdiction.

17. ATTORNEY'S FEES: A Buyer, Seller, Listing Broker, Other Broker, or escrow agent who prevails in any legal proceeding related to this contract is entitled to recover reasonable attorney's fees and all costs of such proceeding.

18. ESCROW:
   A. ESCROW: The escrow agent is not (i) a party to this contract and does not have liability for the performance or nonperformance of any party to this contract, (ii) liable for interest on the earnest money and (iii) liable for the loss of any earnest money caused by the failure of any financial institution in which the earnest money has been deposited unless the financial institution is acting as escrow agent.
   B. EXPENSES: At closing, the earnest money must be applied first to any cash down payment, then to Buyer's Expenses and any excess refunded to Buyer. If no closing occurs, escrow agent may: (i) require a written release of liability of the escrow agent from all parties, (ii) require payment of unpaid expenses incurred on behalf of a party, and (iii) only deduct from the earnest money the amount of unpaid expenses incurred on behalf of the party receiving the earnest money.
   C. DEMAND: Upon termination of this contract, either party or the escrow agent may send a release of earnest money to each party and the parties shall execute counterparts of the release and deliver same to the escrow agent. If either party fails to execute the release, either party may make a written demand to the escrow agent for the earnest money. If only one party makes written demand for the earnest money, escrow agent shall promptly provide a copy of the demand to the other party. If escrow agent does not receive written objection to the demand from the other party within 15 days, escrow agent may disburse the earnest money to the party making demand reduced by the amount of unpaid expenses incurred on behalf of the party receiving the earnest money and escrow agent may pay the same to the creditors. If escrow agent complies with the provisions of this paragraph, each party hereby releases escrow agent from all adverse claims related to the disbursal of the earnest money.
   D. DAMAGES: Any party who wrongfully fails or refuses to sign a release acceptable to the escrow agent within 7 days of receipt of the request will be liable to the other party for (i) damages; (ii) the earnest money; (iii) reasonable attorney's fees; and (iv) all costs of suit.
   E. NOTICES: Escrow agent's notices will be effective when sent in compliance with Paragraph 21. Notice of objection to the demand will be deemed effective upon receipt by escrow agent.

19. REPRESENTATIONS: All covenants, representations and warranties in this contract survive closing. If any representation of Seller in this contract is untrue on the Closing Date, Seller will be in default. Unless expressly prohibited by written agreement, Seller may continue to show the Property and receive, negotiate and accept back up offers.

20. FEDERAL TAX REQUIREMENTS: If Seller is a "foreign person," as defined by Internal Revenue Code and its regulations, or if Seller fails to deliver an affidavit or a certificate of non-foreign status to Buyer that Seller is not a "foreign person," then Buyer shall withhold from the sales proceeds an amount sufficient to comply with applicable tax law and deliver the same to the Internal Revenue Service together with appropriate tax forms. Internal Revenue Service regulations require filing written reports if currency in excess of specified amounts is received in the transaction.

21. NOTICES: All notices from one party to the other must be in writing and are effective when mailed to, hand-delivered at, or transmitted by fax or electronic transmission as follows:

To Buyer	**To Seller**
at: _____	at: _____
_____	_____
Phone: ( ) _____	Phone: ( ) _____
Fax: ( ) _____	Fax: ( ) _____
E-mail: _____	E-mail: _____

Initialed for identification by Buyer_____ _____ and Seller _____ _____   TREC NO. 30-13

121

22. AGREEMENT OF PARTIES: This contract contains the entire agreement of the parties and cannot be changed except by their written agreement. Addenda which are a part of this contract are (check all applicable boxes):

❏ Third Party Financing Addendum

❏ Loan Assumption Addendum

❏ Buyer's Temporary Residential Lease

❏ Seller's Temporary Residential Lease

❏ Addendum for Sale of Other Property by Buyer

❏ Addendum for "Back-Up" Contract

❏ Seller Financing Addendum

❏ Addendum for Coastal Area Property

❏ Short Sale Addendum

❏ Addendum for Seller's Disclosure of Information on Lead-based Paint and Lead-based Paint Hazards as Required by Federal Law

❏ Addendum for Authorizing Hydrostatic Testing

❏ Addendum Concerning Right to Terminate Due to Lender's Appraisal

❏ Environmental Assessment, Threatened or Endangered Species and Wetlands Addendum

❏ Addendum for Property Located Seaward of the Gulf Intracoastal Waterway

❏ Addendum for Release of Liability on Assumption of FHA, VA, or Conventional Loan Restoration of Seller's Entitlement for VA Guaranteed Loan

❏ Addendum for Property in a Propane Gas System Service Area

❏ Other (list):_____

_____

_____

_____

_____

_____

_____

23. TERMINATION OPTION: For nominal consideration, the receipt of which is hereby acknowledged by Seller, and Buyer's agreement to pay Seller $_____ (Option Fee) within 3 days after the Effective Date of this contract, Seller grants Buyer the unrestricted right to terminate this contract by giving notice of termination to Seller within _____ days after the Effective Date of this contract (Option Period). Notices under this paragraph must be given by 5:00 p.m. (local time where the Property is located) by the date specified. If no dollar amount is stated as the Option Fee or if Buyer fails to pay the Option Fee to Seller within the time prescribed, this paragraph will not be a part of this contract and Buyer shall not have the unrestricted right to terminate this contract. If Buyer gives notice of termination within the time prescribed, the Option Fee will not be refunded; however, any earnest money will be refunded to Buyer. The Option Fee ❏will ❏will not be credited to the Sales Price at closing. **Time is of the essence for this paragraph and strict compliance with the time for performance is required.**

24. CONSULT AN ATTORNEY BEFORE SIGNING: TREC rules prohibit real estate license holders from giving legal advice. READ THIS CONTRACT CAREFULLY.

Buyer's Attorney is: _____	Seller's Attorney is: _____
_____	_____
Phone: ( ) _____	Phone: ( ) _____
Fax: ( ) _____	Fax: ( ) _____
E-mail: _____	E-mail: _____

EXECUTED the _____ day of _____, 20_____ (Effective Date).
(BROKER: FILL IN THE DATE OF FINAL ACCEPTANCE.)

_____   _____
Buyer   Seller

_____   _____
Buyer   Seller

TREC NO. 30-13

BROKER INFORMATION
(Print name(s) only. Do not sign)

| Other Broker Firm | License No. | Listing Broker Firm | License No. |

represents ☐ Buyer only as Buyer's agent
            ☐ Seller as Listing Broker's subagent

represents ☐ Seller and Buyer as an intermediary
            ☐ Seller only as Seller's agent

Associate's Name   License No.

Listing Associate's Name   License No.

Associate's Email Address   Phone

Listing Associate's Email Address   Phone

Licensed Supervisor of Associate   License No.

Licensed Supervisor of Listing Associate   License No.

Other Broker's Address   Phone

Listing Broker's Office Address   Phone

City   State   Zip

City   State   Zip

Selling Associate's Name   License No.

Selling Associate's Email Address   Phone

Licensed Supervisor of Selling Associate   License No.

Selling Associate's Office Address

City   State   Zip

Listing Broker has agreed to pay Other Broker _____ of the total sales price when the Listing Broker's fee is received. Escrow agent is authorized and directed to pay Other Broker from Listing Broker's fee at closing.

TREC NO. 30-13

123

OPTION FEE RECEIPT

Receipt of $ _____ (Option Fee) in the form of _____
is acknowledged.

_____   _____
Seller or Listing Broker   Date

EARNEST MONEY RECEIPT

Receipt of $ _____ Earnest Money in the form of _____
is acknowledged.

_____   _____   _____   _____
Escrow Agent   Received by   Email Address   Date/Time

_____   _____
Address   Phone

_____   _____   _____   _____
City   State   Zip   Fax

CONTRACT RECEIPT

Receipt of the Contract is acknowledged.

_____   _____   _____   _____
Escrow Agent   Received by   Email Address   Date

_____   _____
Address   Phone

_____   _____   _____   _____
City   State   Zip   Fax

ADDITIONAL EARNEST MONEY RECEIPT

Receipt of $ _____ additional Earnest Money in the form of _____
is acknowledged.

_____   _____   _____   _____
Escrow Agent   Received by   Email Address   Date/Time

_____   _____
Address   Phone

_____   _____   _____   _____
City   State   Zip   Fax

TREC NO. 30-13

FARM AND RANCH CONTRACT

1. PARTIES: The parties to this contract are _____ _____ (Buyer). Seller agrees to (Seller) and sell and convey to Buyer and Buyer agrees to buy from Seller the Property defined below.

2. PROPERTY: The land, improvements, accessories and crops except for the exclusions and reservations, are collectively referred to as the "Property".

A. LAND: The land situated in the County of _____, Texas, described as follows:_____

_____
or as described on attached exhibit, also known as _____ (address/zip code), together with all rights, privileges, and appurtenances pertaining thereto, including but not limited to: water rights, claims, permits, strips and gores, easements, and cooperative or association memberships.

B. IMPROVEMENTS:
(1) FARM and RANCH IMPROVEMENTS: The following **permanently installed and built-in items**, if any: windmills, tanks, barns, pens, fences, gates, sheds, outbuildings, and corrals.
(2) RESIDENTIAL IMPROVEMENTS: The house, garage, and all other fixtures and improvements attached to the above-described real property, including without limitation, the following **permanently installed and built-in items,** if any: all equipment and appliances, valances, screens, shutters, awnings, wall-to-wall carpeting, mirrors, ceiling fans, attic fans, mail boxes, television antennas, mounts and brackets for televisions and speakers, heating and air-conditioning units, security and fire detection equipment, wiring, plumbing and lighting fixtures, chandeliers, water softener system, kitchen equipment, garage door openers, cleaning equipment, shrubbery, landscaping, outdoor cooking equipment, and all other property owned by Seller and attached to the above described real property.

C. ACCESSORIES:
(1) FARM AND RANCH ACCESSORIES: The following described related accessories: (check boxes of conveyed accessories) ❑ portable buildings ❑ hunting blinds ❑ game feeders ❑ livestock feeders and troughs ❑ irrigation equipment ❑ fuel tanks ❑ submersible pumps ❑ pressure tanks ❑ corrals ❑ gates ❑ chutes ❑ other:_____

_____
(2) RESIDENTIAL ACCESSORIES: The following described related accessories, if any: window air conditioning units, stove, fireplace screens, curtains and rods, blinds, window shades, draperies and rods, door keys, mailbox keys, above ground pool, swimming pool equipment and maintenance accessories, artificial fireplace logs, and controls for:
(i) garages, (ii) entry gates, and (iii) other improvements and accessories.

D. CROPS: Unless otherwise agreed in writing, Seller has the right to harvest all growing crops until delivery of possession of the Property.

E. EXCLUSIONS: The following improvements, accessories, and crops will be retained by Seller and must be removed prior to delivery of possession: _____

_____.

F. RESERVATIONS: Any reservation for oil, gas, or other minerals, water, timber, or other interests is made in accordance with an attached addendum.

3. SALES PRICE:
A. Cash portion of Sales Price payable by Buyer at closing .... $_____
B. Sum of all financing described in the attached: ❑   Third Party Financing Addendum, ❑   Loan Assumption Addendum, ❑   Seller Financing Addendum ... $_____
C. Sales Price (Sum of A and B) .... $_____
D. The Sales Price ❑ will ❑ will not be adjusted based on the survey required by Paragraph 6C. If the Sales Price is adjusted, the Sales Price will be calculated on the basis of $ _____ per acre. If the Sales Price is adjusted by more than 10%, either party may terminate this contract by providing written notice to the other party within _____ days after the terminating party receives the survey. If neither party terminates this contract or if the variance is 10% or less, the adjustment will be made to the amount in ❑ 3A ❑ 3B ❑ proportionately to 3A and 3B.

4. LICENSE HOLDER DISCLOSURE: Texas Law requires a real estate license holder who is a party to a transaction or acting on behalf of a spouse, parent, child, business entity in which the license holder owns more than 10%, or a trust for which the license holder acts as trustee or of which the license holder or the license holder's spouse, parent or child is a beneficiary, to notify the other party in writing before entering into a contract of sale. Disclose if applicable:_____

_____.

5. EARNEST   MONEY: Within 3 days after the Effective Date, Buyer must deliver $_____ as earnest money to,_____, as escrow agent, at _____(address). Buyer shall deliver additional earnest money of $_____ to escrow agent within _____ days after the Effective Date of this contract. If Buyer fails to deliver the earnest money within the time required, Seller may terminate this contract or exercise Seller's remedies under Paragraph 15, or both, by providing notice to Buyer before Buyer delivers the earnest money. If the last day to deliver the earnest money falls on a Saturday, Sunday, or legal holiday, the time to deliver the earnest money is extended until the end of the next day that is not a Saturday, Sunday, or legal holiday. **Time is of the essence for this paragraph.**

Initialed for identification by Buyer_____ _____ and Seller _____ _____   TREC NO. 25-12

6. TITLE POLICY AND SURVEY:

A. TITLE POLICY: Seller shall furnish to Buyer at ❑Seller's ❑Buyer's expense an owner policy of title insurance (Title Policy) issued by: _____ (Title Company) in the amount of the Sales Price, dated at or after closing, insuring Buyer against loss under the provisions of the Title Policy, subject to the promulgated exclusions (including existing building and zoning ordinances) and the following exceptions:
(1) The standard printed exception for standby fees, taxes and assessments.
(2) Liens created as part of the financing described in Paragraph 3.
(3) Reservations or exceptions otherwise permitted by this contract or as may be approved by Buyer in writing.
(4) The standard printed exception as to marital rights.
(5) The standard printed exception as to waters, tidelands, beaches, streams, and related matters.
(6) The standard printed exception as to discrepancies, conflicts, shortages in area or boundary lines, encroachments or protrusions, or overlapping improvements:
❑(i) will not be amended or deleted from the title policy; or
❑(ii) will be amended to read, "shortages in area" at the expense of ❑Buyer ❑Seller.
(7) The exception or exclusion regarding minerals approved by the Texas Department of Insurance.

B. COMMITMENT: Within 20 days after the Title Company receives a copy of this contract, Seller shall furnish to Buyer a commitment for title insurance (Commitment) and, at Buyer's expense, legible copies of restrictive covenants and documents evidencing exceptions in the Commitment (Exception Documents) other than the standard printed exceptions. Seller authorizes the Title Company to deliver the Commitment and Exception Documents to Buyer at Buyer's address shown in Paragraph 21. If the Commitment and Exception Documents are not delivered to Buyer within the specified time, the time for delivery will be automatically extended up to 15 days or 3 days before the Closing Date, whichever is earlier. If the Commitment and Exception Documents are not delivered within the time required, Buyer may terminate this contract and the earnest money will be refunded to Buyer.

C. SURVEY: The survey must be made by a registered professional land surveyor acceptable to the Title Company and Buyer's lender(s). (Check one box only):
❑ (1) Within _____ days after the Effective Date of this contract, Seller shall furnish to Buyer and Title Company Seller's existing survey of the Property and a Residential Real Property Affidavit promulgated by the Texas Department of Insurance (T-47 Affidavit). **If Seller fails to furnish the existing survey or affidavit within the time prescribed, Buyer shall obtain a new survey at Seller's expense no later than 3 days prior to Closing Date.** The existing survey ❑ will ❑ will not be recertified to a date subsequent to the Effective Date of this contract at the expense of ❑ Buyer ❑ Seller. If the existing survey is not approved by the Title Company or Buyer's lender(s), a new survey will be obtained at the expense of ❑ Buyer ❑ Seller no later than 3 days prior to Closing Date.
❑ (2) Within _____ days after the Effective Date of this contract, Buyer shall obtain a new survey at Buyer's expense. Buyer is deemed to receive the survey on the date of actual receipt or the date specified in this paragraph, whichever is earlier.
❑ (3) Within _____ days after the Effective Date of this contract, Seller, at Seller's expense shall furnish a new survey to Buyer.
❑ (4) No survey is required.

D. OBJECTIONS: Buyer may object in writing to (i) defects, exceptions, or encumbrances to title disclosed on the survey other than items 6A(1) through (5) above; or disclosed in the Commitment other than items 6A(1) through (7) above; (ii) any portion of the Property lying in a special flood hazard area (Zone V or A) as shown on the current Federal Emergency Management Agency map; or (iii) any exceptions which prohibit the following use or activity:

_____.
Buyer must object the earlier of (i) the Closing Date or (ii) _____ days after Buyer receives the Commitment, Exception Documents, and the survey. Buyer's failure to object within the time allowed will constitute a waiver of Buyer's right to object; except that the requirements in Schedule C of the Commitment are not waived by Buyer. Provided Seller is not obligated to incur any expense, Seller shall cure any timely objections of Buyer or any third party lender within 15 days after Seller receives the objections (Cure Period) and the Closing Date will be extended as necessary. If objections are not cured within the Cure Period, Buyer may, by delivering notice to Seller within 5 days after the end of the Cure Period: (i) terminate this contract and the earnest money will be refunded to Buyer; or (ii) waive the objections. If Buyer does not terminate within the time required, Buyer shall be deemed to have waived the objections. If the Commitment or Survey is revised or any new Exception Document(s) is delivered, Buyer may object to any new matter revealed in the revised Commitment or Survey or new Exception Document(s) within the same time stated in this paragraph to make objections beginning when the revised Commitment, Survey, or Exception Document(s) is delivered to Buyer.

E. EXCEPTION DOCUMENTS: Prior to the execution of the contract, Seller has provided Buyer with copies of the Exception Documents listed below or on the attached exhibit. Matters reflected in the Exception Documents listed below or on the attached exhibit will be permitted exceptions in the Title Policy and will not be a basis for objection to title:

Initialed for identification by Buyer_____ _____ and Seller _____ _____   TREC NO. 25-12

Document	Date	Recording Reference
_____	_____	_____
_____	_____	_____
_____	_____	_____

F. SURFACE LEASES: Prior to the execution of the contract, Seller has provided Buyer with copies of written leases and given notice of oral leases (Leases) listed below or on the attached exhibit. The following Leases will be permitted exceptions in the Title Policy and will not be a basis for objection to title:_____
_____

G. TITLE NOTICES:
(1) ABSTRACT OR TITLE POLICY: Broker advises Buyer to have an abstract of title covering the Property examined by an attorney of Buyer's selection, or Buyer should be furnished with or obtain a Title Policy. If a Title Policy is furnished, the Commitment should be promptly reviewed by an attorney of Buyer's choice due to the time limitations on Buyer's right to object.
(2) STATUTORY TAX DISTRICTS: If the Property is situated in a utility or other statutorily created district providing water, sewer, drainage, or flood control facilities and services, Chapter 49, Texas Water Code, requires Seller to deliver and Buyer to sign the statutory notice relating to the tax rate, bonded indebtedness, or standby fee of the district prior to final execution of this contract.
(3) TIDE WATERS: If the Property abuts the tidally influenced waters of the state, §33.135, Texas Natural Resources Code, requires a notice regarding coastal area property to be included in the contract. An addendum containing the notice promulgated by TREC or required by the parties must be used.
(4) ANNEXATION: If the Property is located outside the limits of a municipality, Seller notifies Buyer under §5.011, Texas Property Code, that the Property may now or later be included in the extraterritorial jurisdiction of a municipality and may now or later be subject to annexation by the municipality. Each municipality maintains a map that depicts its boundaries and extraterritorial jurisdiction. To determine if the Property is located within a municipality's extraterritorial jurisdiction or is likely to be located within a municipality's extraterritorial jurisdiction, contact all municipalities located in the general proximity of the Property for further information.
(5) PROPERTY LOCATED IN A CERTIFICATED SERVICE AREA OF A UTILITY SERVICE PROVIDER: Notice required by §13.257, Water Code: The real property, described in Paragraph 2, that you are about to purchase may be located in a certificated water or sewer service area, which is authorized by law to provide water or sewer service to the properties in the certificated area. If your property is located in a certificated area there may be special costs or charges that you will be required to pay before you can receive water or sewer service. There may be a period required to construct lines or other facilities necessary to provide water or sewer service to your property. You are advised to determine if the property is in a certificated area and contact the utility service provider to determine the cost that you will be required to pay and the period, if any, that is required to provide water or sewer service to your property. The undersigned Buyer hereby acknowledges receipt of the foregoing notice at or before the execution of a binding contract for the purchase of the real property described in Paragraph 2 or at closing of purchase of the real property.
(6) PUBLIC IMPROVEMENT DISTRICTS: If the Property is in a public improvement district, §5.014, Property Code, requires Seller to notify Buyer as follows: As a purchaser of this parcel of real property you are obligated to pay an assessment to a municipality or county for an improvement project undertaken by a public improvement district under Chapter 372, Local Government Code. The assessment may be due annually or in periodic installments. More information concerning the amount of the assessment and the due dates of that assessment may be obtained from the municipality or county levying the assessment. The amount of the assessments is subject to change. Your failure to pay the assessments could result in a lien on and the foreclosure of your property.
(7) TEXAS AGRICULTURAL DEVELOPMENT DISTRICT: The Property ❑ is ❑ is not located in a Texas Agricultural Development District. For additional information contact the Texas Department of Agriculture
(8) TRANSFER FEES: If the Property is subject to a private transfer fee obligation, §5.205, Property Code, requires Seller to notify Buyer as follows: The private transfer fee obligation may be governed by Chapter 5, Subchapter G of the Texas Property Code.
(9) PROPANE GAS SYSTEM SERVICE AREA: If the Property is located in a propane gas system service area owned by a distribution system retailer, Seller must give Buyer written notice as required by §141.010, Texas Utilities Code. An addendum containing the notice approved by TREC or required by the parties should be used.
(10) NOTICE OF WATER LEVEL FLUCTUATIONS: If the Property adjoins an impoundment of water, including a reservoir or lake, constructed and maintained under Chapter 11, Water Code,

Initialed for identification by Buyer_____ _____ and Seller _____ _____   TREC NO. 25-12

that has a storage capacity of at least 5,000 acre-feet at the impoundment's normal operating level, Seller hereby notifies Buyer: "The water level of the impoundment of water adjoining the Property fluctuates for various reasons, including as a result of: (1) an entity lawfully exercising its right to use the water stored in the impoundment; or (2) drought or flood conditions."

7. PROPERTY CONDITION:

A. ACCESS, INSPECTIONS AND UTILITIES: Seller shall permit Buyer and Buyer's agents access to the Property at reasonable times. Buyer may have the Property inspected by inspectors selected by Buyer and licensed by TREC or otherwise permitted by law to make inspections. Any hydrostatic testing must be separately authorized by Seller in writing. Seller at Seller's expense shall immediately cause existing utilities to be turned on and shall keep the utilities on during the time this contract is in effect .

NOTICE: Buyer should determine the availability of utilities to the Property suitable to satisfy Buyer's needs.

B. SELLER'S DISCLOSURE NOTICE PURSUANT TO §5.008, TEXAS PROPERTY CODE (Notice): (Check one box only)

❑ (1) Buyer has received the Notice

❑ (2) Buyer has not received the Notice. Within _____ days after the Effective Date of this contract, Seller shall deliver the Notice to Buyer. If Buyer does not receive the Notice, Buyer may terminate this contract at any time prior to the closing and the earnest money will be refunded to Buyer. If Seller delivers the Notice, Buyer may terminate this contract for any reason within 7 days after Buyer receives the Notice or prior to the closing, whichever first occurs, and the earnest money will be refunded to Buyer.

❑ (3) The Texas Property Code does not require this Seller to furnish the Notice.

C. SELLER'S DISCLOSURE OF LEAD-BASED PAINT AND LEAD-BASED PAINT HAZARDS is required by Federal law for a residential dwelling constructed prior to 1978.

D. ACCEPTANCE OF PROPERTY CONDITION: "As Is" means the present condition of the Property with any and all defects and without warranty except for the warranties of title and the warranties in this contract. Buyer's agreement to accept the Property As Is under Paragraph 7D (1) or (2) does not preclude Buyer from inspecting the Property under Paragraph 7A, from negotiating repairs or treatments in a subsequent amendment, or from terminating this contract during the Option Period, if any.

(Check one box only)

❑ (1) Buyer accepts the Property As Is.

❑ (2) Buyer accepts the Property As Is provided Seller, at Seller's expense, shall complete the following specific repairs and treatments: _____
_____ .
(Do not insert general phrases, such as "subject to inspections," that do not identify specific repairs and treatments.)

E. COMPLETION OF REPAIRS: Unless otherwise agreed in writing: (i) Seller shall complete all agreed repairs and treatments prior to the Closing Date; and (ii) all required permits must be obtained, and repairs and treatments must be performed by persons who are licensed to provide such repairs or treatments or, if no license is required by law, are commercially engaged in the trade of providing such repairs or treatments. At Buyer's election, any transferable warranties received by Seller with respect to the repairs will be transferred to Buyer at Buyer's expense. If Seller fails to complete any agreed repairs prior to the Closing Date, Buyer may exercise remedies under Paragraph 15 or extend the Closing Date up to 5 days if necessary for Seller to complete repairs.

F. LENDER REQUIRED REPAIRS AND TREATMENTS: Unless otherwise agreed in writing, neither party is obligated to pay for lender required repairs, which includes treatment for wood destroying insects. If the parties do not agree to pay for the lender required repairs or treatments, this contract will terminate and the earnest money will be refunded to Buyer. If the cost of lender required repairs and treatments exceeds 5% of the Sales Price, Buyer may terminate this contract and the earnest money will be refunded to Buyer.

G. ENVIRONMENTAL MATTERS: Buyer is advised that the presence of wetlands, toxic substances, including asbestos and wastes or other environmental hazards, or the presence of a threatened or endangered species or its habitat may affect Buyer's intended use of the Property. If Buyer is concerned about these matters, an addendum promulgated by TREC or required by the parties should be used.

H. SELLER'S DISCLOSURES: Except as otherwise disclosed in this contract, Seller has no knowledge of the following:

(1) any flooding of the Property which has had a material adverse effect on the use of the Property;

(2) any pending or threatened litigation, condemnation, or special assessment affecting the Property;

(3) any environmental hazards that materially and adversely affect the Property;

(4) any dumpsite, landfill, or underground tanks or containers now or previously located on the Property;

(5) any wetlands, as defined by federal or state law or regulation, affecting the Property; or

(6) any threatened or endangered species or their habitat affecting the Property.

Initialed for identification by Buyer_____ _____ and Seller _____ _____   TREC NO. 25-12

I. RESIDENTIAL SERVICE CONTRACTS: Buyer may purchase a residential service contract from a residential service company licensed by TREC. If Buyer purchases a residential service contract, Seller shall reimburse Buyer at closing for the cost of the residential service contract in an amount not exceeding $_____. Buyer should review any residential service contract for the scope of coverage, exclusions and limitations. **The purchase of a residential service contract is optional. Similar coverage may be purchased from various companies authorized to do business in Texas.**

J. GOVERNMENT PROGRAMS: The Property is subject to the government programs listed below or on the attached exhibit:_____.
Seller shall provide Buyer with copies of all governmental program agreements. Any allocation or proration of payment under governmental programs is made by separate agreement between the parties which will survive closing.

8. BROKERS' FEES: All obligations of the parties for payment of brokers' fees are contained in separate written agreements.

9. CLOSING:
A. The closing of the sale will be on or before _____, 20_____, or within 7 days after objections made under Paragraph 6D have been cured or waived, whichever date is later (Closing Date). If either party fails to close the sale by the Closing Date, the non-defaulting party may exercise the remedies contained in Paragraph 15.
B. At closing:
(1) Seller shall execute and deliver a general warranty deed conveying title to the Property to Buyer and showing no additional exceptions to those permitted in Paragraph 6, an assignment of Leases, and furnish tax statements or certificates showing no delinquent taxes on the Property.
(2) Buyer shall pay the Sales Price in good funds acceptable to the escrow agent.
(3) Seller and Buyer shall execute and deliver any notices, statements, certificates, affidavits, releases, loan documents and other documents reasonably required for the closing of the sale and the issuance of the Title Policy.
(4) There will be no liens, assessments, or security interests against the Property which will not be satisfied out of the sales proceeds unless securing the payment of any loans assumed by Buyer and assumed loans will not be in default.
(5) If the Property is subject to a residential lease, Seller shall transfer security deposits (as defined under §92.102, Property Code), if any, to Buyer. In such an event, Buyer shall deliver to the tenant a signed statement acknowledging that the Buyer has acquired the Property and is responsible for the return of the security deposit, and specifying the exact dollar amount of the security deposit.

10. POSSESSION:
A. Buyer's Possession: Seller shall deliver to Buyer possession of the Property in its present or required condition, ordinary wear and tear excepted: ❑ upon closing and funding ❑ according to a temporary residential lease form promulgated by TREC or other written lease required by the parties. Any possession by Buyer prior to closing or by Seller after closing which is not authorized by a written lease will establish a tenancy at sufferance relationship between the parties. **Consult your insurance agent prior to change of ownership and possession because insurance coverage may be limited or terminated. The absence of a written lease or appropriate insurance coverage may expose the parties to economic loss.**
B. Leases:
(1) After the Effective Date, Seller may not execute any lease (including but not limited to mineral leases) or convey any interest in the Property without Buyer's written consent.
(2) If the Property is subject to any lease to which Seller is a party, Seller shall deliver to Buyer copies of the lease(s) and any move-in condition form signed by the tenant within 7 days after the Effective Date of the contract.

11. SPECIAL PROVISIONS: (Insert only factual statements and business details applicable to the sale. TREC rules prohibit license holders from adding factual statements or business details for which a contract addendum or other form has been promulgated by TREC for mandatory use.)

Initialed for identification by Buyer_____ _____ and Seller _____ _____   TREC NO. 25-12

12. **SETTLEMENT AND OTHER EXPENSES:**
   A. The following expenses must be paid at or prior to closing:
   (1) Expenses payable by Seller (Seller's Expenses):
   (a) Releases of existing liens, including prepayment penalties and recording fees; release of Seller's loan liability; tax statements or certificates; preparation of deed; one-half of escrow fee; and other expenses payable by Seller under this contract.
   (b) Seller shall also pay an amount not to exceed $ _____ to be applied in the following order: Buyer's Expenses which Buyer is prohibited from paying by FHA, VA, Texas Veterans Land Board or other governmental loan programs, and then to other Buyer's Expenses as allowed by the lender.
   (2) Expenses payable by Buyer (Buyer's Expenses) Appraisal fees; loan application fees; origination charges; credit reports; preparation of loan documents; interest on the notes from date of disbursement to one month prior to dates of first monthly payments; recording fees; copies of easements and restrictions; loan title policy with endorsements required by lender; loan-related inspection fees; photos; amortization schedules; one-half of escrow fee; all prepaid items, including required premiums for flood and hazard insurance, reserve deposits for insurance, ad valorem taxes and special governmental assessments; final compliance inspection; courier fee; repair inspection; underwriting fee; wire transfer fee; expenses incident to any loan; Private Mortgage Insurance Premium (PMI), VA Loan Funding Fee, or FHA Mortgage Insurance Premium (MIP) as required by the lender; and other expenses payable by Buyer under this contract.
   B. If any expense exceeds an amount expressly stated in this contract for such expense to be paid by a party, that party may terminate this contract unless the other party agrees to pay such excess. Buyer may not pay charges and fees expressly prohibited by FHA, VA, Texas Veterans Land Board or other governmental loan program regulations.

13. **PRORATIONS AND ROLLBACK TAXES:**
   A. PRORATIONS: Taxes for the current year, interest, maintenance fees, assessments, dues and rents will be prorated through the Closing Date. The tax proration may be calculated taking into consideration any change in exemptions that will affect the current year's taxes. If taxes for the current year vary from the amount prorated at closing, the parties shall adjust the prorations when tax statements for the current year are available. If taxes are not paid at or prior to closing, Buyer shall pay taxes for the current year. Rentals which are unknown at time of closing will be prorated between Buyer and Seller when they become known.
   B. ROLLBACK TAXES: If this sale or Buyer's use of the Property after closing results in the assessment of additional taxes, penalties or interest (Assessments) for periods prior to closing, the Assessments will be the obligation of Buyer. If Assessments are imposed because of Seller's use or change in use of the Property prior to closing, the Assessments will be the obligation of Seller. Obligations imposed by this paragraph will survive closing.

14. **CASUALTY LOSS:** If any part of the Property is damaged or destroyed by fire or other casualty after the Effective Date of this contract, Seller shall restore the Property to its previous condition as soon as reasonably possible, but in any event by the Closing Date. If Seller fails to do so due to factors beyond Seller's control, Buyer may (a) terminate this contract and the earnest money will be refunded to Buyer, (b) extend the time for performance up to 15 days and the Closing Date will be extended as necessary or (c) accept the Property in its damaged condition with an assignment of insurance proceeds, if permitted by Seller's insurance carrier, and receive credit from Seller at closing in the amount of the deductible under the insurance policy. Seller's obligations under this paragraph are independent of any other obligations of Seller under this contract.

15. **DEFAULT:** If Buyer fails to comply with this contract, Buyer will be in default, and Seller may (a) enforce specific performance, seek such other relief as may be provided by law, or both, or (b) terminate this contract and receive the earnest money as liquidated damages, thereby releasing both parties from this contract. If Seller fails to comply with this contract for any other reason, Seller will be in default and Buyer may (a) enforce specific performance, seek such other relief as may be provided by law, or both, or (b) terminate this contract and receive the earnest money, thereby releasing both parties from this contract.

16. **MEDIATION:** It is the policy of the State of Texas to encourage resolution of disputes through alternative dispute resolution procedures such as mediation. Any dispute between Seller and Buyer related to this contract which is not resolved through informal discussion will be submitted to a mutually acceptable mediation service or provider. The parties to the mediation shall bear the mediation costs equally. This paragraph does not preclude a party from seeking equitable relief from a court of competent jurisdiction.

17. **ATTORNEY'S FEES:** A Buyer, Seller, Listing Broker, Other Broker, or escrow agent who prevails in any legal proceeding related to this contract is entitled to recover reasonable attorney's fees and all costs of such proceeding.

Initialed for identification by Buyer_____ _____ and Seller _____ _____   TREC NO. 25-12

130

18. ESCROW:

    A. ESCROW: The escrow agent is not (i) a party to this contract and does not have liability for the performance or nonperformance of any party to this contract, (ii) liable for interest on the earnest money and (iii) liable for the loss of any earnest money caused by the failure of any financial institution in which the earnest money has been deposited unless the financial institution is acting as escrow agent.

    B. EXPENSES: At closing, the earnest money must be applied first to any cash down payment, then to Buyer's Expenses and any excess refunded to Buyer. If no closing occurs, escrow agent may: (i) require a written release of liability of the escrow agent from all parties, (ii) require payment of unpaid expenses incurred on behalf of a party, and (iii) only deduct from the earnest money the amount of unpaid expenses incurred on behalf of the party receiving the earnest money.

    C. DEMAND: Upon termination of this contract, either party or the escrow agent may send a release of earnest money to each party and the parties shall execute counterparts of the release and deliver same to the escrow agent. If either party fails to execute the release, either party may make a written demand to the escrow agent for the earnest money. If only one party makes written demand for the earnest money, escrow agent shall promptly provide a copy of the demand to the other party. If escrow agent does not receive written objection to the demand from the other party within 15 days, escrow agent may disburse the earnest money to the party making demand reduced by the amount of unpaid expenses incurred on behalf of the party receiving the earnest money and escrow agent may pay the same to the creditors. If escrow agent complies with the provisions of this paragraph, each party hereby releases escrow agent from all adverse claims related to the disbursal of the earnest money.

    D. DAMAGES: Any party who wrongfully fails or refuses to sign a release acceptable to the escrow agent within 7 days of receipt of the request will be liable to the other party for (i) damages; (ii) the earnest money; (iii) reasonable attorney's fees; and (iv) all costs of suit.

    E. NOTICES: Escrow agent's notices will be effective when sent in compliance with Paragraph 21. Notice of objection to the demand will be deemed effective upon receipt by escrow agent.

19. REPRESENTATIONS: All covenants, representations and warranties in this contract survive closing. If any representation of Seller in this contract is untrue on the Closing Date, Seller will be in default. Unless expressly prohibited by written agreement, Seller may continue to show the Property and receive, negotiate and accept back up offers.

20. FEDERAL TAX REQUIREMENTS: If Seller is a "foreign person," as defined by Internal Revenue Code and its regulations, or if Seller fails to deliver an affidavit or a certificate of non-foreign status to Buyer that Seller is not a "foreign person," then Buyer shall withhold from the sales proceeds an amount sufficient to comply with applicable tax law and deliver the same to the Internal Revenue Service together with appropriate tax forms. Internal Revenue Service regulations require filing written reports if currency in excess of specified amounts is received in the transaction.

21. NOTICES: All notices from one party to the other must be in writing and are effective when mailed to, hand-delivered at, or transmitted by fax or electronic transmission as follows:

To Buyer	**To Seller**
at: _____	at: _____
_____	_____
Phone: (___)_____	Phone: (___)_____
Fax: (___)_____	Fax: (___)_____
E-mail: _____	E-mail: _____

Initialed for identification by Buyer_____ _____ and Seller _____ _____   TREC NO. 25-12

22.AGREEMENT OF PARTIES: This contract contains the entire agreement of the parties and cannot be changed except by their written agreement. Addenda which are a part of this contract are (check all applicable boxes):

❑ Third Party Financing Addendum

❑ Seller Financing Addendum

❑ Addendum for Property Subject to Mandatory Membership in a Property Owners Association

❑ Buyer's Temporary Residential Lease

❑ Loan Assumption Addendum

❑ Addendum for Sale of Other Property by Buyer

❑ Addendum for "Back-Up" Contract

❑ Addendum for Coastal Area Property

❑ Addendum for Authorizing Hydrostatic Testing

❑ Addendum Concerning Right to Terminate Due to Lender's Appraisal

❑ Addendum for Reservation of Oil, Gas and Other Minerals

❑ Environmental Assessment, Threatened or Endangered Species and Wetlands Addendum

❑ Seller's Temporary Residential Lease

❑ Short Sale Addendum

❑ Addendum for Property Located Seaward of the Gulf Intracoastal Waterway

❑ Addendum for Seller's Disclosure of Information on Lead-based Paint and Lead-based Paint Hazards as Required by Federal Law

❑ Addendum for Property in a Propane Gas System Service Area

❑ Other (list): _____
_____
_____
_____
_____
_____

23.TERMINATION OPTION: For nominal consideration, the receipt of which is hereby acknowledged by Seller, and Buyer's agreement to pay Seller $_____ (Option Fee) within 3 days after the Effective Date of this contract, Seller grants Buyer the unrestricted right to terminate this contract by giving notice of termination to Seller within _____ days after the Effective Date of this contract (Option Period). Notices under this paragraph must be given by 5:00 p.m. (local time where the Property is located) by the date specified. If no dollar amount is stated as the Option Fee or if Buyer fails to pay the Option Fee to Seller within the time prescribed, this paragraph will not be a part of this contract and Buyer shall not have the unrestricted right to terminate this contract. If Buyer gives notice of termination within the time prescribed, the Option Fee will not be refunded; however, any earnest money will be refunded to Buyer. The Option Fee ❑will ❑will not be credited to the Sales Price at closing. **Time is of the essence for this paragraph and strict compliance with the time for performance is required.**

24.CONSULT AN ATTORNEY BEFORE SIGNING: TREC rules prohibit real estate license holders from giving legal advice. READ THIS CONTRACT CAREFULLY.

Buyer's Attorney is: _____	Seller's Attorney is: _____
Phone: (_____) _____	Phone: (_____) _____
Fax: (_____) _____	Fax: (_____) _____
E-mail: _____	E-mail: _____

EXECUTED the _____ **day of** _____, 20_____ **(Effective Date).**
(BROKER: FILL IN THE DATE OF FINAL ACCEPTANCE.)

_____   _____
Buyer   Seller

_____   _____
Buyer   Seller

TREC NO. 25-12

RATIFICATION OF FEE

Listing Broker has agreed to pay Other Broker _____ of the total Sales Price when Listing Broker's fee is received. Escrow Agent is authorized and directed to pay Other Broker from Listing Broker's fee at closing.

Other Broker: Listing Broker:

By: _____   By: _____

BROKER INFORMATION AND AGREEMENT FOR PAYMENT OF BROKERS' FEES

| Other Broker | License No. | Listing or Principal Broker | License No. |

| Associate's Name | License No. | Listing Associate's Name | License No. |

| Associate's Email Address | Phone | Listing Associate's Email Address | Phone |

| Licensed Supervisor of Associate | License No. | Licensed Supervisor of Listing Associate | License No. |

| Other Broker's Office Address | Phone | Listing Broker's Office Address | Phone |

| City | State | Zip | City | State | Zip |

represents   ❑ Buyer only as Buyer's agent
             ❑ Seller as Listing Broker's subagent

| Selling Associate | License No. |

| Selling Associate's Email Address | Phone |

| Licensed Supervisor of Selling Associate | License No. |

| Selling Associate's Office Address |

| City | State | Zip |

represents   ❑ Seller only
             ❑ Buyer only
             ❑ Seller and Buyer as an intermediary

Upon closing of the sale by Seller to Buyer of the Property described in the contract to which this fee agreement is attached: (a) ❑ Seller ❑ Buyer will pay Listing/Principal Broker ❑ a cash fee of $_____ or ❑ _____% of the total Sales Price; and (b) ❑ Seller ❑ Buyer will pay Other Broker ❑ a cash fee of $_____ or ❑ _____% of the total Sales Price. Seller/Buyer authorizes and directs Escrow Agent to pay the brokers from the proceeds at closing.

Brokers' fees are negotiable. Brokers' fees or the sharing of fees between brokers are not fixed, controlled, recommended, suggested or maintained by the Texas Real Estate Commission.

_____   _____
Seller   Buyer

_____   _____
Seller   Buyer

Do not sign if there is a separate written agreement for payment of Brokers' fees.

TREC NO. 25-12

OPTION FEE RECEIPT

Receipt of $_____ (Option Fee) in the form of _____
is acknowledged.

_____   _____
Seller or Listing Broker   Date

EARNEST MONEY RECEIPT

Receipt of $_____ Earnest Money in the form of _____
is acknowledged.

_____   _____   _____
Escrow Agent   Received by   Email Address   Date/Time

_____   _____
Address   Phone

_____   _____   _____   _____
City   State   Zip   Fax

CONTRACT RECEIPT

Receipt of the Contract is acknowledged.

_____   _____   _____
Escrow Agent   Received by   Email Address   Date

_____   _____
Address   Phone

_____   _____   _____   _____
City   State   Zip   Fax

ADDITIONAL EARNEST MONEY RECEIPT

Receipt of $_____ additional Earnest Money in the form of _____
is acknowledged.

_____   _____   _____
Escrow Agent   Received by   Email Address   Date/Time

_____   _____
Address   Phone

_____   _____   _____   _____
City   State   Zip   Fax

TREC NO. 25-12

134

NEW HOME CONTRACT
(Completed Construction)
NOTICE: Not For Use For Condominium Transactions or Closings Prior to Completion of Construction

1. PARTIES: The parties to this contract are _____
(Seller) and _____(Buyer). Seller agrees
to sell and convey to Buyer and Buyer agrees to buy from Seller the Property defined below.

2. PROPERTY: Lot _____,Block_____,
_____Addition,
City of_____,County of_____,
Texas, known as _____
(address/zip code), or as described on attached exhibit, together with: (i) improvements,
fixtures and all other property located thereon; and (ii) all rights, privileges and appurtenances
thereto, including but not limited to: permits, easements, and cooperative and association
memberships. All property sold by this contract is called the "Property".

RESERVATIONS: Any reservation for oil, gas, or other minerals, water, timber, or other interests
is made in accordance with an attached addendum.

3. SALES PRICE:
  A. Cash portion of Sales Price payable by Buyer at closing .... $_____
  B. Sum of all financing described in the attached: ❑   Third Party Financing Addendum,
     ❑   Loan Assumption Addendum, ❑   Seller Financing Addendum ...... $_____
  C. Sales Price (Sum of A and B) .... $_____

4. LICENSE HOLDER DISCLOSURE: Texas law requires a real estate license holder who is
a party to a transaction or acting on behalf of a spouse, parent, child, business entity in which
the license holder owns more than 10%, or a trust for which the license holder acts as trustee or
of which the license holder or the license holder's spouse parent or child is a beneficiary, to
notify the other party in writing before entering into a contract of sale. Disclose if applicable:_____
_____.

5. EARNEST MONEY: Within 3 days after the Effective Date, Buyer must deliver
$_____ as earnest money to _____,
as escrow agent, at _____ (address).
Buyer shall deliver additional earnest money of $_____ to escrow agent within
_____ days after the Effective Date of this contract. If Buyer fails to deliver the earnest money
within the time required, Seller may terminate this contract or exercise Seller's remedies under
Paragraph 15, or both, by providing notice to Buyer before Buyer delivers the earnest money. If
the last day to deliver the earnest money falls on a Saturday, Sunday, or legal holiday, the time
to deliver the earnest money is extended until the end of the next day that is not a Saturday,
Sunday, or legal holiday. **Time is of the essence for this paragraph.**

6. TITLE POLICY AND SURVEY:
  A. TITLE POLICY: Seller shall furnish to Buyer at ❑Seller's   ❑Buyer's expense an owner policy of
     title insurance (Title Policy) issued by _____.
     (Title Company) in the amount of the Sales Price, dated at or after closing, insuring Buyer
     against loss under the provisions of the Title Policy, subject to the promulgated exclusions
     (including existing building and zoning ordinances) and the following exceptions:
     (1) Restrictive covenants common to the platted subdivision in which the Property is located.
     (2) The standard printed exception for standby fees, taxes and assessments.
     (3) Liens created as part of the financing described in Paragraph 3.
     (4) Utility easements created by the dedication deed or plat of the subdivision in which the
         Property is located.
     (5) Reservations or exceptions otherwise permitted by this contract or as may be approved by
         Buyer in writing.
     (6) The standard printed exception as to marital rights.
     (7) The standard printed exception as to waters, tidelands, beaches, streams, and related
         matters.
     (8) The standard printed exception as to discrepancies, conflicts, shortages in area or boundary
         lines, encroachments or protrusions, or overlapping improvement:
     ❑(i) will not be amended or deleted from the title policy; or
     ❑(ii) will be amended to read, "shortages in area" at the expense of ❑Buyer ❑Seller.
     (9) The exception or exclusion regarding minerals approved by the Texas Department of
         Insurance.
  B. COMMITMENT: Within 20 days after the Title Company receives a copy of this contract, Seller
     shall furnish to Buyer a commitment for title insurance (Commitment) and, at Buyer's
     expense, legible copies of restrictive covenants and documents evidencing exceptions in the
     Commitment (Exception Documents) other than the standard printed exceptions. Seller
     authorizes the Title Company to deliver the Commitment and Exception Documents to Buyer

Initialed for identification by Buyer_____ _____ and Seller _____ _____   TREC NO. 24-15

at Buyer's address shown in Paragraph 21. If the Commitment and Exception Documents are not delivered to Buyer within the specified time, the time for delivery will be automatically extended up to 15 days or 3 days before the Closing Date, whichever is earlier. If the Commitment and Exception Documents are not delivered within the time required, Buyer may terminate this contract and the earnest money will be refunded to Buyer.

C. SURVEY: The survey must be made by a registered professional land surveyor acceptable to the Title Company and Buyer's lender(s). (Check one box only)

❑ (1) Within _____ days after the Effective Date of this contract, Seller shall furnish to Buyer and Title Company Seller's existing survey of the Property and a Residential Real Property Affidavit promulgated by the Texas Department of Insurance (T-47 Affidavit). **If Seller fails to furnish the existing survey or affidavit within the time prescribed, Buyer shall obtain a new survey at Seller's expense no later than 3 days prior to Closing Date.** If the existing survey or affidavit is not acceptable to Title Company or Buyer's lender(s), Buyer shall obtain a new survey at ❑ Seller's ❑ Buyer's expense no later than 3 days prior to Closing Date.

❑ (2) Within _____ days after the Effective Date of this contract, Buyer shall obtain a new survey at Buyer's expense. Buyer is deemed to receive the survey on the date of actual receipt or the date specified in this paragraph, whichever is earlier.

❑ (3) Within _____ days after the Effective Date of this contract, Seller, at Seller's expense shall furnish a new survey to Buyer.

D. OBJECTIONS: Buyer may object in writing to defects, exceptions, or encumbrances to title: disclosed on the survey other than items 6A(1) through (7) above; disclosed in the Commitment other than items 6A(1) through (9) above; or which prohibit the following use or activity: _____
_____.
Buyer must object the earlier of (i) the Closing Date or (ii) _____ days after Buyer receives the Commitment, Exception Documents, and the survey. Buyer's failure to object within the time allowed will constitute a waiver of Buyer's right to object; except that the requirements in Schedule C of the Commitment are not waived by Buyer. Provided Seller is not obligated to incur any expense, Seller shall cure any timely objections of Buyer or any third party lender within 15 days after Seller receives the objections (Cure Period) and the Closing Date will be extended as necessary. If objections are not cured within the Cure Period, Buyer may, by delivering notice to Seller within 5 days after the end of the Cure Period: (i) terminate this contract and the earnest money will be refunded to Buyer; or (ii) waive the objections. If Buyer does not terminate within the time required, Buyer shall be deemed to have waived the objections. If the Commitment or Survey is revised or any new Exception Document(s) is delivered, Buyer may object to any new matter revealed in the revised Commitment or Survey or new Exception Document(s) within the same time stated in this paragraph to make objections beginning when the revised Commitment, Survey, or Exception Document(s) is delivered to Buyer.

E. TITLE NOTICES:

(1) ABSTRACT OR TITLE POLICY: Broker advises Buyer to have an abstract of title covering the Property examined by an attorney of Buyer's selection, or Buyer should be furnished with or obtain a Title Policy. If a Title Policy is furnished, the Commitment should be promptly reviewed by an attorney of Buyer's choice due to the time limitations on Buyer's right to object.

(2) MEMBERSHIP IN PROPERTY OWNERS ASSOCIATION(S): The Property ❑is ❑is not subject to mandatory membership in a property owners association(s). If the Property is subject to mandatory membership in a property owners association(s), Seller notifies Buyer under §5.012, Texas Property Code, that, as a purchaser of property in the residential community identified in Paragraph 2A in which the Property is located, you are obligated to be a member of the property owners association(s). Restrictive covenants governing the use and occupancy of the Property and all dedicatory instruments governing the establishment, maintenance, and operation of this residential community have been or will be recorded in the Real Property Records of the county in which the Property is located. Copies of the restrictive covenants and dedicatory instruments may be obtained from the county clerk. **You are obligated to pay assessments to the property owners association(s). The amount of the assessments is subject to change. Your failure to pay the assessments could result in enforcement of the association's lien on and the foreclosure of the Property.**
Section 207.003, Property Code, entitles an owner to receive copies of any document that governs the establishment, maintenance, or operation of a subdivision, including, but not limited to, restrictions, bylaws, rules and regulations, and a resale certificate from a property owners' association. A resale certificate contains information including, but not limited to, statements specifying the amount and frequency of regular assessments and the style and cause number of lawsuits to which the property owners' association is a party, other than lawsuits relating to unpaid ad valorem taxes of an individual member of the association. These documents must be made available to you by the property owners' association or the association's agent on your request.

If Buyer is concerned about these matters, the TREC promulgated Addendum for Property Subject to Mandatory Membership in a Property Owners Association should be used.

(3) STATUTORY TAX DISTRICTS: If the Property is situated in a utility or other statutorily created district providing water, sewer, drainage, or flood control facilities and services, Chapter 49, Texas Water Code, requires Seller to deliver and Buyer to sign the statutory notice relating to the tax rate, bonded indebtedness, or standby fee of the district prior to final execution of this contract.

(4) TIDE WATERS: If the Property abuts the tidally influenced waters of the state, §33.135, Texas Natural Resources Code, requires a notice regarding coastal area property to be included in the contract. An addendum containing the notice promulgated by TREC or required by the parties must be used.

(5) ANNEXATION: If the Property is located outside the limits of a municipality, Seller notifies Buyer under §5.011, Texas Property Code, that the Property may now or later be included in the extraterritorial jurisdiction of a municipality and may now or later be subject to annexation by the municipality. Each municipality maintains a map that depicts its boundaries and extraterritorial jurisdiction. To determine if the Property is located within a municipality's extraterritorial jurisdiction or is likely to be located within a municipality's extraterritorial jurisdiction, contact all municipalities located in the general proximity of the Property for further information.

(6) PROPERTY LOCATED IN A CERTIFICATED SERVICE AREA OF A UTILITY SERVICE PROVIDER: Notice required by §13.257, Water Code: The real property, described in Paragraph 2, that you are about to purchase may be located in a certificated water or sewer service area, which is authorized by law to provide water or sewer service to the properties in the certificated area. If your property is located in a certificated area there may be special costs or charges that you will be required to pay before you can receive water or sewer service. There may be a period required to construct lines or other facilities necessary to provide water or sewer service to your property. You are advised to determine if the property is in a certificated area and contact the utility service provider to determine the cost that you will be required to pay and the period, if any, that is required to provide water or sewer service to your property. The undersigned Buyer hereby acknowledges receipt of the foregoing notice at or before the execution of a binding contract for the purchase of the real property described in Paragraph 2 or at closing of purchase of the real property.

(7) PUBLIC IMPROVEMENT DISTRICTS: If the Property is in a public improvement district, §5.014, Property Code, requires Seller to notify Buyer as follows: As a purchaser of this parcel of real property you are obligated to pay an assessment to a municipality or county for an improvement project undertaken by a public improvement district under Chapter 372, Local Government Code. The assessment may be due annually or in periodic installments. More information concerning the amount of the assessment and the due dates of that assessment may be obtained from the municipality or county levying the assessment. The amount of the assessments is subject to change. Your failure to pay the assessments could result in a lien on and the foreclosure of your property.

(8) TRANSFER FEES: If the Property is subject to a private transfer fee obligation, §5.205, Property Code, requires Seller to notify Buyer as follows: The private transfer fee obligation may be governed by Chapter 5, Subchapter G of the Texas Property Code.

(9) PROPANE GAS SYSTEM SERVICE AREA: If the Property is located in a propane gas system service area owned by a distribution system retailer, Seller must give Buyer written notice as required by §141.010, Texas Utilities Code. An addendum containing the notice approved by TREC or required by the parties should be used.

(10) NOTICE OF WATER LEVEL FLUCTUATIONS: If the Property adjoins an impoundment of water, including a reservoir or lake, constructed and maintained under Chapter 11, Water Code, that has a storage capacity of at least 5,000 acre-feet at the impoundment's normal operating level, Seller hereby notifies Buyer: "The water level of the impoundment of water adjoining the Property fluctuates for various reasons, including as a result of: (1) an entity lawfully exercising its right to use the water stored in the impoundment; or (2) drought or flood conditions."

7. PROPERTY CONDITION:

A. ACCESS, INSPECTIONS AND UTILITIES: Seller shall permit Buyer and Buyer's agents access to the Property at reasonable times. Buyer may have the Property inspected by inspectors selected by Buyer and licensed by TREC or otherwise permitted by law to make inspections. Seller at Seller's expense shall immediately cause existing utilities to be turned on and shall keep the utilities on during the time this contract is in effect.

B. ACCEPTANCE OF PROPERTY CONDITION: "As Is" means the present condition of the Property with any and all defects and without warranty except for the warranties of title and the warranties in this contract. Buyer's agreement to accept the Property As Is under Paragraph 7B(1) or (2) does not preclude Buyer from inspecting the Property under Paragraph 7A, from negotiating repairs or treatments in a subsequent amendment, or from terminating this contract during the Option Period, if any.

Initialed for identification by Buyer_____ _____ and Seller _____ _____   TREC NO. 24-15

(Check one box only)
❑ (1)Buyer accepts the Property As Is.
❑ (2)Buyer accepts the Property As Is provided Seller, at Seller's expense, shall complete the following specific repairs and treatments:_____
_____
(Do not insert general phrases, such as "subject to inspections," that do not identify specific repairs and treatments.)

C. WARRANTIES: Except as expressly set forth in this contract, a separate writing, or provided by law, Seller makes no other express warranties. Seller shall assign to Buyer at closing all assignable manufacturer warranties.

D. INSULATION: As required by Federal Trade Commission Regulations, the information relating to the insulation installed or to be installed in the Improvements at the Property is: (check only one box below)
❑ (1) as shown in the attached specifications.
❑ (2) as follows:
   (a) Exterior walls of improved living areas: insulated with _____
      insulation to a thickness of _____ inches which yields an R-Value of _____.
   (b) Walls in other areas of the home: insulated with_____
      insulation to a thickness of _____ inches which yields an R-Value of _____.
   (c) Ceilings in improved living areas: insulated with_____
      insulation to a thickness of _____ inches which yields an R-Value of _____.
   (d) Floors of improved living areas not applied to a slab foundation: insulated with _____
      _____insulation to a thickness of _____ inches which yields an R-Value of _____.
   (e) Other insulated areas: insulated with _____insulation to a thickness of _____ inches which yields an R-Value of _____.
All stated R-Values are based on information provided by the manufacturer of the insulation.

E. LENDER REQUIRED REPAIRS AND TREATMENTS: Unless otherwise agreed in writing, neither party is obligated to pay for lender required repairs, which includes treatment for wood destroying insects. If the parties do not agree to pay for the lender required repairs or treatments, this contract will terminate and the earnest money will be refunded to Buyer. If the cost of lender required repairs and treatments exceeds 5% of the Sales Price, Buyer may terminate this contract and the earnest money will be refunded to Buyer.

F. COMPLETION OF REPAIRS, TREATMENTS, AND IMPROVEMENTS: Unless otherwise agreed in writing: (i) Seller shall complete all agreed repairs, treatments, and improvements (Work) prior to the Closing Date; and (ii) all required permits must be obtained, and Work must be performed by persons who are licensed to provide such Work or, if no license is required by law, are commercially engaged in the trade of providing such Work. At Buyer's election, any transferable warranties received by Seller with respect to the Work will be transferred to Buyer at Buyer's expense. If Seller fails to complete any agreed Work prior to the Closing Date, Buyer may exercise remedies under Paragraph 15 or extend the Closing Date up to 5 days if necessary for Seller to complete Work.

G. ENVIRONMENTAL MATTERS: Buyer is advised that the presence of wetlands, toxic substances, including asbestos and wastes or other environmental hazards or the presence of a threatened or endangered species or its habitat may affect Buyer's intended use of the Property. If Buyer is concerned about these matters, an addendum promulgated by TREC or required by the parties should be used.

H. SELLER'S DISCLOSURE: Except as otherwise disclosed in this contract, Seller has no knowledge of the following:
(1) any flooding of the Property which has had a material adverse effect on the use of the Property;
(2) any pending or threatened litigation, condemnation, or special assessment affecting the Property;
(3) any environmental hazards that materially and adversely affect the Property;
(4) any dumpsite, landfill, or underground tanks or containers now or previously located on the Property;
(5) any wetlands, as defined by federal or state law or regulation, affecting the Property; or
(6) any threatened or endangered species or their habitat affecting the Property.

I. RESIDENTIAL SERVICE CONTRACTS: Buyer may purchase a residential service contract from a residential service company licensed by TREC. If Buyer purchases a residential service contract, Seller shall reimburse Buyer at closing for the cost of the residential service contract in an amount not exceeding $_____. Buyer should review any residential service contract for the scope of coverage, exclusions and limitations. **The purchase of a residential service contract is optional. Similar coverage may be purchased from various companies authorized to do business in Texas.**

8. BROKERS' FEES: All obligations of the parties for payment of brokers' fees are contained in separate written agreements.

Initialed for identification by Buyer_____ _____ and Seller _____ _____   TREC NO. 24-15

138

9. CLOSING:
A. The closing of the sale will be on or before _____, 20_____, or within 7 days after objections made under Paragraph 6D have been cured or waived, whichever date is later (Closing Date). If either party fails to close the sale by the Closing Date, the non-defaulting party may exercise the remedies contained in Paragraph 15.
B. At closing:
  (1) Seller shall execute and deliver a general warranty deed conveying title to the Property to Buyer and showing no additional exceptions to those permitted in Paragraph 6 and furnish tax statements or certificates showing no delinquent taxes on the Property.
  (2) Buyer shall pay the Sales Price in good funds acceptable to the escrow agent.
  (3) Seller and Buyer shall execute and deliver any notices, statements, certificates, affidavits, releases, loan documents and other documents reasonably required for the closing of the sale and the issuance of the Title Policy.
  (4) There will be no liens, assessments, or security interests against the Property which will not be satisfied out of the sales proceeds unless securing the payment of any loans assumed by Buyer and assumed loans will not be in default.

10. POSSESSION:
A. Buyer's Possession: Seller shall deliver to Buyer possession of the Property in its present or required condition, ordinary wear and tear excepted: ❑ upon closing and funding ❑ according to a temporary residential lease form promulgated by TREC or other written lease required by the parties. Any possession by Buyer prior to closing or by Seller after closing which is not authorized by a written lease will establish a tenancy at sufferance relationship between the parties. **Consult your insurance agent prior to change of ownership and possession because insurance coverage may be limited or terminated. The absence of a written lease or appropriate insurance coverage may expose the parties to economic loss.**
B. Leases: After the Effective Date, Seller may not execute any lease (including but not limited to mineral leases) or convey any interest in the Property without Buyer's written consent.

11. SPECIAL PROVISIONS: (Insert only factual statements and business details applicable to the sale. TREC rules prohibit license holders from adding factual statements or business details for which a contract addendum, lease or other form has been promulgated by TREC for mandatory use.)

12. SETTLEMENT AND OTHER EXPENSES:
A. The following expenses must be paid at or prior to closing:
  (1) Expenses payable by Seller (Seller's Expenses):
    (a) Releases of existing liens, including prepayment penalties and recording fees; release of Seller's loan liability; tax statements or certificates; preparation of deed; one-half of escrow fee; and other expenses payable by Seller under this contract.
    (b) Seller shall also pay an amount not to exceed $ _____ to be applied in the following order: Buyer's Expenses which Buyer is prohibited from paying by FHA, VA, Texas Veterans Land Board or other governmental loan programs, and then to other Buyer's Expenses as allowed by the lender.
  (2) Expenses payable by Buyer (Buyer's Expenses): Appraisal fees; loan application fees; origination charges; credit reports; preparation of loan documents; interest on the notes from date of disbursement to one month prior to dates of first monthly payments; recording fees; copies of easements and restrictions; loan title policy with endorsements required by lender; loan-related inspection fees; photos; amortization schedules; one-half of escrow fee; all prepaid items, including required premiums for flood and hazard insurance, reserve deposits for insurance, ad valorem taxes and special governmental assessments; final compliance inspection; courier fee; repair inspection; underwriting fee; wire transfer fee; expenses incident to any loan; Private Mortgage Insurance Premium (PMI), VA Loan Funding Fee, or FHA Mortgage Insurance Premium (MIP) as required by the lender; and other expenses payable by Buyer under this contract.
B. If any expense exceeds an amount expressly stated in this contract for such expense to be paid by a party, that party may terminate this contract unless the other party agrees to pay such excess. Buyer may not pay charges and fees expressly prohibited by FHA, VA, Texas Veterans Land Board or other governmental loan program regulations.

13. PRORATIONS AND ROLLBACK TAXES:
A. PRORATIONS: Taxes for the current year, maintenance fees, assessments, dues and rents will be prorated through the Closing Date. The tax proration may be calculated taking into consideration any change in exemptions that will affect the current year's taxes. If taxes for the current year vary from the amount prorated at closing, the parties shall adjust the prorations when tax statements for the current year are available. If taxes are not paid at or prior to closing, Buyer will be obligated to pay taxes for the current year.

Initialed for identification by Buyer_____ _____ and Seller _____ _____   TREC NO. 24-15

B. ROLLBACK TAXES: If additional taxes, penalties, or interest (Assessments) are imposed because of Seller's use or change in use of the Property prior to closing, the Assessments will be the obligation of Seller. Obligations imposed by this paragraph will survive closing.

14. **CASUALTY LOSS:** If any part of the Property is damaged or destroyed by fire or other casualty after the Effective Date of this contract, Seller shall restore the Property to its previous condition as soon as reasonably possible, but in any event by the Closing Date. If Seller fails to do so due to factors beyond Seller's control, Buyer may (a) terminate this contract and the earnest money will be refunded to Buyer (b) extend the time for performance up to 15 days and the Closing Date will be extended as necessary or (c) accept the Property in its damaged condition with an assignment of insurance proceeds, if permitted by Seller's insurance carrier, and receive credit from Seller at closing in the amount of the deductible under the insurance policy. Seller's obligations under this paragraph are independent of any other obligations of Seller under this contract.

15. **DEFAULT:** If Buyer fails to comply with this contract, Buyer will be in default, and Seller may (a) enforce specific performance, seek such other relief as may be provided by law, or both, or (b) terminate this contract and receive the earnest money as liquidated damages, thereby releasing both parties from this contract. If Seller fails to comply with this contract Seller will be in default and Buyer may (a) enforce specific performance, seek such other relief as may be provided by law, or both, or (b) terminate this contract and receive the earnest money, thereby releasing both parties from this contract.

16. **MEDIATION:** It is the policy of the State of Texas to encourage resolution of disputes through alternative dispute resolution procedures such as mediation. Subject to applicable law, any dispute between Seller and Buyer related to this contract which is not resolved through informal discussion will be submitted to a mutually acceptable mediation service or provider. The parties to the mediation shall bear the mediation costs equally. This paragraph does not preclude a party from seeking equitable relief from a court of competent jurisdiction.

17. **ATTORNEY'S FEES:** A Buyer, Seller, Listing Broker, Other Broker, or escrow agent who prevails in any legal proceeding related to this contract is entitled to recover reasonable attorney's fees and all costs of such proceeding.

18. **ESCROW:**
   A. ESCROW: The escrow agent is not (i) a party to this contract and does not have liability for the performance or nonperformance of any party to this contract, (ii) liable for interest on the earnest money and (iii) liable for the loss of any earnest money caused by the failure of any financial institution in which the earnest money has been deposited unless the financial institution is acting as escrow agent.
   B. EXPENSES: At closing, the earnest money must be applied first to any cash down payment, then to Buyer's Expenses and any excess refunded to Buyer. If no closing occurs, escrow agent may: (i) require a written release of liability of the escrow agent from all parties, (ii) require payment of unpaid expenses incurred on behalf of a party, and (iii) only deduct from the earnest money the amount of unpaid expenses incurred on behalf of the party receiving the earnest money.
   C. DEMAND: Upon termination of this contract, either party or the escrow agent may send a release of earnest money to each party and the parties shall execute counterparts of the release and deliver same to the escrow agent. If either party fails to execute the release, either party may make a written demand to the escrow agent for the earnest money. If only one party makes written demand for the earnest money, escrow agent shall promptly provide a copy of the demand to the other party. If escrow agent does not receive written objection to the demand from the other party within 15 days, escrow agent may disburse the earnest money to the party making demand reduced by the amount of unpaid expenses incurred on behalf of the party receiving the earnest money and escrow agent may pay the same to the creditors. If escrow agent complies with the provisions of this paragraph, each party hereby releases escrow agent from all adverse claims related to the disbursal of the earnest money.
   D. DAMAGES: Any party who wrongfully fails or refuses to sign a release acceptable to the escrow agent within 7 days of receipt of the request will be liable to the other party for (i) damages; (ii) the earnest money; (iii) reasonable attorney's fees; and (iv) all costs of suit.
   E. NOTICES: Escrow agent's notices will be effective when sent in compliance with Paragraph 21. Notice of objection to the demand will be deemed effective upon receipt by escrow agent.

19. **REPRESENTATIONS:** All covenants, representations and warranties in this contract survive closing. If any representation of Seller in this contract is untrue on the Closing Date, Seller will be in default. Unless expressly prohibited by written agreement, Seller may continue to show the Property and receive, negotiate and accept back up offers.

20. **FEDERAL TAX REQUIREMENTS:** If Seller is a "foreign person," as defined by Internal Revenue Code and its regulations, or if Seller fails to deliver an affidavit or a certificate of non-foreign status to Buyer that Seller is not a "foreign person," then Buyer shall withhold from the sales proceeds an amount sufficient to comply with applicable tax law and deliver the same to the Internal Revenue Service together with appropriate tax forms. Internal Revenue Service regulations require filing written reports if currency in excess of specified amounts is received in the transaction.

Initialed for identification by Buyer_____ _____ and Seller _____ _____   TREC NO. 24-15

21. NOTICES: All notices from one party to the other must be in writing and are effective when mailed to, hand-delivered at, or transmitted by fax or electronic transmission as follows:

To Buyer at:	**To Seller** at:
Phone: ( )	Phone: ( )
Fax: ( )	Fax: ( )
E-mail:	E-mail:

22. AGREEMENT OF PARTIES: This contract contains the entire agreement of the parties and cannot be changed except by their written agreement. Addenda which are a part of this contract are (check all applicable boxes):

❑ Third Party Financing Addendum

❑ Seller Financing Addendum

❑ Addendum for Property Subject to Mandatory Membership in a Property Owners Association

❑ Buyer's Temporary Residential Lease

❑ Loan Assumption Addendum

❑ Addendum for Sale of Other Property by Buyer

❑ Addendum for Reservation of Oil, Gas and Other Minerals

❑ Addendum for "Back-Up" Contract

❑ Addendum for Authorizing Hydrostatic Testing

❑ Addendum Concerning Right to Terminate Due to Lender's Appraisal

❑ Addendum for Coastal Area Property

❑ Environmental Assessment, Threatened or Endangered Species and Wetlands Addendum

❑ Seller's Temporary Residential Lease

❑ Short Sale Addendum

❑ Addendum for Property Located Seaward of the Gulf Intracoastal Waterway

❑ Addendum for Property in a Propane Gas System Service Area

❑ Other (list): _____
_____
_____
_____

23. TERMINATION OPTION: For nominal consideration, the receipt of which is hereby acknowledged by Seller, and Buyer's agreement to pay Seller $_____ (Option Fee) within 3 days after the Effective Date of this contract, Seller grants Buyer the unrestricted right to terminate this contract by giving notice of termination to Seller within _____ days after the Effective Date of this contract (Option Period). Notices under this paragraph must be given by 5:00 p.m. (local time where the Property is located) by the date specified. If no dollar amount is stated as the Option Fee or if Buyer fails to pay the Option Fee to Seller within the time prescribed, this paragraph will not be a part of this contract and Buyer shall not have the unrestricted right to terminate this contract. If Buyer gives notice of termination within the time prescribed, the Option Fee will not be refunded; however, any earnest money will be refunded to Buyer. The Option Fee ❑will ❑will not be credited to the Sales Price at closing. **Time is of the essence for this paragraph and strict compliance with the time for performance is required.**

Initialed for identification by Buyer_____ _____ and Seller _____ _____   TREC NO. 24-15

24. CONSULT AN ATTORNEY BEFORE SIGNING: TREC rules prohibit real estate license holders from giving legal advice. READ THIS CONTRACT CAREFULLY.

Buyer's
Attorney is: _____

_____

Phone: (____) _____

Fax: (____) _____

E-mail: _____

Seller's
Attorney is: _____

_____

Phone: (____) _____

Fax: (____) _____

E-mail: _____

EXECUTED the _____ day of _____, 20____ (Effective Date).
(BROKER: FILL IN THE DATE OF FINAL ACCEPTANCE.)

This contract is subject to Chapter 27 of the Texas Property Code. The provisions of that chapter may affect your right to recover damages arising from a construction defect. If you have a complaint concerning a construction defect and that defect has not been corrected as may be required by law or by contract, you must provide the notice required by Chapter 27 of the Texas Property Code to the contractor by certified mail, return receipt requested, not later than the 60th day before the date you file suit to recover damages in a court of law or initiate arbitration. The notice must refer to Chapter 27 of the Texas Property Code and must describe the construction defect. If requested by the contractor, you must provide the contractor an opportunity to inspect and cure the defect as provided by Section 27.004 of the Texas Property Code.

_____
Buyer

_____
Buyer

_____
Seller

_____
Seller

TREC TEXAS REAL ESTATE COMMISSION

TREC NO. 24-15

BROKER INFORMATION
(Print name(s) only. Do not sign)

Other Broker Firm	License No.

represents ☐ Buyer only as Buyer's agent
☐ Seller as Listing Broker's subagent

Associate's Name	License No.

Associate's Email Address	Phone

Licensed Supervisor of Associate	License No.

Other Broker's Address	Phone

City	State	Zip

Listing Broker Firm	License No.

represents ☐ Seller and Buyer as an intermediary
☐ Seller only as Seller's agent

Associate's Name	License No.

Listing Associate's Email Address	Phone

Licensed Supervisor of Listing Associate	License No.

Listing Broker's Office Address	Phone

City	State	Zip

Selling Associate's Name	License No.

Selling Associate's Email Address	Phone

Licensed Supervisor of Selling Associate	License No.

Selling Associate's Office Address	

City	State	Zip

Listing Broker has agreed to pay Other Broker _____ of the total sales price when the Listing Broker's fee is received. Escrow agent is authorized and directed to pay Other Broker from Listing Broker's fee at closing.

TREC NO. 24-15

143

OPTION FEE RECEIPT

Receipt of $_____ (Option Fee) in the form of _____
is acknowledged.

_____   _____
Seller or Listing Broker   Date

EARNEST MONEY RECEIPT

Receipt of $_____ Earnest Money in the form of _____
is acknowledged.

_____   _____ _____
Escrow Agent   Received by   Email Address   Date/Time

_____   _____
Address   Phone

_____   _____ _____   _____
City   State   Zip   Fax

CONTRACT RECEIPT

Receipt of the Contract is acknowledged.

_____   _____ _____
Escrow Agent   Received by   Email Address   Date

_____   _____
Address   Phone

_____   _____ _____   _____
City   State   Zip   Fax

ADDITIONAL EARNEST MONEY RECEIPT

Receipt of $_____ additional Earnest Money in the form of _____
is acknowledged.

_____   _____ _____
Escrow Agent   Received by   Email Address   Date/Time

_____   _____
Address   Phone

_____   _____ _____   _____
City   State   Zip   Fax

TREC NO. 24-15

1. PARTIES: The parties to this contract are _____
(Seller) and _____(Buyer). Seller agrees to sell and convey to Buyer and Buyer agrees to buy from Seller the Property defined below.

2. PROPERTY: Lot _____, Block_____, _____
Addition, City of_____, County of _____Texas, known as _____(address/zip code), or as described on attached exhibit, together with: (i) improvements, fixtures and all other property described in the Construction Documents; and (ii) all rights, privileges and appurtenances thereto, including but not limited to: permits, easements, and cooperative and association memberships. All property sold by this contract is called the "Property".
RESERVATIONS: Any reservation for oil, gas, or other minerals, water, timber, or other interests is made in accordance with an attached addendum.

3. SALES PRICE:
  A. Cash portion of Sales Price payable by Buyer at closing..................... $_____
  B. Sum of all financing described in the attached: ❑   Third Party Financing Addendum,
      ❑   Loan Assumption Addendum, ❑   Seller Financing Addendum ...... $_____
  C. Sales Price (Sum of A and B) .... $_____

4. LICENSE HOLDER DISCLOSURE: Texas law requires a real estate license holder who is a party to a transaction or acting on behalf of a spouse, parent, child, business entity in which the license holder owns more than 10%, or a trust for which the license holder acts as trustee or of which the license holder or the license holder's spouse, parent or child is a beneficiary, to notify the other party in writing before entering into a contract of sale. Disclose if applicable:____
_____.

5. EARNEST MONEY: Within 3 days after the Effective Date, Buyer must deliver $_____ as earnest money to _____, as escrow agent, at _____(address).
Buyer shall deliver additional earnest money of $_____ to escrow agent within _____ days after the Effective Date of this contract. If Buyer fails to deliver the earnest money within the time required, Seller may terminate this contract or exercise Seller's remedies under Paragraph 15, or both, by providing notice to Buyer before Buyer delivers the earnest money. If the last day to deliver the earnest money falls on a Saturday, Sunday, or legal holiday, the time to deliver the earnest money is extended until the end of the next day that is not a Saturday, Sunday, or legal holiday. **Time is of the essence for this paragraph.**

6. TITLE POLICY AND SURVEY:
  A. TITLE POLICY: Seller shall furnish to Buyer at ❑Seller's ❑Buyer's expense an owner policy of title insurance (Title Policy) issued by _____(Title Company) in the amount of the Sales Price, dated at or after closing, insuring Buyer against loss under the provisions of the Title Policy, subject to the promulgated exclusions (including existing building and zoning ordinances) and the following exceptions:
    (1) Restrictive covenants common to the platted subdivision in which the Property is located.
    (2) The standard printed exception for standby fees, taxes and assessments.
    (3) Liens created as part of the financing described in Paragraph 3.
    (4) Utility easements created by the dedication deed or plat of the subdivision in which the Property is located.
    (5) Reservations or exceptions otherwise permitted by this contract or as may be approved by Buyer in writing.
    (6) The standard printed exception as to marital rights.
    (7) The standard printed exception as to waters, tidelands, beaches, streams, and related matters.
    (8) The standard printed exception as to discrepancies, conflicts, shortages in area or boundary lines, encroachments or protrusions, or overlapping improvements:
    ❑ (i) will not be amended or deleted from the title policy; or
    ❑(ii) will be amended to read, "shortages in area" at the expense of ❑Buyer ❑Seller.
    (9) The exception or exclusion regarding minerals approved by the Texas Department of Insurance.
  B. COMMITMENT: Within 20 days after the Title Company receives a copy of this contract, Seller shall furnish to Buyer a commitment for title insurance (Commitment) and, at Buyer's expense, legible copies of restrictive covenants and documents evidencing exceptions in the Commitment (Exception Documents) other than the standard printed exceptions. Seller authorizes the Title Company to deliver the Commitment and Exception Documents to Buyer at Buyer's address shown in Paragraph 21. If the Commitment and Exception Documents are not delivered to Buyer within the specified time, the time for delivery will be automatically extended up to 15 days or 3 days before the Closing Date, whichever is earlier. If the Commitment and Exception Documents are not delivered within the time required, Buyer may terminate this contract and the earnest money will be refunded to Buyer.

Initialed for identification by Buyer_____ _____ and Seller _____ _____   TREC NO. 23-15

C. SURVEY: The survey must be made after the Substantial Completion Date by a registered professional land surveyor acceptable to the Title Company and Buyer's lender(s). (Check one box only)
❑ (1)At least _____ days prior to the Closing Date, Seller, at Seller's expense, shall provide a new survey to Buyer.
❑ (2)At least _____ days prior to the Closing Date, Buyer, at Buyer's expense, shall obtain a new survey. Buyer is deemed to receive the survey on the date of actual receipt or the date specified in this paragraph, whichever is earlier.
D. OBJECTIONS: Buyer may object in writing to defects, exceptions, or encumbrances to title: disclosed on the survey other than items 6A(1) through (7) above; disclosed in the Commitment other than items 6A(1) through (9) above; or which prohibit the following use or activity: _____.
_____
Buyer must object the earlier of (i) the Closing Date or (ii) _____ days after Buyer receives the Commitment, Exception Documents, and the survey. Buyer's failure to object within the time allowed will constitute a waiver of Buyer's right to object; except that the requirements in Schedule C of the Commitment are not waived by Buyer. Provided Seller is not obligated to incur any expense, Seller shall cure any timely objections of Buyer or any third party lender within 15 days after Seller receives the objections (Cure Period) and the Closing Date will be extended as necessary. If objections are not cured within the Cure Period, Buyer may, by delivering notice to Seller within 5 days after the end of the Cure Period: (i) terminate this contract and the earnest money will be refunded to Buyer; or (ii) waive the objections. If Buyer does not terminate within the time required, Buyer shall be deemed to have waived the objections. If the Commitment or Survey is revised or any new Exception Document(s) is delivered, Buyer may object to any new matter revealed in the revised Commitment or Survey or new Exception Document(s) within the same time stated in this paragraph to make objections beginning when the revised Commitment, Survey, or Exception Document(s) is delivered to Buyer.
E. TITLE NOTICES:
(1)ABSTRACT OR TITLE POLICY: Broker advises Buyer to have an abstract of title covering the Property examined by an attorney of Buyer's selection, or Buyer should be furnished with or obtain a Title Policy. If a Title Policy is furnished, the Commitment should be promptly reviewed by an attorney of Buyer's choice due to the time limitations on Buyer's right to object.
(2)MEMBERSHIP IN PROPERTY OWNERS ASSOCIATION(S): The Property ❑is ❑is not subject to mandatory membership in a property owners association(s). If the Property is subject to mandatory membership in a property owners association(s), Seller notifies Buyer under §5.012, Texas Property Code, that, as a purchaser of property in the residential community identified in Paragraph 2A in which the Property is located, you are obligated to be a member of the property owners association(s). Restrictive covenants governing the use and occupancy of the Property and all dedicatory instruments governing the establishment, maintenance, and operation of this residential community have been or will be recorded in the Real Property Records of the county in which the Property is located. Copies of the restrictive covenants and dedicatory instruments may be obtained from the county clerk. **You are obligated to pay assessments to the property owners association(s). The amount of the assessments is subject to change. Your failure to pay the assessments could result in enforcement of the association's lien on and the foreclosure of the Property.**
Section 207.003, Property Code, entitles an owner to receive copies of any document that governs the establishment, maintenance, or operation of a subdivision, including, but not limited to, restrictions, bylaws, rules and regulations, and a resale certificate from a property owners' association. A resale certificate contains information including, but not limited to, statements specifying the amount and frequency of regular assessments and the style and cause number of lawsuits to which the property owners' association is a party, other than lawsuits relating to unpaid ad valorem taxes of an individual member of the association.   These documents must be made available to you by the property owners' association or the association's agent on your request.
If Buyer is concerned about these matters, the TREC promulgated Addendum for Property Subject to Mandatory Membership in a Property Owners Association should be used.
(3)STATUTORY TAX DISTRICTS: If the Property is situated in a utility or other statutorily created district providing water, sewer, drainage, or flood control facilities and services, Chapter 49, Texas Water Code, requires Seller to deliver and Buyer to sign the statutory notice relating to the tax rate, bonded indebtedness, or standby fee of the district prior to final execution of this contract.
(4)TIDE WATERS: If the Property abuts the tidally influenced waters of the state, §33.135, Texas Natural Resources Code, requires a notice regarding coastal area property to be included in the contract. An addendum containing the notice promulgated by TREC or required by the parties must be used.

(5) ANNEXATION: If the Property is located outside the limits of a municipality, Seller notifies Buyer under §5.011, Texas Property Code, that the Property may now or later be included in the extraterritorial jurisdiction of a municipality and may now or later be subject to annexation by the municipality. Each municipality maintains a map that depicts its boundaries and extraterritorial jurisdiction. To determine if the Property is located within a municipality's extraterritorial jurisdiction or is likely to be located within a municipality's extraterritorial jurisdiction, contact all municipalities located in the general proximity of the Property for further information.

(6) PROPERTY LOCATED IN A CERTIFICATED SERVICE AREA OF A UTILITY SERVICE PROVIDER: Notice required by §13.257, Water Code: The real property, described in Paragraph 2, that you are about to purchase may be located in a certificated water or sewer service area, which is authorized by law to provide water or sewer service to the properties in the certificated area. If your property is located in a certificated area there may be special costs or charges that you will be required to pay before you can receive water or sewer service. There may be a period required to construct lines or other facilities necessary to provide water or sewer service to your property. You are advised to determine if the property is in a certificated area and contact the utility service provider to determine the cost that you will be required to pay and the period, if any, that is required to provide water or sewer service to your property. The undersigned Buyer hereby acknowledges receipt of the foregoing notice at or before the execution of a binding contract for the purchase of the real property described in Paragraph 2 or at closing of purchase of the real property.

(7) PUBLIC IMPROVEMENT DISTRICTS: If the Property is in a public improvement district, §5.014, Property Code, requires Seller to notify Buyer as follows: As a purchaser of this parcel of real property you are obligated to pay an assessment to a municipality or county for an improvement project undertaken by a public improvement district under Chapter 372, Local Government Code. The assessment may be due annually or in periodic installments. More information concerning the amount of the assessment and the due dates of that assessment may be obtained from the municipality or county levying the assessment. The amount of the assessments is subject to change. Your failure to pay the assessments could result in a lien on and the foreclosure of your property.

(8) TRANSFER FEES: If the Property is subject to a private transfer fee obligation, §5.205, Property Code, requires Seller to notify Buyer as follows: The private transfer fee obligation may be governed by Chapter 5, Subchapter G of the Texas Property Code.

(9) PROPANE GAS SYSTEM SERVICE AREA: If the Property is located in a propane gas system service area owned by a distribution system retailer, Seller must give Buyer written notice as required by §141.010, Texas Utilities Code. An addendum containing the notice approved by TREC or required by the parties should be used.

(10) NOTICE OF WATER LEVEL FLUCTUATIONS: If the Property adjoins an impoundment of water, including a reservoir or lake, constructed and maintained under Chapter 11, Water Code, that has a storage capacity of at least 5,000 acre-feet at the impoundment's normal operating level, Seller hereby notifies Buyer: "The water level of the impoundment of water adjoining the Property fluctuates for various reasons, including as a result of: (1) an entity lawfully exercising its right to use the water stored in the impoundment; or (2) drought or flood conditions."

7. PROPERTY CONDITION:
A. ACCESS AND INSPECTIONS: Seller shall permit Buyer and Buyer's agents access to the Property at reasonable times. Buyer may have the Property inspected by inspectors selected by Buyer and licensed by TREC or otherwise permitted by law to make inspections.

B. CONSTRUCTION DOCUMENTS: Seller shall complete all improvements to the Property with due diligence in accordance with the Construction Documents. "Construction Documents" means the plans and specifications, the finish out schedules, any change orders, and any allowances related to the plans and specifications, finish out schedules, and change orders. The Construction Documents have been signed by the parties and are incorporated into this contract by reference.

C. COST ADJUSTMENTS: All change orders must be in writing. Increase in costs resulting from change orders or items selected by Buyer which exceed the allowances specified in the Construction Documents will be paid by Buyer as follows:_____

_____.
A decrease in costs resulting from change orders and unused allowances will reduce the Sales Price, with proportionate adjustments to the amounts in Paragraphs 3A and 3B as required by lender.

D. BUYER'S SELECTIONS: If the Construction Documents permit selections by Buyer, Buyer's selections will conform to Seller's normal standards as set out in the Construction Documents or will not, in Seller's judgment, adversely affect the marketability of the Property. Buyer will make required selections within _____ days after notice from Seller.

E. COMPLETION: Seller must commence construction no later than _____ days after the Effective Date of this contract. The improvements will be substantially completed in accordance with the Construction Documents and ready for occupancy not later than _____, 20____ . The improvements will be deemed to be substantially completed in accordance with the Construction Documents upon the final inspection and approval by all applicable governmental authorities and any lender (Substantial Completion Date). Construction delays caused by acts of God, fire or other casualty, strikes, boycotts or nonavailability of materials for which no substitute of comparable quality and price is available will be added to the time allowed for substantial completion of the construction. However, in no event may the time for substantial completion extend beyond the Closing Date. Seller may substitute materials, equipment and appliances of comparable quality for those specified in the Construction Documents.

F. WARRANTIES: Except as expressly set forth in this contract, a separate writing, or provided by law, Seller makes no other express warranties. Seller shall assign to Buyer at closing all assignable manufacturer warranties.

G. INSULATION: As required by Federal Trade Commission Regulations, the information relating to the insulation installed or to be installed in the Improvements at the Property is: (check only one box below)

☐ (1) as shown in the attached specifications.
☐ (2) as follows:
    (a) Exterior walls of improved living areas: insulated with _____ insulation to a thickness of _____ inches which yields an R-Value of _____.
    (b) Walls in other areas of the home: insulated with_____ insulation to a thickness of _____ inches which yields an R-Value of _____.
    (c) Ceilings in improved living areas: insulated with_____ insulation to a thickness of _____ inches which yields an R-Value of _____.
    (d) Floors of improved living areas not applied to a slab foundation: insulated with_____ _____insulation to a thickness of _____ inches   which   yields   an R-Value of _____.
    (e) Other insulated areas: insulated with _____insulation to a thickness of _____ inches which yields an R-Value of _____.
    All stated R-Values are based on information provided by the manufacturer of the insulation.

H. ENVIRONMENTAL MATTERS: Buyer is advised that the presence of wetlands, toxic substances, including asbestos and wastes or other environmental hazards, or the presence of a threatened or endangered species or its habitat may affect Buyer's intended use of the Property. If Buyer is concerned about these matters, an addendum promulgated by TREC or required by the parties should be used.

I. SELLER'S DISCLOSURE: Except as otherwise disclosed in this contract, Seller has no knowledge of the following:
    (1) any flooding of the Property which has had a material adverse effect on the use of the Property;
    (2) any pending or threatened litigation, condemnation, or special assessment affecting the Property;
    (3) any environmental hazards that materially and adversely affect the Property;
    (4) any dumpsite, landfill, or underground tanks or containers now or previously located on the Property;
    (5) any wetlands, as defined by federal or state law or regulation, affecting the Property; or any threatened or endangered species or their habitat affecting the Property.

8. BROKERS' FEES: All obligations of the parties for payment of brokers' fees are contained in separate written agreements.

9. CLOSING:

A. The closing of the sale will be on or before _____, 20_____, or within 7 days after objections made under Paragraph 6D have been cured or waived, whichever date is later (Closing Date). If either party fails to close the sale by the Closing Date, the non-defaulting party may exercise the remedies contained in Paragraph 15.

B. At closing:
    (1) Seller shall execute and deliver a general warranty deed conveying title to the Property to Buyer and showing no additional exceptions to those permitted in Paragraph 6 and furnish tax statements or certificates showing no delinquent taxes on the Property.
    (2) Buyer shall pay the Sales Price in good funds acceptable to the escrow agent.
    (3) Seller and Buyer shall execute and deliver any notices, statements, certificates, affidavits, releases, loan documents and other documents reasonably required for the closing of the sale and the issuance of the Title Policy.
    (4) There will be no liens, assessments, or security interests against the Property which will not be satisfied out of the sales proceeds unless securing payment of any loans assumed by Buyer and assumed loans will not be in default.

10. POSSESSION:

A. Buyer's Possession: Seller shall deliver to Buyer possession of the Property: ☐ upon closing and funding ☐ according to a temporary residential lease form promulgated by TREC or other written lease required by the parties. Any possession by Buyer prior to closing or by Seller after closing which is not authorized by a written lease will establish a tenancy at sufferance relationship between the parties. **Consult your insurance agent prior to change of ownership and possession because insurance coverage may be limited or terminated. The absence of a written lease or appropriate insurance coverage may expose the parties to economic loss.**

B. Leases: After the Effective Date, Seller may not execute any lease (including but not limited to mineral leases) or convey any interest in the Property without Buyer's written consent.

11.SPECIAL PROVISIONS: (Insert only factual statements and business details applicable to the sale. TREC rules prohibit license holders from adding factual statements or business details for which a contract addendum, lease or other form has been promulgated by TREC for mandatory use.)

12.SETTLEMENT AND OTHER EXPENSES:
   A. The following expenses must be paid at or prior to closing:
      (1)Expenses payable by Seller (Seller's Expenses):
         (a)Releases of existing liens, including prepayment penalties and recording fees; release of Seller's loan liability; tax statements or certificates; preparation of deed; one-half of escrow fee; and other expenses payable by Seller under this contract.
         (b)Seller shall also pay an amount not to exceed $ _____ to be applied in the following order: Buyer's Expenses which Buyer is prohibited from paying by FHA, VA, Texas Veterans Land Board or other governmental loan programs, and then to other Buyer's Expenses as allowed by the lender.
      (2) Expenses payable by Buyer (Buyer's Expenses): Appraisal fees; loan application fees; origination charges; credit reports; preparation of loan documents; interest on the notes from date of disbursement to one month prior to dates of first monthly payments; recording fees; copies of easements and restrictions; loan title policy with endorsements required by lender; loan-related inspection fees; photos; amortization schedules; one-half of escrow fee; all prepaid items, including required premiums for flood and hazard insurance, reserve deposits for insurance, ad valorem taxes and special governmental assessments; final compliance inspection; courier fee; repair inspection; underwriting fee; wire transfer fee; expenses incident to any loan; Private Mortgage Insurance Premium (PMI), VA Loan Funding Fee, or FHA Mortgage Insurance Premium (MIP) as required by the lender; and other expenses payable by Buyer under this contract.
   B. If any expense exceeds an amount expressly stated in this contract for such expense to be paid by a party, that party may terminate this contract unless the other party agrees to pay such excess. Buyer may not pay charges and fees expressly prohibited by FHA, VA, Texas Veterans Land Board or other governmental loan program regulations.

13.PRORATIONS AND ROLLBACK TAXES:
   A. PRORATIONS: Taxes for the current year, maintenance fees, assessments, dues and rents will be prorated through the Closing Date. The tax proration may be calculated taking into consideration any change in exemptions that will affect the current year's taxes. If taxes for the current year vary from the amount prorated at closing, the parties shall adjust the prorations when tax statements for the current year are available. If taxes are not paid at or prior to closing, Buyer will be obligated to pay taxes for the current year.
   B. ROLLBACK TAXES: If additional taxes, penalties, or interest (Assessments) are imposed because of Seller's use or change in use of the Property prior to closing, the Assessments will be the obligation of Seller. Obligations imposed by this paragraph will survive closing.

14.CASUALTY LOSS: If any part of the Property is damaged or destroyed by fire or other casualty after the Effective Date of this contract, Seller shall restore the Property to its previous condition as soon as reasonably possible, but in any event by the Closing Date. If Seller fails to do so due to factors beyond Seller's control, Buyer may (a) terminate this contract and the earnest money will be refunded to Buyer (b) extend the time for performance up to 45 days and the Closing Date will be extended as necessary or (c) accept the Property in its damaged condition with an assignment of insurance proceeds, if permitted by Seller's insurance carrier, and receive credit from Seller at closing in the amount of the deductible under the insurance policy. Seller's obligations under this paragraph are independent of any other obligations of Seller under this contract.

15.DEFAULT: If Buyer fails to comply with this contract, Buyer will be in default, and Seller may (a) enforce specific performance, seek such other relief as may be provided by law, or both, or (b) terminate this contract and receive the earnest money as liquidated damages, thereby releasing both parties from this contract. If Seller fails to comply with this contract Seller will be in default and Buyer may (a) enforce specific performance, seek such other relief as may be provided by law, or both, or (b) terminate this contract and receive the earnest money, thereby releasing both parties from this contract.

16.MEDIATION: It is the policy of the State of Texas to encourage resolution of disputes through alternative dispute resolution procedures such as mediation. Subject to applicable law, any dispute between Seller and Buyer related to this contract which is not resolved through informal

Initialed for identification by Buyer_____ _____ and Seller _____ _____   TREC NO. 23-15

discussion will be submitted to a mutually acceptable mediation service or provider. The parties to the mediation shall bear the mediation costs equally. This paragraph does not preclude a party from seeking equitable relief from a court of competent jurisdiction.

17. ATTORNEY'S FEES: A Buyer, Seller, Listing Broker, Other Broker, or escrow agent who prevails in any legal proceeding related to this contract is entitled to recover reasonable attorney's fees and all costs of such proceeding.

18. ESCROW:
  A. ESCROW: The escrow agent is not (i) a party to this contract and does not have liability for the performance or nonperformance of any party to this contract, (ii) liable for interest on the earnest money and (iii) liable for the loss of any earnest money caused by the failure of any financial institution in which the earnest money has been deposited unless the financial institution is acting as escrow agent.
  B. EXPENSES: At closing, the earnest money must be applied first to any cash down payment, then to Buyer's Expenses and any excess refunded to Buyer. If no closing occurs, escrow agent may: (i) require a written release of liability of the escrow agent from all parties, (ii) require payment of unpaid expenses incurred on behalf of a party, and (iii) only deduct from the earnest money the amount of unpaid expenses incurred on behalf of the party receiving the earnest money.
  C. DEMAND: Upon termination of this contract, either party or the escrow agent may send a release of earnest money to each party and the parties shall execute counterparts of the release and deliver same to the escrow agent. If either party fails to execute the release, either party may make a written demand to the escrow agent for the earnest money. If only one party makes written demand for the earnest money, escrow agent shall promptly provide a copy of the demand to the other party. If escrow agent does not receive written objection to the demand from the other party within 15 days, escrow agent may disburse the earnest money to the party making demand reduced by the amount of unpaid expenses incurred on behalf of the party receiving the earnest money and escrow agent may pay the same to the creditors. If escrow agent complies with the provisions of this paragraph, each party hereby releases escrow agent from all adverse claims related to the disbursal of the earnest money.
  D. DAMAGES: Any party who wrongfully fails or refuses to sign a release acceptable to the escrow agent within 7 days of receipt of the request will be liable to the other party for (i) damages (ii) the earnest money; (iii) reasonable attorney's fees; and (iv) all costs of suit.
  E. NOTICES: Escrow agent's notices will be effective when sent in compliance with Paragraph 21. Notice of objection to the demand will be deemed effective upon receipt by escrow agent.

19. REPRESENTATIONS: All covenants, representations and warranties in this contract survive closing. If any representation of Seller in this contract is untrue on the Closing Date, Seller will be in default. Unless expressly prohibited by written agreement, Seller may continue to show the Property and receive, negotiate and accept back up offers.

20. FEDERAL TAX REQUIREMENTS: If Seller is a "foreign person," as defined by Internal Revenue Code and its regulations, or if Seller fails to deliver an affidavit or a certificate of non-foreign status to Buyer that Seller is not a "foreign person," then Buyer shall withhold from the sales proceeds an amount sufficient to comply with applicable tax law and deliver the same to the Internal Revenue Service together with appropriate tax forms. Internal Revenue Service regulations require filing written reports if currency in excess of specified amounts is received in the transaction.

21. NOTICES: All notices from one party to the other must be in writing and are effective when mailed to, hand-delivered at, or transmitted by fax or electronic transmission as follows:

To Buyer at: _____	**To Seller** at: _____
_____	_____
Phone: ( ) _____	Phone: ( ) _____
Fax: ( ) _____	Fax: ( ) _____
E-mail: _____	E-mail: _____

Initialed for identification by Buyer_____ _____ and Seller _____ _____   TREC NO. 23-15

22. AGREEMENT OF PARTIES: This contract contains the entire agreement of the parties and cannot be changed except by their written agreement. Addenda which are a part of this contract are (check all applicable boxes):

☐ Third Party Financing Addendum

☐ Seller Financing Addendum

☐ Addendum for Property Subject to Mandatory Membership in a Property Owners Association

☐ Buyer's Temporary Residential Lease

☐ Loan Assumption Addendum

☐ Addendum for Sale of Other Property by Buyer

☐ Addendum for Reservation of Oil, Gas and Other Minerals

☐ Addendum for "Back-Up" Contract

☐ Addendum Concerning Right to Terminate Due to Lender's Appraisal

☐ Addendum for Coastal Area Property

☐ Environmental Assessment, Threatened or Endangered Species and Wetlands Addendum

☐ Seller's Temporary Residential Lease

☐ Short Sale Addendum

☐ Addendum for Property Located Seaward of the Gulf Intracoastal Waterway

☐ Addendum for Property in a Propane Gas System Service Area

☐ Other (list): _____
_____
_____
_____
_____
_____

23. TERMINATION OPTION: For nominal consideration, the receipt of which is hereby acknowledged by Seller, and Buyer's agreement to pay Seller $_____ (Option Fee) within 3 days after the Effective Date of this contract, Seller grants Buyer the unrestricted right to terminate this contract by giving notice of termination to Seller within _____ days after the Effective Date of this contract (Option Period). Notices under this paragraph must be given by 5:00 p.m. (local time where the Property is located) by the date specified. If no dollar amount is stated as the Option Fee or if Buyer fails to pay the Option Fee to Seller within the time prescribed, this paragraph will not be a part of this contract and Buyer shall not have the unrestricted right to terminate this contract. If Buyer gives notice of termination within the time prescribed, the Option Fee will not be refunded; however, any earnest money will be refunded to Buyer. The Option Fee ☐ will ☐ will not be credited to the Sales Price at closing. **Time is of the essence for this paragraph and strict compliance with the time for performance is required.**

24. CONSULT AN ATTORNEY BEFORE SIGNING: TREC rules prohibit real estate license holders from giving legal advice. READ THIS CONTRACT CAREFULLY.

Buyer's
Attorney is: _____

_____

Phone: (   ) _____

Fax: (   ) _____

E-mail: _____

Seller's
Attorney is: _____

_____

Phone: (   ) _____

Fax: (   ) _____

E-mail: _____

Initialed for identification by Buyer_____ _____ and Seller _____ _____   TREC NO. 23-15

151

EXECUTED the _____ day of _____, 20_____ (Effective Date).
(BROKER: FILL IN THE DATE OF FINAL ACCEPTANCE.)

This contract is subject to Chapter 27 of the Texas Property Code. The provisions of that chapter may affect your right to recover damages arising from a construction defect. If you have a complaint concerning a construction defect and that defect has not been corrected as may be required by law or by contract, you must provide the notice required by Chapter 27 of the Texas Property Code to the contractor by certified mail, return receipt requested, not later than the 60th day before the date you file suit to recover damages in a court of law or initiate arbitration. The notice must refer to Chapter 27 of the Texas Property Code and must describe the construction defect. If requested by the contractor, you must provide the contractor an opportunity to inspect and cure the defect as provided by Section 27.004 of the Texas Property Code.

_____
Buyer

_____
Buyer

_____
Seller

_____
Seller

TREC NO. 23-15

BROKER INFORMATION
(Print name(s) only. Do not sign)

Other Broker Firm	License No.

represents ❏ Buyer only as Buyer's agent
❏ Seller as Listing Broker's subagent

Associate's Name	License No.

Associate's Email Address	Phone

Licensed Supervisor of Associate	License No.

Other Broker's Address	Phone

City	State	Zip

Listing Broker Firm	License No.

represents ❏ Seller and Buyer as an intermediary
❏ Seller only as Seller's agent

Listing Associate's Name	License No.

Listing Associate's Email Address	Phone

Licensed Supervisor of Listing Associate	License No.

Listing Broker's Office Address	Phone

City	State	Zip

Selling Associate's Name	License No.

Selling Associate's Email Address	Phone

Licensed Supervisor of Selling Associate	License No.

Selling Associate's Office Address	

City	State	Zip

Listing Broker has agreed to pay Other Broker _____ of the total sales price when the Listing Broker's fee is received. Escrow agent is authorized and directed to pay Other Broker from Listing Broker's fee at closing.

TREC NO. 23-15

153

OPTION FEE RECEIPT

Receipt of $_____ (Option Fee) in the form of _____
is acknowledged.

_____   _____
Seller or Listing Broker   Date

EARNEST MONEY RECEIPT

Receipt of $_____ Earnest Money in the form of _____
is acknowledged.

_____   _____   _____   _____
Escrow Agent   Received by   Email Address   Date/Time

_____   _____
Address   Phone

_____   _____   _____   _____
City   State   Zip   Fax

CONTRACT RECEIPT

Receipt of the Contract is acknowledged.

_____   _____   _____   _____
Escrow Agent   Received by   Email Address   Date

_____   _____
Address   Phone

_____   _____   _____   _____
City   State   Zip   Fax

ADDITIONAL EARNEST MONEY RECEIPT

Receipt of $_____ additional Earnest Money in the form of _____
is acknowledged.

_____   _____   _____   _____
Escrow Agent   Received by   Email Address   Date/Time

_____   _____
Address   Phone

_____   _____   _____   _____
City   State   Zip   Fax

TREC NO. 23-15

UNIMPROVED PROPERTY CONTRACT
NOTICE: Not For Use For Condominium Transactions

1. PARTIES: The parties to this contract are _____(Seller) and _____(Buyer). Seller agrees to sell and convey to Buyer and Buyer agrees to buy from Seller the Property defined below.

2. PROPERTY: Lot _____, Block _____,
_____Addition,
City of _____, County of_____,
Texas, known as_____
(address/zip code), or as described on attached exhibit together with all rights, privileges and appurtenances pertaining thereto, including but not limited to: water rights, claims, permits, strips and gores, easements, and cooperative or association memberships (the Property). RESERVATIONS: Any reservation for oil, gas, or other minerals, water, timber, or other interests is made in accordance with an attached addendum.

3. SALES PRICE:
   A. Cash portion of Sales Price payable by Buyer at closing ....$_____
   B. Sum of all financing described in the attached: ❏ Third Party Financing Addendum,
       ❏ Loan Assumption Addendum, ❏ Seller Financing Addendum ....$_____
   C. Sales Price (Sum of A and B) ....$_____

4. LICENSE HOLDER DISCLOSURE: Texas law requires a real estate license holder who is a party to a transaction or acting on behalf of a spouse, parent, child, business entity in which the license holder owns more than 10%, or a trust for which the license holder acts as trustee or of which the license holder or the license holder's spouse, parent or child is a beneficiary, to notify the other party in writing before entering into a contract of sale. Disclose if applicable:_____
_____.

5. EARNEST   MONEY: Within 3 days after the Effective Date, Buyer must deliver $_____ as earnest money to _____, as escrow agent, at _____(address). Buyer shall deliver additional   earnest money of $_____ to escrow agent within _____ days after the Effective Date of this contract. If Buyer fails to deliver the earnest money within the time required, Seller may terminate this contract or exercise Seller's remedies under Paragraph 15, or both, by providing notice to Buyer before Buyer delivers the earnest money. If the last day to deliver the earnest money falls on a Saturday, Sunday, or legal holiday, the time to deliver the earnest money is extended until the end of the next day that is not a Saturday, Sunday, or legal holiday. **Time is of the essence for this paragraph.**

6. TITLE POLICY AND SURVEY:
   A. TITLE POLICY: Seller shall furnish to Buyer at ❏Seller's ❏Buyer's expense an owner's policy of title insurance (Title Policy) issued by_____
   (Title Company) in the amount of the Sales Price, dated at or after closing, insuring Buyer against loss under the provisions of the Title Policy, subject to the promulgated exclusions (including existing building and zoning ordinances) and the following exceptions:
   (1) Restrictive covenants common to the platted subdivision in which the Property is located.
   (2) The standard printed exception for standby fees, taxes and assessments.
   (3) Liens created as part of the financing described in Paragraph 3.
   (4) Utility easements created by the dedication deed or plat of the subdivision in which the Property is located.
   (5) Reservations or exceptions otherwise permitted by this contract or as may be approved by Buyer in writing.
   (6) The standard printed exception as to marital rights.
   (7) The standard printed exception as to waters, tidelands, beaches, streams, and related matters.
   (8) The standard printed exception as to discrepancies, conflicts, shortages in area or boundary lines, encroachments or protrusions, or overlapping improvements:
   ❏(i) will not be amended or deleted from the title policy; or
   ❏(ii) will be amended to read, "shortages in area" at the expense of ❏Buyer ❏Seller.
   (9) The exception or exclusion regarding minerals approved by the Texas Department of Insurance.
   B. COMMITMENT: Within 20 days after the Title Company receives a copy of this contract, Seller shall furnish to Buyer a commitment for title insurance (Commitment) and, at Buyer's expense, legible copies of restrictive covenants and documents evidencing exceptions in the Commitment (Exception Documents) other than the standard printed exceptions. Seller authorizes the Title Company to deliver the Commitment and Exception Documents to Buyer at Buyer's address

shown in Paragraph 21. If the Commitment and Exception Documents are not delivered to Buyer within the specified time, the time for delivery will be automatically extended up to 15 days or 3 days before the Closing Date, whichever is earlier. If the Commitment and Exception Documents are not delivered within the time required, Buyer may terminate this contract and the earnest money will be refunded to Buyer.

C. SURVEY: The survey must be made by a registered professional land surveyor acceptable to the Title Company and Buyer's lender(s). (Check one box only)

❑ (1) Within _____ days after the Effective Date of this contract, Seller shall furnish to Buyer and Title Company Seller's existing survey of the Property and a Residential Real Property Affidavit promulgated by the Texas Department of Insurance (T-47 Affidavit). **If Seller fails to furnish the existing survey or affidavit within the time prescribed, Buyer shall obtain a new survey at Seller's expense no later than 3 days prior to Closing Date.** If the existing survey or affidavit is not acceptable to Title Company or Buyer's lender(s), Buyer shall obtain a new survey at ❑ Seller's ❑Buyer's expense no later than 3 days prior to Closing Date.

❑ (2) Within _____ days after the Effective Date of this contract, Buyer shall obtain a new survey at Buyer's expense. Buyer is deemed to receive the survey on the date of actual receipt or the date specified in this paragraph, whichever is earlier.

❑ (3) Within _____ days after the Effective Date of this contract, Seller, at Seller's expense shall furnish a new survey to Buyer.

D. OBJECTIONS: Buyer may object in writing to (i) defects, exceptions, or encumbrances to title: disclosed on the survey other than items 6A(1) through (7) above; or disclosed in the Commitment other than items 6A(1) through (9) above; (ii) any portion of the Property lying in a special flood hazard area (Zone V or A) as shown on the current Federal Emergency Management Agency map; or (iii) any exceptions which prohibit the following use or activity: _____ .
Buyer must object the earlier of (i) the Closing Date or (ii) _____ days after Buyer receives the Commitment, Exception Documents, and the survey. Buyer's failure to object within the time allowed will constitute a waiver of Buyer's right to object; except that the requirements in Schedule C of the Commitment are not waived. Provided Seller is not obligated to incur any expense, Seller shall cure any timely objections of Buyer or any third party lender within 15 days after Seller receives the objections (Cure Period) and the Closing Date will be extended as necessary. If objections are not cured within the Cure Period, Buyer may, by delivering notice to Seller within 5 days after the end of the Cure Period: (i) terminate this contract and the earnest money will be refunded to Buyer; or (ii) waive the objections. If Buyer does not terminate within the time required, Buyer shall be deemed to have waived the objections. If the Commitment or Survey is revised or any new Exception Document(s) is delivered, Buyer may object to any new matter revealed in the revised Commitment or Survey or new Exception Document(s) within the same time stated in this paragraph to make objections beginning when the revised Commitment, Survey, or Exception Document(s) is delivered to Buyer.

E. TITLE NOTICES:
(1) ABSTRACT OR TITLE POLICY: Broker advises Buyer to have an abstract of title covering the Property examined by an attorney of Buyer's selection, or Buyer should be furnished with or obtain a Title Policy. If a Title Policy is furnished, the Commitment should be promptly reviewed by an attorney of Buyer's choice due to the time limitations on Buyer's right to object.

(2) MEMBERSHIP IN PROPERTY OWNERS ASSOCIATION(S): The Property ❑is ❑is not subject to mandatory membership in a property owners association(s). If the Property is subject to mandatory membership in a property owners association(s), Seller notifies Buyer under §5.012, Texas Property Code, that, as a purchaser of property in the residential community identified in Paragraph 2 in which the Property is located, you are obligated to be a member of the property owners association(s). Restrictive covenants governing the use and occupancy of the Property and all dedicatory instruments governing the establishment, maintenance, and operation of this residential community have been or will be recorded in the Real Property Records of the county in which the Property is located. Copies of the restrictive covenants and dedicatory instruments may be obtained from the county clerk. **You are obligated to pay assessments to the property owners association(s). The amount of the assessments is subject to change. Your failure to pay the assessments could result in enforcement of the association's lien on and the foreclosure of the Property.**
Section 207.003, Property Code, entitles an owner to receive copies of any document that governs the establishment, maintenance, or operation of a subdivision, including, but not limited to, restrictions, bylaws, rules and regulations, and a resale certificate from a property owners' association. A resale certificate contains information including, but not limited to, statements specifying the amount and frequency of regular assessments and the style and cause number of lawsuits to which the property owners' association is a party, other than lawsuits relating to unpaid ad valorem taxes of an individual member of the association. These documents must be made available to you by the property owners' association or the association's agent on your request.
If Buyer is concerned about these matters, the TREC promulgated Addendum for Property Subject to Mandatory Membership in a Property Owners Association should be used.

Initialed for identification by Buyer_____ _____ and Seller _____ _____   TREC NO. 9–13

(3) STATUTORY TAX DISTRICTS: If the Property is situated in a utility or other statutorily created district providing water, sewer, drainage, or flood control facilities and services, Chapter 49, Texas Water Code, requires Seller to deliver and Buyer to sign the statutory notice relating to the tax rate, bonded indebtedness, or standby fee of the district prior to final execution of this contract.

(4) TIDE WATERS: If the Property abuts the tidally influenced waters of the state, §33.135, Texas Natural Resources Code, requires a notice regarding coastal area property to be included in the contract. An addendum containing the notice promulgated by TREC or required by the parties must be used.

(5) ANNEXATION: If the Property is located outside the limits of a municipality, Seller notifies Buyer under §5.011, Texas Property Code, that the Property may now or later be included in the extraterritorial jurisdiction of a municipality and may now or later be subject to annexation by the municipality. Each municipality maintains a map that depicts its boundaries and extraterritorial jurisdiction. To determine if the Property is located within a municipality's extraterritorial jurisdiction or is likely to be located within a municipality's extraterritorial jurisdiction, contact all municipalities located in the general proximity of the Property for further information.

(6) PROPERTY LOCATED IN A CERTIFICATED SERVICE AREA OF A UTILITY SERVICE PROVIDER: Notice required by §13.257, Water Code: The real property, described in Paragraph 2, that you are about to purchase may be located in a certificated water or sewer service area, which is authorized by law to provide water or sewer service to the properties in the certificated area. If your property is located in a certificated area there may be special costs or charges that you will be required to pay before you can receive water or sewer service. There may be a period required to construct lines or other facilities necessary to provide water or sewer service to your property. You are advised to determine if the property is in a certificated area and contact the utility service provider to determine the cost that you will be required to pay and the period, if any, that is required to provide water or sewer service to your property. The undersigned Buyer hereby acknowledges receipt of the foregoing notice at or before the execution of a binding contract for the purchase of the real property described in Paragraph 2 or at closing of purchase of the real property.

(7) PUBLIC IMPROVEMENT DISTRICTS: If the Property is in a public improvement district, §5.014, Property Code, requires Seller to notify Buyer as follows: As a purchaser of this parcel of real property you are obligated to pay an assessment to a municipality or county for an improvement project undertaken by a public improvement district under Chapter 372, Local Government Code. The assessment may be due annually or in periodic installments. More information concerning the amount of the assessment and the due dates of that assessment may be obtained from the municipality or county levying the assessment. The amount of the assessments is subject to change. Your failure to pay the assessments could result in a lien on and the foreclosure of your property.

(8) TEXAS AGRICULTURAL DEVELOPMENT DISTRICT: The Property ❑ is ❑ is not located in a Texas Agricultural Development District. For additional information, contact the Texas Department of Agriculture.

(9) TRANSFER FEES: If the Property is subject to a private transfer fee obligation, §5.205, Property Code requires Seller to notify Buyer as follows: The private transfer fee obligation may be governed by Chapter 5, Subchapter G of the Texas Property Code.

(10) PROPANE GAS SYSTEM SERVICE AREA: If the Property is located in a propane gas system service area owned by a distribution system retailer, Seller must give Buyer written notice as required by §141.010, Texas Utilities Code. An addendum containing the notice approved by TREC or required by the parties should be used.

(11) NOTICE OF WATER LEVEL FLUCTUATIONS: If the Property adjoins an impoundment of water, including a reservoir or lake, constructed and maintained under Chapter 11, Water Code, that has a storage capacity of at least 5,000 acre-feet at the impoundment's normal operating level, Seller hereby notifies Buyer: "The water level of the impoundment of water adjoining the Property fluctuates for various reasons, including as a result of: (1) an entity lawfully exercising its right to use the water stored in the impoundment; or (2) drought or flood conditions."

7. PROPERTY CONDITION:
A. ACCESS, INSPECTIONS AND UTILITIES: Seller shall permit Buyer and Buyer's agents access to the Property at reasonable times. Buyer may have the Property inspected by inspectors selected by Buyer and licensed by TREC or otherwise permitted by law to make inspections. Seller at Seller's expense shall immediately cause existing utilities to be turned on and shall keep the utilities on during the time this contract is in effect.
   NOTICE: Buyer should determine the availability of utilities to the Property suitable to satisfy Buyer's needs.
B. ACCEPTANCE OF PROPERTY CONDITION: "As Is" means the present condition of the Property with any and all defects and without warranty except for the warranties of title and the warranties in this contract. Buyer's agreement to accept the Property As Is under Paragraph 7B (1) or (2) does not preclude Buyer from inspecting the Property under Paragraph 7A, from negotiating repairs or treatments in a subsequent amendment, or from terminating this contract during the Option Period, if any.

(Check one box only)
❑ (1) Buyer accepts the Property As Is.
❑ (2) Buyer accepts the Property As Is provided Seller, at Seller's expense, shall complete the following specific repairs and treatments: _____.

_____.

(Do not insert general phrases, such as "subject to inspections" that do not identify specific repairs and treatments.)

C. COMPLETION OF REPAIRS: Unless otherwise agreed in writing: (i) Seller shall complete all agreed repairs and treatments prior to the Closing Date; and (ii) all required permits must be obtained, and repairs and treatments must be performed by persons who are licensed to provide such repairs or treatments or, if no license is required by law, are commercially engaged in the trade of providing such repairs or treatments. At Buyer's election, any transferable warranties received by Seller with respect to the repairs and treatments will be transferred to Buyer at Buyer's expense. If Seller fails to complete any agreed repairs and treatments prior to the Closing Date, Buyer may exercise remedies under Paragraph 15 or extend the Closing Date up to 5 days, if necessary, for Seller to complete repairs and treatments.

D. ENVIRONMENTAL MATTERS: Buyer is advised that the presence of wetlands, toxic substances, including asbestos and wastes or other environmental hazards, or the presence of a threatened or endangered species or its habitat may affect Buyer's intended use of the Property. If Buyer is concerned about these matters, an addendum promulgated by TREC or required by the parties should be used.

E. SELLER'S DISCLOSURES: Except as otherwise disclosed in this contract, Seller has no knowledge of the following:
(1) any flooding of the Property which has had a material adverse effect on the use of the Property;
(2) any pending or threatened litigation, condemnation, or special assessment affecting the Property;
(3) any environmental hazards that materially and adversely affect the Property;
(4) any dumpsite, landfill, or underground tanks or containers now or previously located on the Property;
(5) any wetlands, as defined by federal or state law or regulation, affecting the Property; or
(6) any threatened or endangered species or their habitat affecting the Property.

8. BROKERS' FEES: All obligations of the parties for payment of brokers' fees are contained in separate written agreements.

9. CLOSING:
A. The closing of the sale will be on or before _____, 20_____, or within 7 days after objections made under Paragraph 6D have been cured or waived, whichever date is later (Closing Date). If either party fails to close the sale by the Closing Date, the non-defaulting party may exercise the remedies contained in Paragraph 15.
B. At closing:
(1) Seller shall execute and deliver a general warranty deed conveying title to the Property to Buyer and showing no additional exceptions to those permitted in Paragraph 6 and furnish tax statements or certificates showing no delinquent taxes on the Property.
(2) Buyer shall pay the Sales Price in good funds acceptable to the escrow agent.
(3) Seller and Buyer shall execute and deliver any notices, statements, certificates, affidavits, releases, loan documents and other documents reasonably required for the closing of the sale and the issuance of the Title Policy.
(4) There will be no liens, assessments, or security interests against the Property which will not be satisfied out of the sales proceeds unless securing the payment of any loans assumed by Buyer and assumed loans will not be in default.

10. POSSESSION:
A. Buyer's Possession: Seller shall deliver to Buyer possession of the Property in its present or required condition upon closing and funding.
B. Leases:
(1) After the Effective Date, Seller may not execute any lease (including but not limited to mineral leases) or convey any interest in the Property without Buyer's written consent.
(2) If the Property is subject to any lease to which Seller is a party, Seller shall deliver to Buyer copies of the lease(s) and any move-in condition form signed by the tenant within 7 days after the Effective Date of the contract.

11. SPECIAL PROVISIONS: (Insert only factual statements and business details applicable to the sale. TREC rules prohibit license holders from adding factual statements or business details for which a contract addendum or other form has been promulgated by TREC for mandatory use.)

12. SETTLEMENT AND OTHER EXPENSES:
    A. The following expenses must be paid at or prior to closing:
       (1)Expenses payable by Seller (Seller's Expenses):
         (a) Releases of existing liens, including prepayment penalties and recording fees; release of Seller's loan liability; tax statements or certificates; preparation of deed; one-half of escrow fee; and other expenses payable by Seller under this contract.
         (b) Seller shall also pay an amount not to exceed $ _____ to be applied in the following order: Buyer's Expenses which Buyer is prohibited from paying by FHA, VA, Texas Veterans Land Board or other governmental loan programs, and then to other Buyer's Expenses as allowed by the lender.
       (2) Expenses payable by Buyer (Buyer's Expenses): Appraisal fees; loan application fees; origination charges; credit reports; preparation of loan documents; interest on the notes from date of disbursement to one month prior to dates of first monthly payments; recording fees; copies of easements and restrictions; loan title policy with endorsements required by lender; loan-related inspection fees; photos; amortization schedules; one-half of escrow fee; all prepaid items, including required premiums for flood and hazard insurance, reserve deposits for insurance, ad valorem taxes and special governmental assessments; final compliance inspection; courier fee; repair inspection; underwriting fee; wire transfer fee; expenses incident to any loan; Private Mortgage Insurance Premium (PMI), VA Loan Funding Fee, or FHA Mortgage Insurance Premium (MIP) as required by the lender; and other expenses payable by Buyer under this contract.
    B. If any expense exceeds an amount expressly stated in this contract for such expense to be paid by a party, that party may terminate this contract unless the other party agrees to pay such excess. Buyer may not pay charges and fees expressly prohibited by FHA, VA, Texas Veterans Land Board or other governmental loan program regulations.

13. PRORATIONS AND ROLLBACK TAXES:
    A. PRORATIONS: Taxes for the current year, interest, maintenance fees, assessments, dues and rents will be prorated through the Closing Date. The tax proration may be calculated taking into consideration any change in exemptions that will affect the current year's taxes. If taxes for the current year vary from the amount prorated at closing, the parties shall adjust the prorations when tax statements for the current year are available. If taxes are not paid at or prior to closing, Buyer shall pay taxes for the current year.
    B. ROLLBACK TAXES: If this sale or Buyer's use of the Property after closing results in the assessment of additional taxes, penalties or interest (Assessments) for periods prior to closing, the Assessments will be the obligation of Buyer. If Assessments are imposed because of Seller's use or change in use of the Property prior to closing, the Assessments will be the obligation of Seller. Obligations imposed by this paragraph will survive closing.

14. CASUALTY LOSS: If any part of the Property is damaged or destroyed by fire or other casualty after the Effective Date of this contract, Seller shall restore the Property to its previous condition as soon as reasonably possible, but in any event by the Closing Date. If Seller fails to do so due to factors beyond Seller's control, Buyer may (a) terminate this contract and the earnest money will be refunded to Buyer (b) extend the time for performance up to 15 days and the Closing Date will be extended as necessary or (c) accept the Property in its damaged condition with an assignment of insurance proceeds, if permitted by Seller's insurance carrier, and receive credit from Seller at closing in the amount of the deductible under the insurance policy. Seller's obligations under this paragraph are independent of any other obligations of Seller under this contract.

15. DEFAULT: If Buyer fails to comply with this contract, Buyer will be in default, and Seller may (a) enforce specific performance, seek such other relief as may be provided by law, or both, or (b) terminate this contract and receive the earnest money as liquidated damages, thereby releasing both parties from this contract. If Seller fails to comply with this contract, Seller will be in default and Buyer may (a) enforce specific performance, seek such other relief as may be provided by law, or both, or (b) terminate this contract and receive the earnest money, thereby releasing both parties from this contract.

16. MEDIATION: It is the policy of the State of Texas to encourage resolution of disputes through alternative dispute resolution procedures such as mediation. Any dispute between Seller and Buyer related to this contract which is not resolved through informal discussion will be submitted to a mutually acceptable mediation service or provider. The parties to the mediation shall bear the mediation costs equally. This paragraph does not preclude a party from seeking equitable relief from a court of competent jurisdiction.

17. ATTORNEY'S FEES: A Buyer, Seller, Listing Broker, Other Broker, or escrow agent who prevails in any legal proceeding related to this contract is entitled to recover reasonable attorney's fees and all costs of such proceeding.

18. ESCROW:
    A. ESCROW: The escrow agent is not (i) a party to this contract and does not have liability for the performance or nonperformance of any party to this contract, (ii) liable for interest on the earnest money and (iii) liable for the loss of any earnest money caused by the failure of any financial institution in which the earnest money has been deposited unless the financial institution is acting as escrow agent.
    B. EXPENSES: At closing, the earnest money must be applied first to any cash down payment, then to Buyer's Expenses and any excess refunded to Buyer. If no closing occurs, escrow

agent may: (i) require a written release of liability of the escrow agent from all parties, (ii) require payment of unpaid expenses incurred on behalf of a party, and (iii) only deduct from the earnest money the amount of unpaid expenses incurred on behalf of the party receiving the earnest money.

C. DEMAND: Upon termination of this contract, either party or the escrow agent may send a release of earnest money to each party and the parties shall execute counterparts of the release and deliver same to the escrow agent. If either party fails to execute the release, either party may make a written demand to the escrow agent for the earnest money. If only one party makes written demand for the earnest money, escrow agent shall promptly provide a copy of the demand to the other party. If escrow agent does not receive written objection to the demand from the other party within 15 days, escrow agent may disburse the earnest money to the party making demand reduced by the amount of unpaid expenses incurred on behalf of the party receiving the earnest money and escrow agent may pay the same to the creditors. If escrow agent complies with the provisions of this paragraph, each party hereby releases escrow agent from all adverse claims related to the disbursal of the earnest money.

D. DAMAGES: Any party who wrongfully fails or refuses to sign a release acceptable to the escrow agent within 7 days of receipt of the request will be liable to the other party for (i) damages; (ii) the earnest money; (iii) reasonable attorney's fees; and (iv) all costs of suit.

E. NOTICES: Escrow agent's notices will be effective when sent in compliance with Paragraph 21. Notice of objection to the demand will be deemed effective upon receipt by escrow agent.

19.REPRESENTATIONS: All covenants, representations and warranties in this contract survive closing. If any representation of Seller in this contract is untrue on the Closing Date, Seller will be in default. Unless expressly prohibited by written agreement, Seller may continue to show the Property and receive, negotiate and accept back up offers.

20.FEDERAL TAX REQUIREMENTS: If Seller is a "foreign person," as defined by Internal Revenue Code and its regulations, or if Seller fails to deliver an affidavit or a certificate of non-foreign status to Buyer that Seller is not a "foreign person," then Buyer shall withhold from the sales proceeds an amount sufficient to comply with applicable tax law and deliver the same to the Internal Revenue Service together with appropriate tax forms. Internal Revenue Service regulations require filing written reports if currency in excess of specified amounts is received in the transaction.

21.NOTICES: All notices from one party to the other must be in writing and are effective when mailed to, hand-delivered at, or transmitted by fax or electronic transmission as follows:

To Buyer	**To Seller**
at: _____	at: _____
_____	_____
Phone: ( ) _____	Phone: ( ) _____
Fax: ( ) _____	Fax: ( ) _____
E-mail: _____	E-mail: _____

22.AGREEMENT OF PARTIES: This contract contains the entire agreement of the parties and cannot be changed except by their written agreement. Addenda which are a part of this contract are (check all applicable boxes):

❏ Third Party Financing Addendum

❏ Seller Financing Addendum

❏ Addendum for Property Subject to Mandatory Membership in a Property Owners Association

❏ Buyer's Temporary Residential Lease

❏ Seller's Temporary Residential Lease

❏ Addendum for Reservation of Oil, Gas and Other Minerals

❏ Addendum for "Back-Up" Contract

❏ Addendum Concerning Right to Terminate Due to Lender's Appraisal

❏ Addendum for Coastal Area Property

❏ Environmental Assessment, Threatened or Endangered Species and Wetlands Addendum

❏ Addendum for Property Located Seaward of the Gulf Intracoastal Waterway

❏ Addendum for Sale of Other Property by Buyer

❏ Addendum for Property in a Propane Gas System Service Area

❏ Other (list): _____
_____
_____
_____
_____

Initialed for identification by Buyer_____ _____ and Seller _____ _____   TREC NO. 9–13

23. **TERMINATION OPTION:** For nominal consideration, the receipt of which is hereby acknowledged by Seller, and Buyer's agreement to pay Seller $_____ (Option Fee) within 3 days after the Effective Date of this contract, Seller grants Buyer the unrestricted right to terminate this contract by giving notice of termination to Seller within _____ days after the Effective Date of this contract (Option Period). Notices under this paragraph must be given by 5:00 p.m. (local time where the Property is located) by the date specified. If no dollar amount is stated as the Option Fee or if Buyer fails to pay the Option Fee to Seller within the time prescribed, this paragraph will not be a part of this contract and Buyer shall not have the unrestricted right to terminate this contract. If Buyer gives notice of termination within the time prescribed, the Option Fee will not be refunded; however, any earnest money will be refunded to Buyer. The Option Fee ❑will ❑will not be credited to the Sales Price at closing. **Time is of the essence for this paragraph and strict compliance with the time for performance is required.**

24. **CONSULT AN ATTORNEY BEFORE SIGNING:** TREC rules prohibit real estate license holders from giving legal advice. READ THIS CONTRACT CAREFULLY.

Buyer's
Attorney is: _____

Seller's
Attorney is: _____

_____

_____

Phone: (____) _____

Phone: (____) _____

Fax: (____) _____

Fax: (____) _____

E-mail: _____

E-mail: _____

EXECUTED the _____ day of _____, 20_____ (Effective Date).
(BROKER: FILL IN THE DATE OF FINAL ACCEPTANCE.)

_____
Buyer

_____
Seller

_____
Buyer

_____
Seller

Initialed for identification by Buyer_____ _____ and Seller _____ _____   TREC NO. 9-13

BROKER INFORMATION
(Print name(s) only. Do not sign)

Other Broker Firm _____ License No. _____

represents ☐ Buyer only as Buyer's agent
☐ Seller as Listing Broker's subagent

Associate's Name _____ License No. _____

Associate's Email Address _____ Phone _____

Licensed Supervisor of Associate _____ License No. _____

Other Broker's Address _____ Phone _____

City _____ State _____ Zip _____

Listing Broker Firm _____ License No. _____

represents ☐ Seller and Buyer as an intermediary
☐ Seller only as Seller's agent

Listing Associate's Name _____ License No. _____

Listing Associate's Email Address _____ Phone _____

Licensed Supervisor of Listing Associate _____ License No. _____

Listing Broker's Office Address _____ Phone _____

City _____ State _____ Zip _____

Selling Associate's Name _____ License No. _____

Selling Associate's Email Address _____ Phone _____

Licensed Supervisor of Selling Associate _____ License No. _____

Selling Associate's Office Address _____

City _____ State _____ Zip _____

Listing Broker has agreed to pay Other Broker_____ of the total sales price when the Listing Broker's fee is received. Escrow agent is authorized and directed to pay Other Broker from Listing Broker's fee at closing.

TREC NO. 9-13

OPTION FEE RECEIPT

Receipt of $_____ (Option Fee) in the form of _____
is acknowledged.

_____   _____
Seller or Listing Broker   Date

EARNEST MONEY RECEIPT

Receipt of $_____ Earnest Money in the form of _____
is acknowledged.

_____   _____   _____   _____
Escrow Agent   Received by   Email Address   Date/Time

_____   _____
Address   Phone

_____   _____   _____   _____
City   State   Zip   Fax

CONTRACT RECEIPT

Receipt of the Contract is acknowledged.

_____   _____   _____   _____
Escrow Agent   Received by   Email Address   Date

_____   _____
Address   Phone

_____   _____   _____   _____
City   State   Zip   Fax

ADDITIONAL EARNEST MONEY RECEIPT

Receipt of $_____ additional Earnest Money in the form of _____
is acknowledged.

_____   _____   _____   _____
Escrow Agent   Received by   Email Address   Date/Time

_____   _____
Address   Phone

_____   _____   _____   _____
City   State   Zip   Fax

TREC NO. 9-13

163

PROMULGATED BY THE TEXAS REAL ESTATE COMMISSION (TREC)

11-15-18

NOTICE OF BUYER'S TERMINATION OF CONTRACT

CONCERNING THE CONTRACT FOR THE SALE OF THE PROPERTY AT

EQUAL HOUSING OPPORTUNITY

_____
(Street Address and City)

BETWEEN THE UNDERSIGNED BUYER AND_____

_____ (SELLER)

Buyer notifies Seller that the contract is terminated pursuant to the following:

❑(1) The unrestricted right of Buyer to terminate the contract under Paragraph 23 of the contract.

❑(2) Buyer cannot obtain Buyer Approval in accordance with the Third Party Financing Addendum to the contract.

❑(3) The Property does not satisfy Property Approval in accordance with the Third Party Financing Addendum to the contract. Buyer has delivered to Seller lender's written statement setting forth the reason(s) for lender's determination.

❑(4) Buyer elects to terminate under Paragraph A of the Addendum for Property Subject to Mandatory Membership in a Property Owners' Association.

❑(5) Buyer elects to terminate under Paragraph 7B(2) of the contract relating to the Seller's Disclosure Notice.

❑(6) Buyer elects to terminate under Paragraph (3) of the Addendum Concerning Right to Terminate Due to Lender's Appraisal. Buyer has delivered a copy of the Appraisal to Seller.

❑(7) Buyer elects to terminate under Paragraph 6.D. of the contract (6.C. for Residential Condominium Contract) because timely objections were not cured by the end of the Cure Period.

❑(8) Other _(identify the paragraph number of contract or the addendum)_: _____

_____

_____

_____

_____

NOTE: This notice is not an election of remedies. Release of the earnest money is governed by the contract.

CONSULT AN ATTORNEY BEFORE SIGNING: TREC rules prohibit real estate license holders from giving legal advice. READ THIS FORM CAREFULLY.

_____   _____
Buyer   Date   Buyer   Date

This form has been approved by the Texas Real Estate Commission for use with similarly approved or promulgated contract forms. Such approval relates to this form only. TREC forms are intended for use only by trained real estate license holders. No representation is made as to the legal validity or adequacy of any provision in any specific transactions. It is not suitable for complex transactions. Texas Real Estate Commission, P.O. Box 12188, Austin, TX 78711-2188, (512) 936-3000 (http://www.trec.texas.gov) TREC No. 38-6. This form replaces TREC No. 38-5.

TREC No. 38-6

Made in the USA
San Bernardino, CA
05 December 2019